Michael Barnes's *The Real Duke of Hazzard* is a wonderful contribution to the lore of Hazzard County. But it is more than a story of good ol' boys, fast cars, and moonshining. It is the true story of Jerry Rushing, on whom our show was based. It is also a story of the struggle of a man who won his life's biggest battle, overcoming the demons within him and finding God right back at home, in the beautiful hills of North Carolina.

—Ben "Cooter" Jones

Jerry Rushing is an amazing man who has led an amazing life. Without him, John Schneider as "Bo Duke" never would have existed. Thanks for loaning me your life, Jerry!

—John "Bo Duke" Schneider

THE REAL DUKE OF HAZZARD
THE JERRY RUSHING STORY

Michael D. Barnes

with Jerry Rushing

CREATION HOUSE
A STRANG COMPANY

THE REAL DUKE OF HAZZARD by Michael D. Barnes with Jerry Rushing
Published by Creation House
A Strang Company
600 Rinehart Road
Lake Mary, Florida 32746
www.creationhouse.com

All Scripture quotations are from the King James Version of the Bible.

Cover design by Terry Clifton

Photos by Billy Wilcox and Jerry Rushing

Library of Congress Control Number: 2005930405
International Standard Book Number: 1-59185-899-2

First Edition

05 06 07 08 09 — 987654321
Printed in the United States of America

Soli Deo Gloria

Acknowledgments

THANKS TO THE original Duke of Hazzard, Jerry Elijah Rushing, for his help, for his assistance, and for the hours of taping his stories and reliving the past for the sake of fans and readers. I appreciate his belief and trust in me that I could embrace his past to portray accurately his life and the change God brought about in his soul, and for his understanding of God's timing—that the time had come to tell his story.

A special thanks to Jerry's wife, Shelby Dean Rushing, for accepting our persistence to get the stories of the past accurate, and for enduring the pain of reliving some of the darkest moments of her life. She has my gratitude for her undying care, concern, and prayers for her bootlegger husband—without whom there would be no story.

My thanks to Darlene Tarlton, Jerry's daughter, for sharing stories that led to a better understanding of the "loving father" that was under the harsh exterior of the moonshiner and bootlegger.

My loving appreciation to my wife, Candice Barnes, for being there for me and with me, encouraging me when I was tired, and for believing in me when I lost faith. I also thank her for sharing me for almost two years as I plunged headlong into my research and writing. She knew the passion and burden God placed within me for this work. I thank her for enduring the times when my obsession for it was overwhelming.

A big appreciative thanks to my own children—Juliette, Gabriel, Kimberly, and Marielle—for sharing their father with his computer nearly every night for well over a year as the book was taking shape.

My thanks to Betty Reeder, my typist, for her faithful transcription of Jerry's many tapes. And to Robert Caggiano at Creation House for his insightful editing.

Lastly, my heartfelt appreciation to God and the Holy Spirit for inspiring me, for providing the strength to endure the dry times, for anointing the words on the page, for directing this entire work, for sending His Son to save the bootlegger and his family, and for His saving grace offered to all mankind. And yes…to you, the reader.

Contents

Introduction

THIS IS THE true story of a legendary moonshiner and bootlegger by the name of Jerry Elijah Rushing, who ultimately ran over two million gallons of bootleg moonshine whiskey through the hills of North Carolina. This is also the true story behind the TV show *The Dukes of Hazzard*, a comedy that debuted on January 26, 1979 and ran until August 16, 1985. Though no one expected much from *The Dukes of Hazzard*, especially CBS, it became an instant hit. The network aired the series as a mid-season replacement, and it eventually became one of the hottest comedies of the early 1980s.

Although the Dodge Charger was a popular car, winning twenty-two of fifty-four races during the 1969 NASCAR season, the most popular and recognizable Charger at the beginning of the eighties was not even running NASCAR races—it was setting all kinds of records for the CBS television network.

The show was very simple. It was just an old-fashioned western, but with fast cars and good-looking young folk who were always running from crazy and crooked lawmen. The program was written as

1

a slapstick comedy. The good guys were the bootleggers and moon-shiners who were always at odds with the bad guys, who happened to be the lawmen.

The Dukes of Hazzard centered on the Duke family, cousins Bo, Luke, and Daisy. They lived with their Uncle Jessie and fought the system to run their bootleg whiskey. They were surrounded by the corrupt practices of Hazzard County Commissioner Boss Hogg and his bumbling sheriff, Roscoe P. Coltrane. The show never failed to win its timeslot during the original run on CBS.

But where exactly did *The Dukes of Hazzard* have its roots? Let's go back to an article in *Brute Force* magazine:[1]

> We begin our story with the familiar Friday night scenario.... The bright orange Dodge Charger, Stars and Bars emblazed proudly on its roof and the numbers "01" in bold black fixed to its side, sails deftly through the air landing mag-ically and unscathed across a creek from the pursuing sher-iff. This scene is repeated weekly on television sets across the nation tuned into *The Dukes of Hazzard*. Wild? Unbelievable? The quirk of some lunatic imagination? No. The TV exploits are largely based on the true-life adventures of a country boy named Jerry Rushing.
>
> An article on Rushing in the *National Enquirer* noted, "Rush-ing and his brother once ran moonshine liquor with a pretty cousin who wore shorts and had an Uncle Dooley who was a bit of a philosopher like Uncle Jessie on the television show."

Jerry Rushing was not only a bootlegger and moonshine runner, but he loved country music and wrote many songs. One song that was slightly autobiographical was his song about a North Carolina bootlegger, "that finally went down." It goes something like this:

> So many stories have been written about the big rigs up and
>   down the line,
> That I'd like to tell the story about this ol' rig of mine.
> It's not a big diesel with twin stacks,
> But an old three-quarter flatbed with a camper on back.

1. *Brute Force*, Volume 13, Number 5, July/August 1983

So they're haulin' and I'm doin' the same,
Wild and reckless and hard to tame.

They'll tell you about the pretty waitresses that they've left
    behind.
Well they've left theirs and I've left mine.
They'll tell you about Mary and Betty and Sue,
But I got Judy, Donna, and Pat and Clara, too.
They're a'lovin' and I'm doin' the same,
Wild and reckless and hard to tame.

They'll tell you about the big loads they've pulled up and down
    the hills,
But me, I'm just a plain ol' country boy, workin' these moon-
    shine stills.
Got a fist of iron and foot of lead,
Haulin' that booze on a three-quarter flatbed.
But I'm a'haulin' just the same,
Just wild and reckless and hard to tame.

Late one night they come knockin' on my door.
It was a U.S. Marshall with eight or ten more.
I knew this was the end of my good luck,
When they put on the cuffs and confiscated my truck.
But I'm a'haulin' just the same,
Just wild and reckless and hard to tame.

I'm goin' to miss them gals for three years or four,
But I've got their names written on the jailhouse door.
I'm not too wild and almost tame,
Number four-eight-one, yep that's my name.
Well, I hail from a place called Monroe Town,
A North Carolina bootlegger that finally went down.

—© Jerry E. Rushing

The same *Brute Force* article had this to say:

Prompted into taking the moonshining song to an agent, Jerry
told some of the story behind the song, and the agent was so
impressed that he asked Jerry to carry a tape recorder home and

relate as many of his experiences as possible. From this tape came a Hollywood motion picture called *Moonrunners*, which was the actual story of Jerry Rushing's life. Starring in the movie were Jim Mitchum and Jerry Rushing, playing in a motion picture about his life.

Guy Waldron was a producer and director born in Lennoxburg, Kentucky, and raised in the nearby town of Falmouth. Similar to Jerry Rushing, he grew up in an area where much of the local culture revolved around the automobile, modified stock cars, and running moonshine. Waldron attended the University of Georgia and was hired at a local television station in Atlanta. He had always wanted to write and produce movies that portrayed the backwoods culture of the moonshiner and bootlegger. After he started on the script, Bob Clark, a writer-producer he was collaborating with, suggested they talk to a real-life moonshiner named Jerry Rushing.

According to Rushing, "Bob Clark told me that they were working on a movie script and wanted me to write down the experiences I had both as a moonshiner and a bootlegger. I had been in prison several times and had been in multiple wrecks running moonshine, but I had never been caught running moonshine. I had also raced in a number of the early stock car races and decided that this might be fun. I did not necessarily want to talk to an agent, so I talked into a tape recorder instead and collaborated with him on the movie *Moonrunners*."

According to David Hofstede in the book *The Unofficial Companion of The Dukes of Hazzard,* "This time, the script made it into production, and the film *Moonrunners* was shot in Griffin, Georgia, and released by United Artists in April 1975. Guy Waldron directed the movie and Bob Clark was the executive producer. Jerry Rushing served as the technical advisor and also preformed much of the stunt driving."

The opening credits of *Moonrunners* stated, "Although the characters herein are fictitious, some of the events are based upon incidents in the life of Jerry Rushing, who also served as technical advisor."

The movie *Moonrunners* ultimately attracted the attention of Phil Mandelker, producer at Warner Brothers Television. Mandelker was interested in Waldron writing a TV show with the identical flavor of

Moonrunners, but as a comedy. The family would be the good guys, though they were all on probation because they used to be moonshine runners, and the bad guys would be the law. There was a complete flip-flopping in what normally would be the public expectation—the moonrunners being the bad folk and the law being the good guys. The TV program was an immediate hit.

Consider the following similarities between the life of Jerry Rushing and *The Dukes of Hazzard:*

✱ The original moonrunners were Jerry Rushing and his brother Johnny. In the TV program they were cousins Bo Duke and Luke Duke.

✱ Uncle Dooley was the family moonshiner, who had passed down his craft from previous generations. He was a type of philosopher. In *The Dukes of Hazzard,* this character is Uncle Jessie who was also the philosopher and original moonshiner of the family.

✱ Jerry and Johnny Rushing had a cousin named Dixie who occasionally assisted them in getting out of trouble, and loved to hang around the old moonshiners and bootleggers listening to their wild stories. In *The Dukes of Hazzard,* this was Daisy Duke, played by Catherine Bach.

✱ There was a beer joint by the name of the Pig Pen, which became famous for selling illegal moonshine and also dealing in drugs and prostitution. *The Dukes of Hazzard* had a place called the Boar's Nest, the truck stop where Daisy Duke worked.

✱ In real life, the pit was run by D. Jay Bailey, nicknamed Hog Jaw. He was portrayed as the character Jefferson Davis (JD) Hogg by the actor Sorrell Booke in *The Dukes of Hazzard.*

✱ Another interesting similarity is the fact that Jerry and Johnny had both been in prison for some of their moonshine activities and were on probation. This meant they could not own a firearm and could only carry a bow and arrow. One might remember that Bo and Luke were also on probation in the TV series and never carried a firearm, but used their bows.

★ The most amazing similarity between the life of Jerry Rushing and *The Dukes of Hazzard* TV show was the car. *The Dukes of Hazzard* car was a 1969 Dodge Charger painted orange and named the *General Lee*. In the real life of Jerry Rushing, he had a favorite car named *Traveler*. The real car was not orange, but white.

The *Brute Force* article picks up the story:

It was not called the *General Lee,* either. It was called *Traveler,* the name of General Robert E. Lee's horse. And it was not a Dodge Charger. It was a Chrysler, and not just any Chrysler, but a 1958 Chrysler 300-D. And not just any 300-D, it had been especially prepared as a moonrunner to run moonshine liquor.

The bottom of the rear seat had been removed to allow cases of moonshine to be loaded into the back and into the trunk. Tubes running from under the rear bumper to the tank in the trunk held oil for releasing an oil slick into the path of the pursuing federal agents. A switch under the dash allowed the driver to cut off the brake lights when navigating steep mountain turns. It was an excellent device for dissuading federal agents from following close and taking steep turns while following the brake lights ahead.

While Chrysler Corporation was busy selling the 300-D by racing their cars under carefully prepared stock car rules, *Traveler* had been outrunning federal agents for years under far from ideal conditions and its speed far in excess of Chrysler's claims for top speeds. Many times, *Traveler* topped 140 miles per hour on the two-lane mountain highways and the dirt farm roads of North Carolina.

Throughout these pages, you will learn of a man torn between the love of his family and his love for racing—and the loves of his life, moonshining and bootlegging. You will witness the tragedies in the home and on the road, the disastrous accidents in which Jerry Rushing nearly lost his life, and the dark side of the bootleggers life—separation from his family while behind bars.

This is the spiritual adventure of a man that not only ran whiskey but also ran another race. Jerry Rushing ran from God for nearly forty years. You will experience the grace of God that spared his life time and time again. You will also experience the love of a wife that stood by her man and the love of a daughter who loved her daddy despite the life he led.

You will hear his cry for help when he reached the depths of the deep, dark pit of sin. Then you will stand and shout when the bootlegger had a spiritual transformation and accepted Jesus Christ as his Savior. It was only through spiritual rebirthing that God was able to replace the anger in Jerry with His love and replace the hate in Jerry's heart with His grace and forgiveness.

Hang onto your boots and enjoy the ride; in the meantime, my prayer is that God will richly bless you and change your life as you run the hills of Carolina with Jerry Elijah Rushing.

Buckle up and jump in!

CHAPTER 1

Inheriting the Moonshine Legacy

LIL' OLD SNAKE

THE GENTLE EVENING breeze rustled through the oak trees out front of the little cabin. Nestled back into the trees off the rural route in Monroe, the cabin was nearly hidden from view. Those twisted oak limbs had stretched far up into the heavens as long as any member of the Rushing family could remember. They had supported many old tire swings, and the little tots of several generations of the family had taken their turns swinging in those old oak trees.

It was autumn. Autumn was beautiful in North Carolina, from the eastern coastline, through the Piedmont, right up to the great Blue Ridge Mountains. North Carolina was a true, proud Southern state that had pledged all its men and most of its wealth wholeheartedly to the Confederacy. Right about the center of the state between the waves of the Atlantic and the peaks of the Blue Ridge was Union County. Near the very center of Union County was the county seat, the rural town of Monroe. Situated twenty-five miles southeast of Charlotte, Monroe was a little town comprised of good, hard-working people.

So in the center of the state was Union County, and in the center of Union County was the town of Monroe, and in the town of Monroe lived a little boy who was about to go on his very first moonshine run. He was no taller than three feet and could not have weighed much more than a wet potato sack. He had disheveled reddish-brown hair that hung in long strands over his ears and collar, and he was dressed in his favorite pair of overalls.

In fact, it was his only pair of overalls.

He was always a skinny kid. His long, lean arms hung down well below his trouser pockets, and his scrawny legs were no bigger around than his arms. He was kidded a lot by his family because he was by far the skinniest youngster born into the family. He may even have been the skinniest kid in the whole county. They used to say he was skinnier than a long, lanky woods possum and ganglier than a North Carolina rattler. In fact, that was exactly how this little boy got the nickname that stuck with him throughout his childhood . . . "Snake."

"Hey, Snake, we're running out tonight," his daddy yelled. Snake answered well to his name. It was not a proper or nice-sounding name, but it fit his tall, wiry appearance, and, in a strange way, it fit the rural country of these parts of North Carolina.

It was chilly that autumn night, and his dad had already warmed up the old 1938 Ford. "Snake, let's go," his daddy yelled again from the front porch. Snake ran out to the truck and pulled his cap down over his ears. Where other young boys in Monroe played stickball or kick the can, Snake was different. He was a third-generation moonshiner. His grandpa made and sold bootleg whisky. His daddy made and ran the stuff through the hills of North Carolina. Now, the youngest of the Rushings walked in the footsteps of his forefathers.

Though only four years old on that chilly night, Snake never forgot it. That evening's experience was his first real recollection of the moonshine business that shaped and molded his life for many years. His daddy pulled the '38 Ford closer to the house and blew the horn loud and long.

"Come on, son," he yelled again as Snake jumped into the front seat and smiled at his dad. Being included was significant to Snake. He felt important and loved, something that did not come easy in 1930s Union County—especially in the Rushing household. Life was hard, and only the tough survived. Snake knew early on that he too would have to be tough and hard one day. He also knew that he was a survivor, and survive he would.

The Ford sped away and threw gravel at each turn as they headed out for some more sugar, yeast, wheat bran, cornmeal, and anything else needed for another batch of illegal moonshine whiskey. There was an old man's house down the country road a bit, and they often loaded up their supplies from him. Sugar and yeast bought in bulk had to be kept undercover because it pointed to a backwoods still that sat on top of a fire, next to a stream, and dripped its newly condensed batch of whisky into gallon jugs ready to be run to a countryside thirsty for that old mountain dew.

Some called it moonshine.

But little Snake heard it referred to by many a strange name. Some called it "corn liquor," while others referred to it as "white lightning" or "sugar whiskey." However, in an attempt to hide their moonshining from the law, many moonshiners and bootleggers had special code words they used to discuss their specialized business. This was almost a special language, a lingo of sorts, within their own moonshine culture: "skull cracker," "ruckus juice," "rotgut," "catdaddy," "tiger's sweat," "happy sally," or even "hillbilly pop." But it made no difference what they called the fire-biting stuff. It was all the same—illegal, homemade, backwoods alcohol that burned when it went down and knocked down the largest of men.

Snake stood around intently and watched his daddy and the old man as they loaded the sacks of sugar, yeast, and an assortment of other moonshine goodies into the back of the old Ford. They finished loading their supplies and tossed in a couple of old buckets and a few wooden kegs. After they squared up with the old man and promised to pay for the goods after the next bootleg run, Snake and his daddy took off toward home again. That was his life.

THE THREE GENERATIONS

Snake's real name was Jerry Elijah Rushing. Born in Monroe, North Carolina to a family of notorious bootleggers, little Jerry was actually a third-generation bootlegger. One might say he was a Christmas present that year since he was born on a cold, snowy day just six days before Christmas on December 19, 1936. His daddy was Espy Rushing, the next to youngest boy in the Rushing family of eleven children. Jerry's daddy made whiskey with his father, Atlas Rushing, throughout Prohibition.

No one ever knew where Granddaddy Atlas got his money. He was a farmer and had a lot of money for those days, especially in Union County. Most people were farmers after the Civil War tore through the heart of North Carolina. They remained farmers down to Granddaddy Atlas's days. He was married to Melissa Jane Rushing. A stingy woman of sorts.

"Grandma doesn't really like me much," lil' Snake shared with his friends.

Snake and his family lived some with his grandpa and grandma, but Snake had no real family connection with Grandma Melissa Jane.

"She's an awfully stingy granny," Snake said. Why he felt his grandma was stingy, he doesn't really know. But that was not the case with his granddaddy. Actually, Granddaddy Atlas bought his children a farm in the county. Perhaps, some thought, Atlas got his money from farming. But maybe the hard-to-come-by cash in his pockets came from his private moonshine still. One of Union County's largest moonshine whiskey operations was hidden back in the hill country.

A still of ten gallons was quite large during Prohibition. But Granddaddy Atlas had a specially built fifty-gallon still that turned out some of the best-tastin' cornmash whiskey in the region. He sold his whiskey by word of mouth. When the word got out, the whiskey ran. Perhaps he was Monroe's first bootleg whiskey-financed land buyer and developer. Regardless of how Granddaddy Atlas amassed his fortune, several offspring acquired one hundred acres each. No wonder the desire to make that sweet burning firewater just seemed to be in old Snake's bones. It ran through his system like the blood in his veins.

Moonshinin' was not a desire to break the law or do something bad. It was a generational thing. It was Snake's legacy—an inheritance, a birthright—and his Southern-born and -bred heritage. His granddaddy Atlas made moonshine, and his daddy, Espy Rushing, made moonshine. Old Snake's earliest recollections of both his daddy and granddaddy were the trips to pick up that old wheat bran stuff and then trucking the wheat bran into the woods—deep into the woods where the fire ran under the kettle and the moon would shine all night.

It was a hard life back there for Snake, living in the Rushing household. His daddy was a very hard man. Perhaps he learned the "hardness" of his ways from his daddy. Day after day, night after night, Espy would come home drunk. Some people made moonshine only to sell. It became a manufacturing and retailing operation for them. But others, like Snake's daddy, would make a jug to sell and then make a jug to drink.

Jerry knew, as he grew up, that his daddy was rough, hot-tempered, and often ready for a fight. He was never interested in making whiskey on a large scale, but he made enough of the stuff to pay the bills. It was a cycle he never grew out of. Most in the county knew Espy as the moonshiner that would end up drinking more of his homemade 'shine than he sold. You might say he was closer to his whiskey than he was to his little boy.

Snake hated when his daddy got all liquored up. Espy often embarrassed the entire family when he had been drinking, such as the time he and Snake went into town for some simple supplies. Espy had been sipping on the moonshine for a couple of days straight when he and his son headed for town.

"Daddy, what are we going to town for?" little Snake asked.

"Mama needs some thangs from th'store, and I needs ta run me a few errands," his daddy replied, with that all-too-familiar slur that accompanied his sipping escapades.

Oh, Lord, Snake thought to himself, *I just hope Daddy doesn't cause a scene. He always gets into fights and makes me feel so stupid and embarrassed.*

Well, that prayer did not seem to work. They were not in the store for more than a minute or two when Espy started yelling at the supply clerk.

"Whattaya mean, you don't have any of these? You should keep these on the shelf. Now I can't finish muh work. How'd you like a good old-fashioned butt-kickin'?" Espy yelled, as he continued to back the little store clerk into a corner.

About that time, Snake ran out the front door and onto the wooden front porch of the store. It happened again, and young Snake had trouble handling the humiliation. He did not like the scene his daddy caused, and silently, standing alone outside the store, little Jerry wondered why his prayer had not worked.

So, like many times before, Snake prayed the prayer he had prayed many times before on occasions like this one. In fact, this was one of Snake's very first prayers, *Lord, please kill me. I'm so embarrassed. Go ahead and let me die . . . take my life . . . do it anyway You want to do it. It's just too hard to live with all of this. I can't keep facing the kids at school. I'm just too embarrassed. I'm too tired of this. I'm just too tired. Let me die . . . let me die . . . let me die, please.*

Fortunately for Snake, God did not answer his sad little prayer. But there were many days in Snake's young life when he repeated this prayer over and over standing outside that rundown country store, life's heavy burdens weighing on his little shoulders and his troubled spirit. What a terrible prayer for any child to pray. What a heavy burden to carry for the little tyke.

The burden grew heavier each day for Snake as his daddy yelled, cussed, and screamed at him. Snake just tried to survive. He was just a little fellow and could barely handle the pressure of these daily struggles. Each day had enough brawls and scrapes for an entire lifetime.

Most of young Snake's life was difficult, but his daddy's cussing hurt the most. It was like long sharp arrows pierced his soul and landed— bull's-eye—squarely on his sensitive little heart. Snake carries those wounds of his childhood with him—wounds of a moonshine drinkin' father are slow to heal, especially when he grew up without the childhood love and concern most children receive.

Snake rarely shared his innermost feelings with those around him, but there were many days when he headed out to the deep, dark woods, his sanctuary of sorts, and felt the breeze, talked to the trees, and soaked in the beauty of the forest. It was in a moment like that when the little boy's thoughts were drawn to the harshness of his life and the hardness of his father. On one such occasion, young Snake sat down and leaned back into an old oak while thinking about his father.

Why doesn't he love me? Snake asked the stately trees that sheltered him from the hot summer sun. *Why doesn't my daddy ever say he loves me?* Those questions never left Snake. To this day, he cannot remember his daddy ever telling him he loved him. Why do men become so hard in life, especially to those around them that they should care for and love?

Espy was a hard man in general, but he was especially hard on young Snake. One summer day, Espy told Snake to sit still and keep an eye on their dog. Jerry was only three or four years old as he sat on the front porch step and watched the dog slumber in the grass. But he was little, and the entire world called out for an adventurer to run the hills and explore the valleys. Explore he did—until Daddy came back. When Espy saw the dog running wild without the watchful eye of young Snake, he ran through the yard and found the little boy skipping stones in the pond. He grabbed Snake by the ear and began wildly beating him. Arms flailing, Snake screamed as he took a beating from his father that no animal should have to endure.

"Dad, stop!" the young boy screamed while little tears raced down his dirty cheeks. "Stop, you're hurting me! You're going to kill me!"

"Don't ever disobey me again!" Espy screamed. "Never again . . . never again . . . never, never!"

Young Snake never really knew why he took such beatings. He just knew that when he did, he could not sit down for an entire week. The red hand and switch markings turned into whelps, and the whelps turned into blue-green bruises just under his skin.

Slowly, all signs of physical pain vanished while the hurt of being unloved cut deep into the soul of the little boy from Union County. As he grew up, he found that those emotional wounds took longer to heal than the physical ones. Espy beat him more and more until the day a caring "family hand" witnessed a harsh beating and told him, "Enough is enough, Espy. If you don't stop losing your temper, one day you could kill that kid. You've gotta stop it. It's just not right. It's not at all right."

Well, whether Espy's conscience got the best of him or he just decided to heed the warnings, the beatings did slack off. But the little boy never heard the words he yearned to hear, just three simple words that he would have given the world to hear from his father, "I love you." Funny how the lack of just three little words, just eight little letters, could leave such a void in a little boy's life. Strange how long a little void lingered in a grown man's soul.

Though his daddy was a hard-spirited man, his mama was tender-hearted. She hated the drinking, and she hated when Espy ran out of the house, drinking and driving.

Snake had many rough memories of his daddy drinking and his mother crying. In fact, he grew up with the idea that most daddies drank incessantly while most mamas cried continuously. Why wouldn't he? Most every night started with drinking and ended with crying. He was getting used to it.

One typical Friday night, after supper, there was nothing left on the table but a few empty plates and a bowl of gravy. The empty plates that night held a few rabbit bones and a squirrel bone or two. Little Snake was only five years old and enjoyed playing through the day with some friends who lived close to the farm. For this young country boy, catching frogs and snakes was a start that lead to trapping fox, raccoons, beavers, and muskrats. But that day, the frogs and snakes seemed to be such a prize.

"Hey, Daddy, did you see my pet frog?" Snake sheepishly asked. "I found him hopping around the stone pile in the back. He's a pretty green color, isn't he Daddy?"

"Sure," Espy barked. "Sure it is."

Had the pressures of life in Monroe pressed old Espy into the mold of a cynical and case-hardened man with no real concern for his family? Or had his homemade "catdaddy" and "skullcracker" from his rough-built still finally taken its toll on this second-generation moonshiner? Regardless of the cause of his hardness, it took a toll on the entire Rushing clan.

Espy grabbed his jug sitting beside the rocker and headed to the door.

"Please don't go out drinkin' tonight, Espy . . . please don't go," Snake's mama cried. "You're drinking too much these days, Espy . . . you've gotta stop . . . please."

But Espy had his mind made up. Or, perhaps, the "ruckus juice" had set his mind for him.

"Outta the way, woman!" he spat out. "I gotta go . . . got stuff to do . . . the brew's a brewin'."

Snake watched the scene unfold this night as he had many nights before. Each night played out the same, and tonight would be no different. His mama walked to the sofa and fell back exhausted from the burdens she was carrying.

"I care for the family all day long, and care for Espy, and he just goes out a'drinkin' and cares for nobody or nothing."

She started crying and cried from then on. The old truck sped out of the driveway, and she cried. Espy burned his tires, which screamed like an old hoot owl as he picked up speed. Mama Rushing continued to cry hurtful sobs. Tears and hurt mingled with despair. Snake gazed at his crying mother with fearful eyes; he wanted only to be accepted and loved. But a life composed of a drinking father and a crying mother was his lot—love and acceptance were nowhere to be found.

He wished life would be different, as sometimes his mother cried for a week straight. That night she cried all night long, and the next morning Snake was shocked at what he saw. Wiping the sleep from his eyes, he came into the kitchen hoping for a hug, with other hopes that his mama would have stopped the constant crying from the night before. But his hopes were dashed like waves upon the rocky shore when his eyes met his mother's eyes.

"Mama," Snake cried, "what's wrong with your eyes?"

"Nothing," she replied, trying to hide her swollen eyes. "It must be the allergies."

"Mama . . . what are allergies?" Snake persisted.

"Just puffiness around the eyes. It will go away in a few days. Don't you worry your little head. I'm OK . . . I'm OK." The "I'm OKs" softly, slowly blurred into the morning, replaced by the salty aroma of country ham burning in the frying pan on the stove while his mama continued to cry. She vainly tried to turn the ham, as she watched it through one small slit in her puffed-up left eye.

It was not an allergy. Snake, though young in years, knew better. His mama's eyes were puffed up and inflamed as if she was on the moonshine herself. But moonshine was not her choice. She had cried all night long, and now her tear-burned eyes finally gave up the ghost and closed for the day. She barely made out little Snake's image standing there in the kitchen alone. Snake saw it before and would witness this sad course of events many times over.

At least she *loves me,* he thought, as he pulled himself from his mother's presence and watched her tease the ham with the fork. *At least* she *loves me,* he thought. But he knew he was only kidding himself since he did not remember his mama saying she loved him. *Why is the statement "I love you" so difficult in this Rushing household?* he pondered quietly to himself. As if that was not harm enough for a five-year-old trying to exist within a moonshine and bootleg environment, his mother never even put her arms around him. He had dreams of it happening one day, but they remained dreams and existed only in the wishful imagination of a little boy who merely wanted to be loved.

As his mother cried and the salty pork belly burned, little Snake retreated to the outdoors and into his sanctuary of solitude in the deep, dark woods. In fact, until later in life, this was the only sanctuary he ever found.

The evening ritual continued for years as the events played and replayed like a recurring nightmare. Espy drank and Mama cried. The sun went down and then returned for another day, and Espy continued his affair with his "mistress of the backwoods"—the Rushing bittersweet corn liquor.

The cycle repeated until one cold day when Snake was well into early manhood. Espy was out on a local farmer's pond just paddling about in a small rusty johnboat he borrowed from the shoreline. Later, many that had passed by on that fateful day said they saw old Espy paddling from here to there and back again. But he was not fishing in that little metal boat, and there was nowhere to go on that little pond.

"So what was he doing?" many wondered.

Perhaps he was just relaxing on that cold day, enjoying the warmth of the late-winter sun. Or better yet, perhaps Espy enjoyed another type of warmth on that chilly day. Possibly he was just enjoying the taste of some homemade brew as it burned his tongue and warmed his innards. To this day, no one really knows whether it was the coldness of that winter day, the iciness of the chilled pond water, or the liquor that may have finally poisoned him from within.

A passerby stopped when he saw the man in the boat slip silently over the bow into the dark winter water. He waited for the man to surface. He called for help, and Snake was first on the scene. Even though Snake was now older and stronger, no longer the little boy Espy cussed, Espy was still his dad.

Hoping his dad may have just exited the pond and headed into the nearby woods, Snake hollered, "Dad…Dad…Dad." But there was no answer. Snake dived deep into the cold, dark abyss to search for his father. He felt around the muddy bottom until his lungs burned for air and forced him back to the surface. Once his lungs were revived again, Snake searched the bottom to find his father. Finally, after many attempts, his hand caught the cold, rough hand of the daddy he had wanted to love. His hand caught the hand that had whipped and beaten him repeatedly.

Despite past hurts and troubles, he did not want it to end like this. He grabbed his daddy's arm and kicked hard until he had him back to the surface. But it was too late—Espy was gone.

Forty-five years young, and Espy departed from his life of whiskey drinking, moonshine making, and humiliating Snake inside the country store.

It was an awful thing to find your father at the bottom of a pond. It was a memory that haunted Snake for years. It was another heartbreak in a series of heartbreaks for him. Though Espy was no longer around drinking and sipping his homemade stuff, Snake's mama continued to cry. Now Espy was gone, and it was the void that was left that caused Mama's tears. Snake watched his mother from afar and kept his own feelings, hurts, and pains buried deep inside. Though there were questions as to whether Espy drowned or died of a heart attack, the family doctor said it was a heart attack.

I really don't care if I live or die, Snake would cry within himself. *I really don't give a hoot. It really doesn't make any difference anymore.* And with that, they buried Espy deep in the ground with a small graveside service on a windy, cold day as his son buried his own feelings just as deep.

Early Excitement and Thrills

Though the Rushing household was void of love, it had its share of excitement. Excitement was not a surrogate for parental love and concern, and the occasional thrills and frequent adventures provided sufficient enough excitement to take Snake's mind off his immediate troubles.

His granddaddy Atlas was often sick and had a hard time getting around. Many of the younger Rushings visited their granddaddy and grandma and stayed at their house assisting the older folks with some of the day's simple country chores. Snake liked those visits because they often meant listening to story after story of the earlier moonshining days. His favorite visits were to see his great-granddaddy who must have been ninety-four or ninety-five years old. Jerry's great-granddaddy was the oldest man he ever met. Sometimes Jerry just sat and stared at this very old man. But when his great-granddaddy got started with his stories, little Jerry sat for hours spellbound by the magic of the old man spinnin' tales.

"Ya know that crazy Jessie would come a 'ridin' to your great-great-great-granddaddy's place many years ago. He'd stop by the old homestead jes fer something to eat." His great-granddaddy just loved to brag.

"Jessie?" Snake asked with eyes as big as Morgan silver dollars. "You mean the real Jessie James?"

Snake heard this story on most every trip to see his great-granddaddy. But each story was exciting, and each story seemed to take on a life of its own.

"Yep, and I mean the real McCoy... I heard it straight from my granddaddy. It was a hot summer day and your great-great-great-grandma had just fixed a bunch of those old greens with a chunk of wild boar thrown in fer flavor. They were about to sit down t'eat when Jessie James himself and a group'a his boys came a'ridin' up to the house."

Snake sat still as a statue with both eyes fixed on his great-granddaddy while he continued with his spinnin'.

"He and his boys rode right up to the front porch. In fact, old Jessie's horse actually ran so fast and stopped so quick that both of his front hoofs landed on top of the porch floor while his back hoofs remained glued to the grass in front of the first step. It was a very funny sight. He said the boys were hungry, so they invited the whole bunch of them in for wild boar and greens. They loved it."

Once his great-granddaddy got started and had a captive audience, even if it was just Snake, he seldom slowed down. Sometimes facts got stirred up with a bit of imagination and some fiction—just the right recipe for an exciting afternoon for the little great-grandson.

So great-granddaddy continued, "Jessie and his boys were on their way to visit Rubin James at Marshall, North Carolina. It wasn't the first time they came by, and it wasn't the last. Boy, did I ever tell you of the time Jessie James needed another rider? He needed one more rider when they were headed out of Union County into the northern part of South Carolina to jump a train carrying gold from the mountains back to the Midwest. My granddaddy grabbed his rifle..."

The old man closed his eyes for a moment and yawned a giant yawn.

"He grabbed his rifle..."

Another yawn, larger and longer than the first one, interrupted the fascinating story.

"Boy, I will never forget it. He grabbed..."

With that last breath, his great-granddaddy, full of stories of Jessie James and his boys, quietly drifted into the deep, soft slumber that is mostly reserved for very old men. As the old man drifted, the little boy's eyelids grew heavier and heavier until at last he joined his great-granddaddy in dreamland with Jessie and the boys. They often rode together.

When Snake and his vivid imagination were not riding with his great-granddaddy and the James boys, you might have found him, on a typical day, fetching supplies for the moonshine operation or playing around the stills in the backwoods. He loved playing in the woods where he trapped some of the smaller game or skinny-dipped in a local creek with some buddies. Basically, Snake was just an all-American country boy that loved the outdoors and just happened to be born into a moonshine family.

A Hint of the Gospel

Being a member of the Rushing clan in the time period just after Prohibition, little Snake's inheritance was as much the moonshinin' and the bootleggin' as was his Rushing surname. His heritage was grounded in the Carolina backwoods mystique; he was as Southern as any son of the Confederacy. North Carolina was known for its country corn liquor and was the home of many true-grit confederate soldiers. Even the famous boy colonel, Henry K. Burgwyn Jr., was from this great southern state. But not only was North Carolina known for its role in the great War between the States and its white lightning, it was also the center of the "Bible Belt" of the old South.

The Bible Belt was derived from the Fundamentalist movement during the first part of the twentieth century. It was a conservative Protestant movement that crossed over many denominational lines that had naturally developed as the population grew. The Bible Belt was founded on the literal interpretation of the Bible and ultimately became a strong component of the culture of the South. It stretched from Virginia through the Carolinas into the deeper southern states and through the southern plains into parts of the Midwest.

The Bible Belt's greatest religious influence came about with Prohibition, a temperance movement that gained popularity within church culture of the late nineteenth and early twentieth centuries. Church leaders led their congregations against the evils of drunkenness and attempted to close most of their town's saloons either by prayer or violence, whichever worked. Ultimately many of those states' political candidates helped pass state laws banning saloons, which then led to the Woman's Christian Temperance Union. The WCTU, along with the Anti-Saloon League of America, succeeded in passing the Eighteenth Amendment to the Constitution, which became federal law as the Volstead Act of 1920.

The legislation banned the manufacture, sale, and transportation of alcohol. It was into this anti-drinking, anti-saloon Bible Belt of the South that Snake was born. Though his family tradition was rich in moonshine culture of the day, which was actually perpetuated by the Prohibition laws, his family life and upbringing were void of Bible Belt influences.

Sunday mornings were no different from any other morning. Breakfast, chores, and work to be completed were the agenda for most of the seven days in a typical week. Such was the case one particular Sunday as Snake ran out of the house and started another adventurous day. He was no five or six years old when he began to wonder what church was all about. He saw a friend heading down the road with his family, and Snake immediately ran back into the house to find his mama working in the kitchen. He slammed the front door behind him and ran as little boys do, slipping and sliding on the old wood kitchen floor, until he about knocked his mama over.

"Mama, why do some people get so dressed up on Sundays?" Snake inquired. "I just saw Billy and his family going down the road in some of those fancy things…and his mama had a hat on her head with a pretty pink feather."

"Church stuff is not for us, son. We have too much work around here, and your daddy has never been too up on that church stuff. Besides, your daddy is too liquored up from Saturday to ever make it anywhere on a Sunday morning."

With that said, his mama laughed a forced chuckle as if the sad fact of Espy's drinking held some tiny nugget of humor for her. The truth was, most Sunday mornings would find her still crying from the night before—and the night before that. Most Sunday mornings would find Espy down at his still drinking as much of that Rushing moonshine as he had bottled.

Though Snake was still young, he felt a little bit sorry for his mama, and he even felt a bit of sadness for himself. Somewhere down deep, he wondered what church was all about. Billy had mentioned something about "prayer," which was not something you heard about from the Rushings. In fact, Jerry had never heard any of his family get together and pray. They did not pray before breakfast. They did not pray before lunch or dinner, and they never prayed at night. But there came a day in his life when an older Jerry Rushing needed prayer—a day came when, without the care of a loving and praying wife, his life just might have ended early. Ultimately, Snake's life could have been wrecked, ruined, and finished without the power of prayer. But for now, the little boy from Monroe could only wonder what a church was or what prayer was for.

Fortunately for Snake, his small schoolhouse had a teacher that read exciting adventure stories from the Bible each day. Snake loved adventure and listened attentively as the teacher breathed life into the stories of Noah, Gideon, David, Goliath, and others. One of his favorites was David and Goliath.

"So he really killed that giant with a slingshot?" Snake asked. "Just a slingshot?"

Slingshots were something any kid made with a forked limb, a pocketknife, and some rubber from an old inner tube. Snake related to slingshots because he hunted many rabbits and squirrels with his homemade weapons.

"Just a slingshot…and that big old ugly giant was killed?"

"Well," his teacher often told the children, "never forget that God was with him."

"God was with him," she stressed.

Little Jerry never forgot those Bible stories. He remembered all of them and recounted many of them for his little friends or family if they asked. Somehow he knew his teachers believed in God. They taught about Him. And somehow, Snake knew his mama must have believed in God. That thought came from many instances, like the time he told his mama to "shush."

"Mama, just be quiet," Snake yelled on one occasion from the back room. Well, it took her no time at all to scuttle on over to that side of the house and grab the little one by his ear.

"What did you say?" she asked. "Did you tell me to shush? Boy, that is so disrespectful, I should give you an old-fashioned whippin'."

"No, mama, I'm sorry…please don't whip me."

"Well, then, I'm gonna stand here until you ask the Lord to forgive you for such disrespectin'. Go ahead, tell the Lord yer sorry and you won't do it again," she continued.

As his mama stood over him, with the threat of an oak-switch thrashing, the little boy bowed his head and asked the Lord to forgive him. We do not know how much of this "forgiveness thing" little Snake really understood, but that was a start. In that moonshinin' family that never prayed, there were small spiritual seeds planted by a schoolteacher and a crying mama. The occasional prayer of forgiveness for some childhood silliness coupled with the little Bible stories in school were the foundation God used to ultimately get little Jerry's attention.

God loves the moonshiner and the bootlegger. Despite Espy's drinking and the generations of whiskey making, God loved the Rushing family. Though prayer was never heard, God was always listening.

That's just how God is.

Though no one called on His name, God never stopped being attentive for that call. He could use a mama's tears, a repentant little boy's prayer, or even a simple school Bible story to plant seeds of His love into the heart of this third-generation moonshiner. And plant seeds He did. The seeds of spirituality sat dormant for many years, but the little boy grew up to be a large strapping man grasping at his apparent Rushing birthright to become the fastest and most feared bootlegger in the South. He seized the bootleg legacy of the Rushings that was laid out before him and ran the race with gusto. But somewhere deep within, the seeds were there. God's love was there.

After a long and winding run, and years of dancing with the devil on the backwood roads of his Carolina homeland, those small seeds eventually brought him home.

But it took a long time.

CHAPTER 2

Mountain Moonshine and the First Whiskey Run

IT IS JUST INBRED

FROM AN EARLY age, Snake held a certain fascination for moonshine culture. Making whiskey was more or less a normal family tradition. It just seemed like an ordinary Union County way of life. Having grown up in the Rushing family, it was actually the easiest part of the family inheritance for Snake to take hold of. It seemed as American to the folks of the Carolinas as baseball, mom, and apple pie to the rest of nation.

So what exactly was moonshining, and what was bootlegging? Here are the basics.

A moonshiner was a person who made illegal whiskey, while the bootlegger was a person that sold and distributed the illegal whiskey. Tough farmers and mountaineers, primarily in the mountains and lowcountry hills of Appalachia, made illegal whiskey for generations. Moonshining was very popular in most places in the South during the late nineteenth and early twentieth centuries. It was primarily concentrated in the Blue Ridge Mountains of Tennessee, western South Carolina, and parts of central and western North Carolina.

Jerry and his family were proud to be called moonshiners. The term *moonshiner* was derived from the word *moonlighter*. This term was first used to describe night smugglers of brandy from Holland and France. As early as 1785, illegal brandy was sold from the coasts of Kent and Sussex and referred to as "moonshine." During the early twentieth century in North Carolina, making unlawful whiskey was done at night, hidden in some country woodland corner or secretly concealed up some forgotten trail deep in the Appalachians. The distilling of whiskey needed to be hidden from the law, and that meant being hidden from any light source. The whiskey was made by the light of the moon—in other words, by "moonshine."

Consider one of Snake's earliest experiences making moonshine with his daddy. He was still a little tot and loved helping in the woods. He hiked into the woods with his daddy and followed a stream back to the still. The moon shone brightly on Union County, providing just enough light through the canopy of lofty pine trees that swayed with the wind and provided cover for this clandestine operation. Snake and his daddy had new bottles to fill, and the mash from the day before was ready to be boiled into that clear brew that was so popular among the locals. Mash was a mixture of corn, sugar, and yeast that starts to ferment and was used for producing a fine whiskey brew. Their family recipe was like a magical firey potion, and the Rushings took great pride in their family brand of this brew.

"Fire up that still pot and add a bit more mash into it, Snake," his daddy would yell. "We need more of that oak stack to keep the fire running through the night. Keep it hot, but not too hot. The still needs to run at about 170 degrees."

"Sure, Daddy, I just put some wood on the fire from the wood we stacked last night," Snake responded.

Later, when Snake was a teenager, he liked hanging around the old stills hidden in the woods where he had played as a little boy. But tonight, he stoked the fire, stacked some of the old oak logs, and sat down on another. He watched the sparks rise into the shadowy black sky and burn themselves out. They disappeared as if they were vanishing into the night air so as not to be discovered by a local sheriff or some federal revenuer on the prowl.

The distillation process by which the clear brew was made required heat from a wood-fueled fire to boil the alcoholic liquor from the prepared "mash." The process produced a great deal of smoke and steam that was visible from a long distance, which could give away the location of the still. On a clear night, Snake could actually stack the logs, feed them to the fire, and do it all with no other light source but the illumination of the moon.

Snake stared into the white-hot blaze as the coals glowed and the fire flickered, spitting sparks into the air. It was so quiet as he sat there. Just then a screech owl let loose with a shriek that split the night in two. Snake's troubles seemed worlds away as he sat before the dancing flames. There was no swollen-eyed mama, and his daddy was preoccupied with the stirring of the mash and making the liquor. Espy had no time to scream, holler, or curse the son of his youth.

Snake grew up hunting, fishing, and trapping. He loved being immersed in the natural wilderness. In fact, most of his young life was spent in the woods. He felt at one with nature because it calmed his "buck-wild" nerves and soothed his soul. To a certain extent he liked making liquor because it was an outdoor thing, like hunting. He loved to get out of the house to help put these stills in their hiding spots in the woods.

One often heard Snake bragging on a night like this one, "I don't know what I like best—huntin', trappin', brewin', or just lookin' at the pretty girls in town." He continued, "Shucks, I guess I really like it all. A day with huntin' and trappin' mixed with a night of brewin' would just be heaven."

"Heaven…" he pondered, as he considered what he liked best. "I like all that stuff, but my heart belongs in the fast lane where the whiskey runs through the county and the rubber of my hot runnin' tires squeals while they leave black tread tracks at every one hundred mile per hour turn."

You see, some boys were moonshiners and took great pride in their corn-whiskey manufacturing operation, while others specialized in the actual selling or delivery of the unlawful liquor— or "bootleg-ging." The origin of the term *bootlegging* is still debated. Some believe the expression refers to a time in colonial America when many of the colonists sold the homemade "fire water" to Native Americans. As the story goes, many of the colonists attempted to trade the illegal spirits to Indians for some of the Indian's beadwork. Since many of the Puritan colonists tried to prevent this trade activity, the sellers of the juice often concealed bottles or small jugs of the liquor in the top of their boots. They then covered their bulging boots with the bottom of their pant legs, hence the term, *bootlegger*. Others believe that the term *bootlegger* originated in the Civil War when illegal whiskey trafficking within the federal troops was prevalent. The soldiers, who peddled the unlawful goods, hid the small flasks or bottles in their cowhide bootlegs until a sale or trade took place under the cloak of darkness, during battle, or in a nearby tent.

But to Snake, it made no difference where the term originated. He was a growing young man who loved the adventure of the moonshine business and the bootlegging of those spirits. As long as he could remember, he wanted to be a whiskey runner. Not just the run-of-the-mill Carolina moonrunner, but the best darn runner in the state. He often bragged about his life's ambition to any that would listen.

"Y'all jes wait," Snake bragged to his friends while lounging on the front porch one hot evening. Espy could not help but overhear, and listened quietly through the front window.

Snake took off his hat, pushed back the growing brown locks, and wiped the sweat from his brow as he continued.

"One day, I'll be the best whiskey runner in the whole South. I'll load a fast car up with as much stuff as it'll hold. Bring on some jugs of that corn liquor, stumphole, alley bourbon, cool water, or blue john, it jes won't matter. I'll run it faster than old General Lee's horse *Traveler*. I'll run that see seven-stars, old horse, wildcat, or jes whatever ya got and whatever y'call it, from one side'a the state to the other!"

"Well, uh…what about the law, Snake?" one of his admiring friends sheepishly asked.

"Don't you go worryin' none 'bout no lawman. I'll run faster than the law, faster than the sheriff, and faster than the revenuer. No lawman'll ever catch old Snake, here... you can betcha that one. Jes you wait and see."

Snake loved to blow his own horn. As he grew up, he became quite the storyteller and talked up a country storm when a friend would pull up a chair and listen. About the time Snake was ready to belt out another of his outlandish bootleggin' brags, his daddy came bounding through the front door waving his hat in one hand and shaking his bony bent finger at Snake in the other.

"Don't you go braggin' about such things, Snake. I don't want you growin' up and runnin' any of this crazy 'shine. You're too wild as it is. You've always been wild. A downright wild buck is what you are... always have been. If you grow up and stay in this moonshinin' business, you're likely to jes go crazy. You forget it now, ya hear?"

"Sure, Daddy... yeah," Snake replied and nodded his head to his daddy in agreement while he winked to his buddies. Snake knew better. He wanted to be the best darn 'shinerunner in the state. His youthful mind was already made up. He was just plain fascinated with running from the cops and hiding from the law.

One day I'll be famous, Snake thought, as his daddy retreated into the house to look for some more 'shine for his personal consumption.

"If it was good enough for my granddaddy Atlas and it's been good enough for my daddy, it's good enough for me. Besides, there's nothing else in old Union County for a boy like me to do anyway," he said to his buddies. As Jerry sat on the porch, the Carolina sun continued to drop, melting into the long hazy line of the distant horizon. Jerry closed his eyes and daydreamed about the day when he too would take corners in his own car at speeds over one hundred miles per hour, leaving the law choking in his dust.

One day it will happen, he thought. *One day it will.*

AN ERRAND FOR HIS DADDY: THE FIRST RUN

Snake never forgot the first time he sat behind the wheel and drove at the breakneck speeds he ultimately became addicted to. It was an inner obsession that slowly captivated his every waking hour. Some men have an insatiable need and lust for money that lead them into darkness, where others require power and control over others to feel significance or purpose in life. Snake needed none of these. He was hooked on speed.

Even as a little boy, he wondered what it felt like to be a bootlegger. On occasion, he was in the car when the driver, usually one of his moonshining kin, needed a quick getaway. He remembered the lights of the law, the squealing of the tires, and the stench of the burning rubber. It was as if the sights and sounds woke up the darkness of the Carolina woods like when the carnival came to town. The rhythmic beating of his little heart rapidly started to intensify until he thought he could actually hear the pounding. He remembered placing his tiny hand on his chest and feeling the drum in his chest beating.

He stood up in the rear seat and watched the bright lights behind the car fade into the distance as they grew fainter until they disappeared into the night's fog. It was almost more fun and excitement than the little boy could handle. When they finally reached home, his mama expressed her disappointment with this family activity, as she disapproved of the moonshining and the bootlegging. She especially disliked that her little boy had anything to do with that danger.

It was just a few days after Snake's birthday, during the cold of December, when his daddy first commissioned him to fetch some corn whiskey for his personal pleasure.

"Snake! Where are ya?" Espy hollered throughout the house. Being late in the year, the sun had already vanished from the cold western sky, and there was the familiar chill in the air.

"Here I am, Daddy. I was just helping Mama with the potatoes."

Espy continued, "I need a favor from ya, boy. You know where Uncle Dooley lives, don'cha?"

"Sure, Daddy."

"Do you think you could find your way there in the dark…like tonight?"

"Sure, Daddy…I think I can," Snake replied, with eyes that were growing wider with each question.

"OK, boy. I want ya to make a run for me down to Uncle's place and pick up a bottle of some special 'shine he finished today. Put it under the seat, and be sure to get yerself back here quick, ya hear?" Espy's stern, serious eyes scrutinized his young son and watched his every move and expression. *Could he make this simple run...he's only twelve or so...and such a little boy?* Espy wondered, in a rare display of a father's care. *Is this really the right thing to do?*

He asked his young son not only to break the law, but also to possibly endanger himself in a chase if he were sighted. But the care he sensed was quickly overshadowed by his own personal thirst for the 'shine that gripped his soul. He had an unquenchable appetite for that clear-running liquid that grew with each passing year. As Espy reflected on his selfish request, Snake's response shook him back to reality.

"Sure I'll go, Daddy. I'll be careful and watch for those lawmen at the creekbottom and there in the cutover where the new corn's growing. I remember where they hide."

With that, young Jerry was out of the house and gone before his mama could stop him. She just sat at the table and continued to peel potatoes. As she finished the last one, a small drop of dampness dripped from her sad eyes onto her apron...but nobody noticed.

Snake fired up his daddy's old truck and burned the tires around the first turn like a boy twice his age. He crossed the creek, then the cutover, and eyed each shadow in the wood line. His young imagination transformed every silhouette and dark outline into a lawman or revenuer's car, but there was none on this evening.

He ran up to Uncle Dooley's cabin and quickly knocked on the door.

"Uncle Dooley, Uncle Dooley," he shouted in a soft whisper. The door slowly opened until his uncle could make out the boy on his steps.

"What the heck're you doin' here, boy? Where's yer daddy?"

"Back at the house. He asked me to make the run. Gimme the bottle, fast. I gotta get goin' 'cuz Daddy's expectin' me directly."

Uncle Dooley handed him the package for Espy, carefully wrapped in a soft burlap bag to protect the stuff on the run back home. It came in handy as the lawmen were down in the cornfield just waiting for any 'shinerunner to come by. Uncle Dooley told his nephew to be careful and watched in amazement as young Snake placed the jug in the truck and quietly backed out onto the road to head home. Jerry knew he was just a kid, but he handled the trucks around the farm for years and knew he could drive. In a strange way, as he headed back out into the night, he fantasized about a real run…a real chase with lawmen.

But as his imagination ran with this long-played fantasy, the fantasy mixed with reality as the lights he dreamed about were now brightly flashing behind his truck and following him down the country road. It took him a moment to shift from his dreamlike state back to the evening run at hand. He had passed the cornfield at about seventy miles per hour with no thought or concern for a waiting cop car. Had he forgotten about the cop's hiding spot? Or had he subconsciously wished for a chase as his spinning tires at the curve spit gravel all over the concealed cop car in waiting?

His heart beat wildly like it did when he was just a little tyke riding in the back seat with his daddy and Uncle Dooley. But now it was different. Snake was in the driver's seat, without a license and with an illegal stash of 'shine hidden beneath the seat. Though Snake was only twelve years old, it took him but a second to shift into "running mode," to immediately push the pedal all the way down to the rusty floorboard. He had to lean forward to the front edge of the seat in order to get the pedal down, and he stomped it with such force that he nearly pushed his boot through the thin rusty metal of the front floor.

The speedometer needle made a strange plinking sound as it bumped against the right side of the meter, bounced back to the left, only to bang again to the far right. Snake had exceeded the speed the old truck could even measure. The souped-up carburetor was drinking gas faster than old Espy could down his moonshine.

Snake turned to the right and then to the left as the winding country road tested his reflexes. The tires began to heat up and started their familiar whine as they were stretched passed their limits. Snake noticed that the law vehicle would pull closer to him on the straightaway, but dropped back through the curves.

Snake knew the back roads as well as any lawman and immediately ran to some of those old dirt roads that had nonstop curves. He hugged the shoulder in the right-turning curves hurling dirt, gravel, and grass high into the air. He took the left turns at top speed and cut off the apex of the curve by traveling across the middle of the road that straightened out the sharpest of turns. In the midst of this battle of speed and wits, the young boy never considered that any car might have been coming his way. This type of high-risk driving ultimately became Snake's signature in his bootlegging.

"Crazy, just darn crazy," his daddy would say.

Though the first run only took fifteen minutes or so, it seemed to the twelve year-old country boy that he ran all night. His previous bragging came back to his memory and played time and time again during his first run. *I will not be caught. I will be the best. No lawman will ever catch me.*

As soon as Snake took a few curves and saw the bright headlights of the lawman's car fall behind a few hundred feet, he jerked the steering wheel forcefully to the right. The truck went over a bank and slid into a cut cotton field. He quickly cut his lights as the old truck came to an abrupt stop in the mud. He took his foot off the brake pedal to kill the taillights, and hunkered down into the front seat. His heart continued to beat, and great drops of perspiration dripped from his brow.

As soon as he ducked down in the front seat, the bright lights and red flasher passed the bank and continued chasing the phantom runner down the empty road. Young Jerry could not help himself. He giggled softly, the soft giggle leading to out-loud laughter.

I did it. I really did it! he thought as he poked his head up over the dash and watched the lights disappear down the road.

"I'm the greatest driver of all time. They will never forget my name—Jerry Rushing!" he hollered. Snake continued giggling to himself, having ditched the lawman with some creative curve manipulation, and then ditched the truck up and over a nearby bank. He sat there for nearly fifteen minutes before firing up the old truck and heading back home.

Espy was still on the porch waiting for his moonjuice when Snake hurriedly pulled into the yard. He had really outraced and outrun his very first lawman. Now *he* was an outlaw. He drove like an absolute maniac and nearly risked his young life doing it. This run was the first of many young Snake would make for his daddy. It was as if he was being primed and prepared for the longer and more dangerous runs of a real bootlegger. He was determined to be as wild as he could be. Why not? He heard his daddy on many occasions say, "You're crazy, boy...in fact, you're as wild as a buck deer." That "wild as a buck deer" description stayed with Snake for years to come. As he slammed on the brakes, sliding the old truck in a semi-circle through the grass, Espy just shook his head. Snake hopped out of the truck and ran the 'shine up to his daddy. Espy grabbed the jug with a smirk and, without even saying thank you, he asked, "How was the run? See Uncle Dooley? Everything fine?"

As Snake bounded through the front door looking for dinner he responded, "Jes fine, daddy...the run was jes fine."

Moonshine . . . the First Time

In the late 1940s, thousands of people throughout the Southeast were hooked on the prohibited 'shine. Many of those that were addicted to the stuff were also afflicted with a partial paralysis of the lower extremities from a concoction often referred to as "Jake." Jake was a special brew with a variety of additives that was often dangerous.

Some moonshiners added extra ingredients to their 'shine to make it distinct from the others. Sometimes this additive was intentional, and other times it was accidental due to their distinct distilling process. Often lead or pine pitch seeped into the liquor, depending on the type of materials they used in the still or mash barrels. Some historians suggested that moonshiners might have added bleach, paint thinner, chemical fertilizer, lye, or rubbing alcohol for a variety of reasons.

Some of the lightning would be used up by the moonshiners about as quick as it dripped from the condenser coils. Other jugs might be sold or shared with the locals, including friends and family. Some of the sacred sap might be sold to buyers throughout the state where other cases of the 'shine would occasionally make it out to the shot houses of New York or Chicago. It was the taste, the burn, and the aftereffects that had Southerners and Northerners yearning after the stuff.

One reporter in the early 1900s described the drinking of the illegal beverage like this:

> The instant he swallowed the stuff, he feels as if he were sunburned all over, his head begins to buzz as if a hive of bees had swarmed there, when he closed his eyes, he sees six hundred million torchlight processions all charging at him, ten abreast, and when he opens his eyes, the light blinds him and everything seems dancing about.

It seemed everyone in the South had a favorite family recipe for their 'shine. There was great pride in many of the moonshine families for adhering to a strict recipe and providing high-quality, liquid corn. Though there were many different recipes for concocting the stuff, the following seems to be representative of the basics:

Ingredients: shelled corn, sugar, cornmeal, water, and yeast. (Malt is optional.)

Process:

1. Take the shelled corn and place in a cotton flour sack. Wet the corn with warm water and put in a warm, dark place. Several times a day, wet it again with warm water until, after three of four days, the corn sprouts and grows about two inches long.

2. Spread sprouted corn out to dry, then grind it with a meat grinder and mix with cornmeal.

3. Add the sugar and boil all the ingredients into a sloppy consistency, which the moonshiners referred to as "mash."

4. Add the yeast and lukewarm water and set aside to ferment. Fermentation took ten to fourteen days without yeast, but adding the yeast sped up the process to three or four days. At that time, the fermenting settled down and the mash was very sour.

5. Place the mash into the still cooker and heat the mash to the point of alcohol vaporization, about 173 degrees. The mash produced a clear liquid and then produced a vapor.

6. The vapor condensed as it ran through a tube or coil that was cooled by cold water from a nearby stream.

7. The resulting condensation was the moonshine. If the first runoff was weak, the still pot was cleaned and the mash was redistilled to rid the 'shine of excess water and oil.

8. Keep mash in a container. It is now referred to as "slop." Add more sugar and use again. It can often be used six to seven times before it needs to be replaced.

Snake was only sixteen years old when his uncle Dooley asked him to help with what would be his first whiskey operation. He had occasionally visited the site of an illegal brewer. However, he never actually worked a still until the day his uncle enlisted him to join in this unlawful venture.

Snake was out setting muskrat traps down on one of the nearby creeks. He often spent the evening hours setting trap lines. Ever since he was very little, he had enjoyed both the trapping and the money the pelts brought him. He was ankle deep in the running creek water, setting the underwater traps, when Uncle Dooley saw him from up the bank on the other side.

"Hey, Snake, watcha doin' this time of night there in the creek bottom?" his uncle hollered.

"Runnin' the end of these trap lines. I'm getting' a bunch'a muskrat from this here creek. Must be an entire family or more livin' in these waters. A few more nights like last night's catch, and I might have enough cash for my own runnin' car."

"Well..." his uncle continued, setting his own trap with equal thoughtfulness, "how would you like to make some real money? I mean some real green stuff?"

"Well, sure...whatcha got in mind?"

With that seed planted, Uncle Dooley walked back up the steep bank, waving his hand over his shoulder. "Come on up to the house when you're finished. I'll meet you back there."

Snake quickly turned back to his trap line and secured it to some boulders, working with precision as he carefully positioned each trap. Over the many years he worked the creeks, Jerry had become a skilled and proficient trapper and was held in high esteem among his peers in the county. With a bright full moon that illuminated his steps, Snake made his way through the woods and around the winding creek until he arrived at his uncle's house.

"Uncle Dooley...Uncle Dooley, where are you?"

"Back here working on our new project," his uncle replied.

Snake made his way to the far back room, and his eyes began to grow as he saw his uncle working on the beginnings of a big new still.

"Snake, remember when you told me that the next time I wanted to make more liquor that you wanted in? Well...I want to make more liquor. Are you up for it?"

"Sure am. In fact, I've been wanting to get into the family moonshine business as long as I can remember."

Snake continued, with a wide Rushing smile wrapped from ear to ear, "I can start right now—and I mean tonight!"

With that excitement that began to brew, Snake and his uncle Dooley planned their next operation. This was young Jerry's first real moonshine business operation. They decided they first needed some large wooden whiskey barrels in order to start their mash. They left at sunrise early the next morning, caught breakfast in Charlotte, and bought their barrels before returning home.

Snake was so excited he could hardly sleep the night before. He kept watch on that eastern horizon. In fact, that night, like many when he stayed out the entire night in the woods, he watched as the moon made its way slowly from one side of the sky to the other and then quietly slinked behind some distant tree. The actual daybreak was still thirty minutes away when he jumped into his old 1949 Ford convertible. It was a brisk morning to ride in that old convertible, but Snake was ready. He picked up his uncle, screamed, "Let's go," and headed out for the drive.

Snake now knew he had grown up—that he was a man, no longer a boy. He was not just his uncle's scrawny nephew who trapped and sold pelts to make some extra change. He was a "real-live outlaw," a moonshiner secretly slipping into Charlotte to invest in some whiskey barrels to begin this undercover backwoods operation.

I am a moonshiner, he thought, as he pulled the big old black cowboy hat down on his head to keep it from blowing off during the expedition. *I am a moonshiner.*

He loved being around his uncle Dooley. His uncle was not only a moonshiner, but a religious man, as well. Though one might have had trouble reconciling the two, Uncle Dooley had no problem with it. He believed in God, and he believed in the holy Scriptures. But he also believed he had the right to use his God-given corn any way he wanted. If he wanted to make whiskey, no stuffy white-collar city-guy government official from Washington or anywhere else was going to tell him otherwise. He felt strongly that this was a God-given entitlement, that he was right, and that the tax revenuers were dead wrong.

So Uncle Dooley sometimes made whiskey and sometimes preached. Snake loved to watch him. His uncle got so drunk on the corn-juice that he had seen him jump up on a table, beat on it with his fist, and preach at the top of his voice—all the while drunk as a skunk.

He preached and hollered, took another swig, coughed, wiped his brow, and preached some more. Why, he cut loose a'preachin', and all of the town drunks in the saloon just sat around the tables and chanted, "Mr. Dooley, Mr. Dooley." He got them so wound up that they screamed his name, and all the while he screamed back to them, "You're all goin' to hell...I hope you know it...you're all goin' to hell...you'd bes' be gettin' ready and gettin' your life right...I'm tellin' ya." It went on for hours and hours.

Fortunately, this was not one of those trips. They stayed out of those types of drinking places. There was just too much to do as they continued to discuss the different streams and hiding places for their new operation. Into Charlotte they went, Uncle Dooley in his bibs and young Snake in his big black cowboy hat. They parked outside a diner, had breakfast, bought the barrels, and headed home.

They were quite a sight. They put one of the big barrels into the trunk and Dooley tied it down, and placed the other two barrels in the backseat of the convertible. Out of town they rode, riding high, along with their barrels, Snake's black cowboy hat, and their pride. His dream was to be one of Union County's biggest and baddest outlaws of all time. Obviously, most onlookers must have known what they were up to. But they did not care.

Two rugged country-lookin' desperados ran wide-open, headed back to the woodland hills, and carried three giant wood barrels. Snake just loved it. He remembered in school when the teacher asked the kids what they wanted to be when they grew up. Many answered a cowboy, a fireman, a doctor, a farmer, or the president of the United States. This always brought smiles and nods from both the teachers and the other students. But Snake thought differently. He would not be a simple farmer or doctor. He had no such aspirations to be a governor or the president. Actually, Snake thought he had a higher calling.

When called on, Snake stood up with a big smile plastered on his face and proudly proclaimed, "I want to be a modern-day outlaw, just like Jesse James." The teacher had heard it before and was not surprised. Snickers broke out from around the little classroom. Snake smiled, pointed his finger at some of his friends, and said, "That's right, you jes wait and see. I'll be the wildest outlaw this county has ever seen. Just like Jesse James...just like Jesse James. You'll read about me one day. Just read the paper; one day I'll be there."

Charlotte was only thirty miles northwest of Monroe, and though a bootleggin' trip across the hills could be run in fifteen minutes, a casual stroll would take forty-five minutes or so. Snake and Uncle Dooley arrived back in Monroe and hauled all three barrels back into the woods. Then they carefully dug holes under a fence line and fixed the barrels up so no one could tell they were there. Part of the success of any moonshine venture was the location of the still and mash barrels. Were they hidden from the sight of any revenuer? Could they be seen from the air?

Many of the revenuers flew small planes over an entire area and tried to follow the line of a creek, stream, or branch looking for smoke or the reflection of the sun off one of those shiny copper stills. But

Uncle Dooley had hiked the hills and found another remote area far from the roads and close to a small stream. The cool water from the stream was needed for mixing the mash and the condensing part of the moonshine operation.

They quickly cut a little square hole in the barrels and began toting the water from the nearby stream back to the barrels. Once full, they added their secret ingredients, stirred it up, and then added the yeast to quicken the fermentation process. The toting of the water from the stream to the barrels for mash, and then the toting of the mash back to the still, which needed to be located adjacent to the creek, was a time-consuming process. But what else were country boys going to do in the middle of the night? After they got the mash a bubblin', Uncle Dooley turned to Snake on one dark night and said, "Snake, let's go get the still. Whatcha say?"

"Right now? I mean, sure. I don't have anything else to do. Do you have it hidden in the barn or back in the woods?"

The actual still itself was often made of copper, and because the very shape of it gave it away, it was important to keep it hidden once it was made. The stills often consisted of two separate parts consisting of a large kettle bottom and a copper top. The mash, after it had fully fermented, was poured into the bottom part of the still. That was the part that sat atop the fire. The top was then placed on the bottom part and sealed. Often the pressure built up and a pressure release was built into the still for safety purposes. To accommodate this, sometimes the lap between the top and the bottom was sealed with a water and flour mixture. If too much pressure built up, the seal blew off rather than causing the entire still to explode and injure the moonshiners.

A large copper arm protruded from the top of the still cooker and projected over to the side of the large cooking pot. This often ran out twelve to twenty-four inches and connected to the worm, the condensing part of the still. It was this odd shape, the large size, the two-part connection, and the large copper arm that provided this dead giveaway whether this object was ever seen atop a truck.

Stills were often transported in a truck covered with old tires, a tarp, or some farmer's hay. Seldom were stills ever confiscated out in the open as they were almost always very well hidden. Such was the case with Uncle Dooley's still.

"So where is it?" Snake continued. "Is it in the woods or in your barn under that hay up there in the loft?"

"Nope," Uncle Dooley replied, "it's not in the barn. And it's not in the woods. If fact, you will not believe it. Follow me."

Snake followed his uncle back to the cabin and then over the hill to the small bass pond. It was a beautiful Carolina night, and that bright Union County moon was reflecting right off of that pond in a way that could mesmerize any young country boy. They stood at the bank of the pond, breathing in that cool crisp country air and watching the moon's reflection on the pond surface move about as young bass were hitting small bugs on the surface. After a few minutes, young Snake asked again where the still was hidden.

His uncle just pointed to the pond and started laughing quietly.

"In there, boy. It's at the bottom of my pond. I just figured that they would never find it here." He sat down on the grassy bank of the pond holding his hand over his mouth in a vain attempt to keep the giggles from exploding into the night air.

"Well, how the heck are we going to get that dang thing out of the pond?" Snake asked.

His uncle just pointed to the pond in the direction where he had buried the new still, and Snake knew just what he meant. So within an instant or so, Snake had dropped his trousers, kicked off his boots, and was wading into the dark water to fetch the copper thing. He felt around the muddy bottom pushing his toes into the mushy muck as he ventured further and further from the bank while the water got deeper and deeper. About the time he was about to ask for better instructions, he stubbed his big toe on something big, round, and hard.

"I found it," he yelled in a whisper to his still giggling uncle. What a sight it must have been for his uncle to sit there on that bank and watch his young nephew wading into that dark, watery abyss with only the moonlight as a companion.

"Here it is, here it is!" he shrieked again.

His uncle just sat there with a big smile on his face.

"Well, bring it out slowly, Snake. Be careful. That thing cost me over one hundred gallons of my last run. Push it up here on the bank, and we'll empty it of all the water and get it back there near the stream while it's still dark."

So Snake picked up that big old still and loaded it on his back. The idea that his uncle was also using him for his youth, vigor, and strength never crossed his mind.

With the still balanced on his back, Snake followed his uncle back across the pasture and down the lane next to the pasture. Snake was still barefooted, and his uncle was carrying his shirt. Though the liquor still was heavy, Snake was excited to finally make it as an outlaw. If only his friends could see him now. He was a modern-day outlaw carrying his first real still back into the woods for his very first moonshine operation.

About that time, a spark split open the cold dark night as Snake had hit an electric fence that had a small nearly invisible wire running from post to post next to the pasture lane. As Snake was bragging in his mind about the outlaw thing, he had run right into the electric fence, and it had sparked what looked like a spring lightening bolt. It knocked Snake directly to the ground. The still bounced off his burning back like a basketball and rolled out into the pasture.

"Wow!" Snake yelled. "That just burnt my butt off. Whoo...I'm on fire...hot as..."

Uncle Dooley scowled him for the thunderous outburst.

"Quiet, boy! Good Lord, be quiet. If someone sees us, we'll be in big trouble. Lord, be quiet." Snake picked himself up from the ground.

"I could'a been 'lectricuted," he grumbled. "I was nearly fried...wet and all like I was." He continued to quietly moan as he picked up the still and followed his uncle quietly back into the woods where they had begun the night.

Before 3:00 a.m. or so, they had the fire cooking and the mash loaded into the bottom of the new liquor still. The last of the piping connections were made as the condensing coil was firmly attached to the still arm. Before sunrise, the first drips of the condensing 'shine came dripping into a glass jar. Snake just sat there with his hat pushed back on his head and marveled at the sights and sounds. It was really something to see that first whiskey coming out of the pipe as he breathed in deep breaths of that whiskey smell. The fumes were strong and the moon was shining. *Moonshine...homemade whiskey,* he thought. *I am making my first homemade whiskey.*

As the sun rose on Snake's first Carolina moonshine still, Uncle Dooley was showing him how to proof it and all. Snake understood most of those first instructions that evening, though his uncle needed to repeat some of the early lessons later in the week. When Uncle Dooley turned around with the fifth gallon that morning, there against one of the larger oak trees sat Snake. He was still a bit damp from his pond ordeal and even now had the burn marks from the electric fence on his chest and arms. He had slid down the tree that had been holding him up when his eyelids became too heavy for his will. His big black hat had fallen off and rolled too close to the fire. Barefooted and slumped over like a toy doll, he laid there as if dead with only a soft snore indicating he was still alive. With an unusual touch of compassion, Uncle Dooley put his black hat back upon Snake's head and patted his arm.

"Sleep tight, young nephew," the uncle whispered. "Sleep tight. There will be many more moonlit nights like this one."

A Small Spiritual Seed Planted

The only preaching young Snake ever really heard as a boy was the drunken screaming and screeching that his uncle did from the top of some barroom table when he got drunk on some of that moon juice. But that was not the kind of preaching that could change a young boy's heart. It was not the type of preaching that could open up the secrets of heaven for a moonshine kid. With only the Bible stories from his early school years in his heart, young Snake ventured into the woods and made this moonshine without any pang of conscience at all. It was a generational thing, and he really thought nothing of it.

All three generations of the Rushing clan really did not see any right or wrong in it. In fact, within this moonshine culture most whiskey makers often held on to their passion as some type of inalienable right. As far as being ethically or morally right or wrong, they really saw no wrong in it. Snake had often heard his uncle Dooley say, "If the law can sell liquor and make a lot of money, then we ought to be able to make whiskey and sell it as well. Nothin' wrong about it." So with that, the third-generation Rushing boy launched headlong into the whiskey-making business without a thought regarding right or wrong.

Whether there was any sense of his conscience bothering him, to this day he just cannot remember. If his conscience ever did speak up within him, it was quickly drowned out and smothered by the thrill and exhilaration of building the still, operating the still, smelling that liquor odor coming out of the condensing line, and ultimately the running of that illegal shine. Snake was always looking for excitement and this moonshine business fulfilled his every need.

There was no real spiritual emphasis in the Rushing home. In fact, where some families at least attend a church after the death of family loved ones, this was not even the case in this family. When a family member died, they basically just buried him and life went on. Snake knew there must be a God, but it was not an important part of his life. With the whiskey making and then the running of that shine, there was little time left for God, church, or any other spiritual endeavor.

But through it all, when Snake was quite young, he did have a conscience about one thing. And that one thing was using God's name in vain. He had grown up around the cursing rough moonshine crowd and could cuss the horn off a sailor. When young Snake got mad and lost his temper, watch out, as his cussin' started and someone got hit up the side of the head with his massive fist. One punch from Snake is all that was really needed. He then jumped back into his car and continued cussing up a storm. But when things really spiraled out of control, Snake began using God's name in vain, and that really did bother him.

Somewhere and somehow a deep "respect" for God had been planted within Snake. Whether it was the Bible stories or the drunken preaching of his uncle Dooley, he could never decide. But deep within him was a true admiration for the God of this universe. After a brawl with a local boy who just happened to get in his way, he seldom felt sorry for the whippin' he gave the fellow. Whether he beat him with his fists, hit him with a large stick, cut him with his hunting knife, or shot him with his concealed handgun, nothing bothered the young moonshiner quite like using God's name in vain.

Well, the Scripture states a promise regarding the Word of God in Isaiah 55:11:

> So shall my word be that goeth forth out of my mouth: it shall not return unto me void, but it shall accomplish that which I please, and it shall prosper in the thing whereto I sent it.

That verse does not say that the only Word of God that accomplishes God's intentions is that which is spoken from the pulpit from a professional preacher. It just says that His Word, once spoken, will accomplish His will. Whether the Word of God was from the schoolteacher, clothed within a child's Bible story, or whether it was proclaimed from the mouth of a drunken uncle, the Word came forth and planted a small seed within this young moonshiner. And it was this seed planted from God's Word that ultimately grew a deep-rooted respect for God Himself.

Did Jerry often think of God during his clandestine moonshining? Was God on his mind through his crazy and fast-driving bootlegging or throughout his other outlaw activities? Well, probably not. But God was always there whenever he used God's name in a disrespectful way. It is funny how God will pull on the heartstrings of even the most hard-hearted of men. He can use little Bible stories told during the infancy of a young boy, or He can use a drunken good-hearted man screaming and preaching at the other drunken good-hearted men surrounding him.

So God does work in the hearts of men. That much we know and that much is settled. God did work in the heart of little Jerry. God loved Snake so much, even within the moonshine culture in which he was born. God loved Snake as he ran for the first time for liquor for his father. He loved Snake while he built and ran his very first still. He was watching down from the heavens one night as young

Snake ran directly into that electric fence after having fetched the hidden still buried deep within his uncle's pond.

Had God's hand not been upon Snake, one false turn during his younger whiskey running years would have taken him home well before his prime. And his home would not have been the one with the pearly gates or streets of gold. Likely it would have been the one that Jesus talks about in Scripture—the hell saved for the devil and his workers.

Yet Snake lived through these early dangerous years to ultimately tell about it. God may have used just a simple remembrance of Himself when Snake's conscience was pricked each time he used God's own name in the midst of one of his cursing episodes. But his conscience, in due course, grew hard and cold. As Snake continued in the whiskey business, he got hard and strong and ultimately did not believe in anything and "did not care for nothing," as he used to say. He got so hard-hearted that he could use God's name anyway he desired without feeling anything at all. The conscience was hard now, and it took years for God to soften it up.

How hard did it get? If somebody got in his way, he simply drove to their house at night and opened his machine gun into the side of the house. At other times he took his trusty twelve-gauge shotgun with some buckshot and shot out the house windows, the glass doors, and tried to blow out each of the electric lights in the rooms. He blew out the front picture windows just for fun without considering the consequences of the little children that just might have been playing on some couch lying next to that blown-out window. On other occasions he drove down the road, found his prey in the car ahead of him, and just pulled out the shotgun to blow out their taillights. He shot out all of the car lights and still chased them out of town.

Jerry could often be heard saying, "Boy, are we outlaws or what? Hell-bent on destruction, and nobody is going to stop us. Why, we're bowing down to nobody. That's just the way it's going to be."

With that, young Jerry grew up to be hard Jerry...a modern-day outlaw with a hardened conscience and far from the God that had protected him from so much possible harm when he was young. As he grew older and became more indebted to the way of the outlaw, the Bible stories became distant past memories otherwise lost in the hazardous shadows of his youth.

It would be years until those Bible stories and the truths they held spoke to his heart again.

It was years.

CHAPTER 3

Early Whiskey Runnin'

WRECKIN' DADDY'S CAR

IF YOU PASSED an old country house in the Deep South back in the fifties, you would see as many old cars, trucks, and tractors sitting around the yard as there were little boys, little girls, or farm cats running in and around them. It was as if folks drove them right up to the last breath of life the cars had, only to abandon them the moment they died. The cars were buried just above the ground with only waist-high grass around them to hide them from view.

One of the old cars that Espy Rushing used for running liquor was an old 1942 Chevrolet. It was basically just an old, rundown '42 stock Chevy. It was weathered and rusty and had as many miles on it as most of the other dead or dying "law-fleeing" cars buried about Union County. It had not yet been "souped-up." Souped-up to a bootlegger meant one thing—the engine had been overhauled to provide a lot more horsepower than a typical stock engine. It was not unusual for a hot car to have a new Offenhauser head, three two-barrel carburetors, or even a custom rear set of springs containing twelve to fourteen leaves.

As the sophistication of early auto mechanics grew, techniques became standard in the typical bootlegger car. Many times, the bootleggers themselves or some mechanically oriented friend milled the stock heads or even substituted the newer higher-compression Denver heads. Others dropped in larger engines or bored the cylinder out, increasing the engine displacement. Some mechanics were known to actually bore out the standard intake manifolds and install two or three carburetors to increase the flow of air and fuel, thus drastically increasing the horsepower. But that was not the case with this '42 Chevy. It was just an old Chevy, nothing really special.

But it was fast, it belonged to Espy, and it had a reputation for outrunning the law. On this particular sweltering summer evening, Espy was just too tired to make the last haul of the night, so he turned to his young son. Though the Carolina sun had long since retired behind some low-lying clouds, the heavy heat of the day lingered through the county like a dead man's dying breath. Snake was tired and had grabbed some cool water from the well.

Someday I will be the fastest and the baddest, he thought to himself. *I've just gotta get more driving time... more time running this stuff... more time practicing outrunning the law.*

As if his daddy had reached out beyond the front wall to sense his thoughts, he hollered, "Snake... come here quick, boy. I need ya to do something for me."

Snake jumped as he was shaken from his daydreaming.

"I'm out here on the porch, Daddy. Whatcha want?"

"Hurry up, boy... get yerself in here quick. I've got one more job for ya!"

With that, the wiry young boy crawled off his makeshift bed on the porch and dragged himself into the house. Young Snake could see from his daddy's eyes that he had been dipping too much that day from the family brew. His eyes contained that glassy fogged-over stare that Snake could make out even from across the room.

Snake often wondered if every family was just like his—brewing, drinking, then running and selling what you did not drink, and then starting the cycle all over again. He did not mind the moonshining. It was a culture to which he had become easily addicted. However, he did tire of the drunkenness and was careful of criticizing his father, especially to his face. He knew it certainly meant a beating or at best a long-winded cussing.

It was the dream of bootlegging that had put the fire in his belly, burning from deep within. Just the thought of outrunning the law, spinning and whirling a fast-running car in a dust cloud around the corners of some backwoods dirt road was exciting. The thrill of running homemade whiskey is something that can grab hold of an adventurous young lad. And it had grabbed hold of Snake and his vivid imagination. He was on his way to becoming North Carolina's fastest bootlegger.

Espy continued with his callous pressure on Snake.

"Tomorrow never comes boy. I need you tonight…and right now, tonight."

"Well, Dad—"

He was interrupted by Espy's abrupt burst of anger.

"Boy," he screamed, "you're gonna move it—now. I need a whiskey run, and I need you to make it—now."

Immediately, Snake's frown transformed itself into a giant smile as if the boy were standing before Santa himself on Christmas morning.

"Why Daddy, why didn't you say so? I'd love to run some stuff tonight. Someday, I'm gonna be the king of runners. In fact—"

"Sure, sure," Espy interrupted. "Keys are in the old Chevy. Take the seven cases of fresh brew out in the shed and load them in the back of the car. Take Highway 84 west out of Monroe and then head north on the backroads to Chelsey's Place right south of Charlotte. Chelsey'll be there waiting for you after he closes. You should get there sometime after 1:00 in the morning."

"Yes siree, you can depend on old Snake here." Snake's big old grin continued to swell across his face as his mind was already fantasizing about this midnight outlaw operation. Only the best of the best outlaws would he be.

His daddy studied the silly grin growing on his son's face and continued, "Then get yerself back here quick. I expect you back before morning. And be careful—the law has been on the lookout for cars heading north out of Monroe here. That's why you'll be headin' west and then back up north."

Then, with a stern eye, he warned his son, "Don't get caught... drive hard. I'll tell ya again, don't let those lawmen getcha. Now git, ya hear?"

With that, Snake was out the door in a flash. He carried the cases of the homemade 'shine from the barn and carefully placed them in the trunk and the backseat of the old Chevy. Once loaded, Snake crawled into the driver's seat and headed off for Charlotte, throwing gravel from the driveway back to the old wood porch where moments before he had daydreamed about such a run as this.

In the heat of August there were few really cool nights. But that did not bother Snake on this particular evening as the old Chevy windows were rolled down and a seventy-mile-an-hour wind rushed by. He quickly cooled off as the breeze blew across the perspiration on his head and neck from the frantic loading of the cases minutes earlier.

Snake took off west on Highway 84 just as his daddy had instructed him. Once he was several miles out of Monroe, Snake turned the fast runnin' Chevy north onto the first backroad he could find. He was like Jesse James, one of his childhood heroes, only his horse was the Chevy and his booty was the 'shine, not some bag of banknotes or chest of gold. He had dreamed his entire young life of being just like Jesse—a true-life, modern-day outlaw. Now, in his mind, he was one, too.

Though he was not being chased by any lawman, he liked to practice his rapid hairpin turns at each bend of the country road. Each curve became an obstacle to overcome at the highest speed possible. He pressed the old Chevy to run with all its might. The engine hummed and then sputtered as if giving all its life to accomplish this moonshine run. Snake imagined some lawman on his rear bumper and pressed the old rusty gas pedal farther down until it bounced off the floorboard with each bump of the road. Within just a couple of hours from the time he pulled out of Union County, he was at the rear door of Chelsey's Place.

Snake pulled behind the old cinder-block building and hurriedly hit the lights and killed the engine. A couple of knocks on the rear door quickly brought Chelsey to unlock the rear moonshine delivery door. As with many runs, few words were shared as several of Chelsey's big bouncer types raced to the Chevy and unloaded the illegal juice. Cash changed hands quickly while one of the men stood at the side of the old block building with a loaded twelve-gauge shotgun, keeping a watchful eye on the road and the nearby intersection. On this particular night, however, there were no lawmen to fight and no revenuers to shake.

The unloading was complete and the cash stashed deep within Snake's back right pocket—the pocket with no holes. It was as important to deliver the cash back to Union County as it was to deliver the moonshine. *Job well done,* Snake thought as he picked up speed heading back out of Charlotte toward Monroe. *Easy as pie... apple pie.* It was shortly after 2:00 a.m. and he would easily be back well before dawn. As he raced through Charlotte, Snake pressed down on that old pedal and again hit speeds of eighty to ninety miles per hour while racing back home.

Snake was about five miles outside of Monroe when the first lawman pulled out from the backside of a turn in the road and began pursuing his car. Then a county sheriff car pulled from the next turn and began the chase as well. Snake must have run a good mile or two before he noticed the siren of the quickly approaching officers' cars.

Most young men would be shaken when confronted with such a challenge, but Snake was different. He had practiced for such a time as this. He was a born-and-bred outlaw who took pride in his outlaw heritage. Snake looked in the rearview mirror and smiled that big silly grin his daddy had seen just a few hours before. He then downshifted the old '42 Chevy, pulled into the middle of the road, and took the approaching right turn at eighty miles per hour. The tires squealed from the stress they were enduring just trying to grip the road. The Chevy hit a bump, became airborne for a second or two, and crashed back into the pavement with a squeal of both rear tires.

The revenuers had been staking out this area for some time trying to put a halt to the northern flow of moonshine into the Charlotte area. Young Snake had just accidentally driven right through the stakeout. He continued to bank right and then left again, keeping one eye on the road and one eye on the lawmen behind him. On the straightaways, Snake pushed the old Chevy to nearly one hundred miles per hour trying to escape the siren-blaring patrol cars behind him. Try as he might, the revenuer stayed glued to his rear bumper, sometimes coming within ten to twenty yards, only to fall further behind on the straightaways.

They raced for several minutes without seeing any other oncoming cars. This was fortunate for both of them as they were using both lanes of the roadway, from the far left gravel shoulder to the muddy right embankment. Then Snake remembered the last bark of his old daddy as he had left the house.

"Don't get caught, boy...ya hear me? Don't you let them lawmen get'cha," his daddy had warned him.

With a picture in his mind of old Espy coming into the town's little police headquarters to get his boy out of jail, he quickly made up his mind that this was no picture he wanted to see played out. His daddy could get real mad, and he had taken his share of whippings and beatings from as early as he could remember. With the determination of a man twice his age, young Snake pressed down on the rusty gas pedal and began weaving down the old country road. Gravel shot from behind his old '42 Chevy like a twelve-gauge shotgun shooting buckshot on opening day. As he slid over onto the muddy left bank, he slung red Carolina mud onto the road behind him.

Faster and faster the old Chevy flew down the road, the tires throwing gravel and then mud...more mud and then gravel. They whined as if singing the Carolina state moonshinin' song, if there were such a song. The engine ran fast and purred like an old cat awaiting its evening's milk treat. Just how much heat the old engine could take, Snake was not sure. The engine's tachometer was topping out as the rpms were at their peak. As he pushed faster and faster down the road, dark blue smoke began blowing out the rear tailpipes from a worn piston ring or two. But the revenuer was gaining on him. With a quick pull on the wheel, the Chevy made an abrupt right down a gravel road, only to slide out of control, hitting a stony embankment. Bright red and yellow sparks flew up into the night sky. Snake quickly pulled behind several large rock outcroppings, hitting the key and the lights just as the lawman sped down the road without a clue.

"I did it!" Snake exclaimed to himself. "Man, what a run. That old lawman didn't have a chance—not a chance."

But before he could bask long in this most recent exploit, his mind immediately shot back to the sparks, flashes, and flickers that had lit up the sky and then vanished into the shadowy night air when he had slipped on the muddy bank and sideswiped the rock embankment.

My dad will kill me, he thought. *When he gets hold of me and sees the side of this car, he'll beat me so I will not sit for days.*

As fear began to well up within his soul, he began to feel sick at his stomach. He was too frightened to even look at the twisted and scratched side of the car he just raced. He had just outrun real-life lawmen and should be shouting in victory. But his night of triumph and his feelings of accomplishment had just gone up in smoke like the sparks in the night air.

Now a sense of dread and horror filled soul, though it was only twenty minutes or so. He waited for what seemed like hours before he fired up the old '42. He wanted to make sure the lawman was good and gone. He slowly turned the key, turned the headlights back on, and pulled out from behind the rocks. He turned back onto the gravel road and slowly headed toward Monroe in the direction of his daddy's house.

The homemade 'shine had been successfully delivered on time, and Snake had not been caught. However, the right quarter panel of the Chevy carried home the battle scars of the encounter, and his daddy would not be happy. Snake was no longer in a hurry to get back home.

"Maybe Daddy will be asleep...maybe," he hoped.

It was not until he quietly pulled into the gravel drive of the old homestead and parked the Chevy that he had mustered up the courage to look at the dents and damage caused by oversteering that right turn. He slowly walked through the dark and peaked at the damage done earlier that night.

His daddy would certainly notice the damage to the car. There was not enough time left in the night to attempt any cover-up. He decided to take it like a man. But first he would sneak back into the house, trying not to be noticed, to get at least a couple of hours of sleep before the whippings began. With that thought, Snake slowly opened up the front door and, for once, was happy to find Espy dead drunk and passed out on the floor from too much 'shine. Snake stepped over his daddy's legs, stepped around the empty 'shine bottle, and tiptoed to his room. Though he was tired, his young mind raced, trying to imagine how difficult the thrashing would be when Espy found out. As he imagined his daddy chasing him around the house with a broom handle, a piece of wood, or an oak switch, he quietly drifted off to sleep and began to dream.

In his dream he outran the lawman without wrecking the family car—and returned a hero. He lived for the day that he was the outlaw hero of the Rushing clan, his other friends of the moonshine trade, and the entire county—and not just in his dreams. As he drifted from one moonshine run to another, his dreams carried him from county to county within the Carolina country he loved.

While he dreamed of pulling the Chevy back into the woods at another local still, he was shaken out of his sleep by the deep, dark yell of the family drunk, come back to life from the night before.

"Jerry Rushing," his daddy shouted. "You get yerself out here right now!"

Snake jumped from the bed and wiped the salty, sandy stuff from his eyes.

Don't cry, he told himself. *Men don't cry...don't cry, just don't cry.*

He slowly walked through the front room, watching his mama's eyes on him from her place at the kitchen sink. She had been crying again. Jerry never got used to the hurt he saw deep within her eyes. He glanced her way, forced out a sheepish grin, wiped the moisture from his eyes, and crossed the room while still repeating in his head silently, *Don't cry...just don't cry.*

He watched through the front window as his dad walked back and forth in front of the Chevy, appraising the damage from the night before. The wild back-and-forth shaking of Espy's head along with his violent kicking of the gravel warned Snake of his eventual fate. He fought back his tears and tried to walk through the door like a man. But boys were never meant to walk like men. That is why men start out as little boys. But Snake had never experienced a typical little boy's upbringing. His life seemed to fast-forward from infancy directly into manhood. So with a determined hesitancy, Snake opened the door quickly, trying to prepare himself for whatever pounding was to come his way.

As Snake crossed the porch with whisper-like steps, his daddy was still kicking gravel as he belted out again, "Jerry Rushing, if you don't get yerself out here..." His voice trailed off as he kicked the bent and twisted metal on the right side of the old car.

"Here I am, Dad. I hear ya, I'm right here," Snake responded.

"Let me tell you something, boy. This here car's all banged up. It's terrible. I'm gonna ask ya just once, and you're gonna tell me the truth. Ya hear?"

"Sure, Dad," Snake responded, still trying to choke back the tears. His mama had slowly moved from the sink to the front door and stood in a shadow behind the screen, expecting the worse.

"Snake, I really just drank too much 'shine last night, and somewhere in the night, I even passed out. But before that, I must have gone somewhere and look at this right side...just look at it. Now, you tell me, do you know how I did this? Where did I go last night, and how in the world did I do this? Do ya know?" Espy was now standing right in the boy's face, staring at Snake while his mama watched the drama unfold from a safer distance.

Snake heard the question, but it was obviously not the question he had expected. He asked his daddy again before he answered.

"You want me to tell ya how *you* did this to the car?"

"Yep," Espy responded without blinking.

"Well, Daddy, to tell you the truth, I don't know what you did last night. I wasn't with ya, and I really never quite know what all you do or where you go. Sorry. The car really looks bad, though. Ya must'a hit something really hard."

With that, Snake slowly turned toward the house with a growing grin on his face. His daddy did not even ask him how or if Snake had wrecked the car. He had asked Snake where he himself had gone to do such a thing. And Snake, without lying or even having to stretch the truth, was able to say he really did not know what his daddy had done. As he passed through the front door and brushed against his mother, she whispered, "Why the smile, Snake? What's so funny?"

"Nothin' Mama," Snake quietly replied. "Really nothin'."

That moonshine run and the wreck of his daddy's Chevy was but the first of many in Snake's life and outlaw career. His experience in moonshining and his know-how in fast and wild driving grew with each year. He was a local born-and-bred Union County boy that was growing up untamed. He was unruly and undisciplined, and "rowdy" became his middle name. He was revered for his moonshining abilities and respected by his clan for his driving abilities. But by the revenuers that never caught the boy, he was feared.

In the years after, he drove many cars and named many of his cars.

The Southern Nickname Phenomena

In most states of this great country, a person's name is his name. Bob will be called Bob, Mike will be called Mike, and a Ford truck will be referred to by its owner as "my truck" or "the Ford." However, this is not necessarily so in many of our great southern and rural states. Though life in general is simple in the South, the nickname phenomenon is a strange thing. It is typical for most little boys and girls in the South to grow up with a specific nickname, which is often used by friends and family alike even as they grow up into adulthood.

A nickname can sometimes be a shortened version of a person's proper name. But in the South, the nickname often reflected certain aspects of an individual's personality, body style, body size, or sometimes their distinctive accomplishments. Stonewall Jackson received his nickname, "Stonewall," from the first battle of Bull Run in 1861 where his troops stood their ground against the Union forces "like a stone wall."

Many men have had nicknames that are remembered well after they are gone. Billy the Kid, Buffalo Bill, and Bear Bryant are some examples of famous nicknames that are still popular in referring to those individuals today. Even specific geographical areas can be known by a nickname, such as *Dixie*. The term *Dixie* became the most popular name for the American South, though the actual origin of the term is fairly obscure. Some suggest that it may have come from the French *dix* (meaning ten) inscribed on the backside of the ten dollar bills first issued by the Louisiana Citizens' Bank before the Civil War. Others believe that it may have come from songs sung by slaves about the good life that was experienced by some who worked for Dixie, a kind slaveholder. Still there are some that believe the name Dixie may have come from the Mason-Dixon line, which divided the slave states from the free states. The Mason-Dixon line was the boundary line between Maryland and Pennsylvania and was surveyed by two British astronomers, Charles Mason and Jeremiah Dixon.

Many of the young boys in Union County had nicknames. Some were "Buck," others were called "Termite," "Eagle Eye," or "Deer Hunter"—even "Snake." But in the Deep South, the southerners also gave their mountains, their cabins, their stills, or even their hot-runnin' moonshine cars a unique nickname that often represented their true feelings regarding whatever it was they were naming. Such is the case with Beulah.

The name "Beulah" to many might be a name of a girlfriend, a sweetheart, a wife, or even the mother of their children, but not so with Snake's Beulah. The name Beulah conjured up memories of the sweet thing hidden back in the woods away from the girlfriends, sweethearts, and officers of the law—a big submarine still.

It was in the spring of the year when they began stoke up the fires under old Beulah. One might guess that the size of that old still was suggested in that name. A name like Sally or Suzy might have suggested a tiny, petite still for brewin' a small amount of that mountain 'shine, but not so with a name like Big Beulah.

Inherent in that nickname alone is found the hint of what one would see if they happened upon it back in the deep woods. Old Beulah was a beaut in Jerry's eyes. It was nearly the size of a submarine, and it had been made with two sides of wood and two sides of metal. Snake had always wanted to have the biggest and baddest stills in Union County. He was known for thinkin' big. Some of the locals had occasionally kidded Snake about his big ideas about moonshining and bootlegging: "Snake, slow down, boy. Don't you know you've gotta crawl before you can walk, and you've gotta walk before you can run." But not in Snake's mind. He had an idea to break out running in a very big way, and run he did.

Snake never forgot when he went back to one of the local men that milled lumber for local carpenters and builders.

"Hey, buddy," Snake hollered as he jumped out of his old truck. "We're back and I need you to cut me some long lumber for a new submarine-style still. I've gotta have a couple of big pieces longer than my old truck there."

"What are you talkin' about, boy? I've never seen such a big still before. Why do you need such a big piece of lumber for?" the old man replied, wiping sawdust from his beard and cheeks.

"For the biggest still that this old county has ever seen," Snake replied. "Just cut me some big pieces."

The old man eyed Snake up and down before allowing a smile that gradually ran from one ear to the other.

"Remember when we used to joke you about crawling before you walk and walking before you run?"

"Yeah," Snake replied. "You always teased me about that."

"Well," the old man said as he headed back into the mill to cut the lumber Snake had requested, "you are certainly up and runnin' now, boy... and I mean really up and runnin'."

Snake smiled as he followed the old man back into the mill. And with a rip or two of a big saw, Snake was on his way with the lumber that eventually made out the sides of Old Beulah. And though Beulah was not a beautiful lady to put your arms around and love, Snake loved Beulah. Many a gallon of 'shine came from her for several years.

So boys, men, territories, and even stills had nicknames that reflected their nature or character. The little moonshine boy born into the third generation of old-fashioned moonshiners in the center of Union County was Jerry Rushing. Jerry grew up into a slim, scrawny young man and inherited not only a legacy of moonshining but also the nickname Snake. Snake built Beulah and hid her in the woods to brew some of that good old Rushing 'shine. So goes the use of nicknames in the beloved South, also known as Dixie. Snake named two of his cars "Bluebird" and the "Green Hornet." But before them came one of Snake's first cars. It was an old '49 Ford convertible.

That Old '49 Ford Convertible

Snake was barely out of his teens, and already this moonshinin' boy had a couple of stills hidden way back in the woods. The stills had been carefully built, transported, and assembled under the clandestine cover of darkness. After scouting for several evenings, the liquor stills were finally located under the cover of some large pine trees and oak trees, which acted as a visual blanket hiding it from sight. Even the occasional revenuer in his single-engine spy plane was unable to make out the camouflaged still hidden by the bountiful leaf cover above.

Drip by drip the illegal corn liquor flowed from the condensing coils, which were being cooled by the chilly water from a nearby stream. Slowly the gallon jug became full as the experienced young moonshiner grabbed it quickly and replaced it with another empty jug, being careful that not a drop of that precious backwoods 'shine trickled onto the ground. Bottle after bottle was filled and capped until there were bottles of 'shine sitting all around the still. Some were resting against the trees that were providing the camouflaged cover, and others were being set on top of boxes or within crates ready for delivery.

It didn't really matter what type of car you drove to deliver the illegal stuff, as long as it was fast and had plenty of storage room for the liquor. The larger cars of the forties and fifties were great for bootlegging because they were nearly as big as boats, and, with the passenger seat and the rear seat removed, hundreds of gallons of whiskey could be hauled in one run. Ultimately the runnin' cars became modified stocks with special engines, springs, and tires. But in the beginning, any big fast car sufficed for young Snake's runs.

One of his first cars in his official bootlegging business was an old 1949 Ford convertible. Some of his first big runs were made in that old convertible. On some of the county's cold winter nights, he tightened and strapped down the convertible top after he loaded the 'shine and made the night run with all of the windows up. But some of Snake's favorite early runs were during the cool spring or fall nights when he could make the run with the top completely down. Snake first loaded the space where the rear seat had been removed. Once that area was filled to the top, he loaded the area where the passenger seat had been removed, and then he moved to the trunk. The trunk area in that old '49 Ford was very large and held nearly fifty gallons of the strong, biting liquid.

There were many runs in that old '49 Ford convertible. Snake, "the Union County outlaw," outran every lawman that tried to catch him. He liked to wear a big, old black Stetson hat. When that convertible top was down, Snake pulled the Stetson down tight upon his head until it nearly folded down his ears alongside his head. There was no time to back up and pick up a wind-blown hat if he were in the middle of some bootleg chase.

Snake ran down the road with the convertible wide open, with that big, black Stetson upon his head, looking quite like the outlaw he always pictured. Sometimes he sang to himself; sometimes he wrote a song in his head about his runnin' along the way.

Some Union County boys made money with the moonshine, leaving the dangerous delivery to someone else. However, though Jerry Rushing one day became best known as the fastest runner in the South, he ran a lucrative undercover business both making the 'shine and then running it. Though there was some good money to be made in this business, Snake often reinvested his profits back into his family corn liquor business. But he had to be careful as federal revenue officers were always on the prowl.

It was a common sight to come over the hill, walking to your still early in the morning or evening, only to find it surrounded by revenue officers breaking the jugs and busting up the still operation with hammers, axes, or any other tool they could use to wreak havoc. You then used your profits to buy another still and the needed materials for another condensing coil and start again. Or perhaps on a fast run you had wrecked your souped-up bootleg car. Then the money made from the trip was quickly spent on another vehicle for another run. It was always a cat-and-mouse game.

On one such occasion, Snake and a friend had parked the old convertible up the road and in the woods just a mile or so from one of their still operations. They often backtracked from the car and entered the woods far from the actual path that led to the still. It was a sultry August night and the sliver of the quarter moon had just come up above the horizon. They had made a run just a hundred miles or so outside of Monroe. It had been a good run, and several cases of the high-quality Rushing alcohol had been delivered on time. Happy clients, even in the moonshining business, meant return costumers.

Not all moonshiners took pride in the quality of their corn or sugar liquor stuff. But this was not the case with the Rushing clan. They made the good stuff and never watered down their 'shine or mixed it with dangerous additives. If you bought jugs from any of the Rushings, you could bet that you had the best-tasting stuff in the South.

Well, Snake and his friend were happy about the run that night, another successful one for the Rushings. It was a fast one, and no revenuers were even on the road. However, they were both tired from the run and from the working of the still earlier that evening. They walked quietly through the woods like a doe walking her fawn during the early hunting season. They knew that sometimes the revenuers stopped along the road, got out of the car, and listened to the squeal of the still, the smell of some strong mash, or the lighthearted joking of some moonshiner with too much 'shine for his own good. So they walked along the worn path without saying too much. Occasionally one commented on the run, in a quiet whisper just loud enough for the other to hear. They knew that the dawn was just an hour away.

They had crossed the creek twice as it snaked back and forth along this valley, and, though it was dark, they knew from memory that they had one more crossing, before coming to the still. They had come to that final crossing, and Snake was about to cross the fallen tree that laid across the creek when he stopped dead in his tracks on the fallen rotten trunk. Snake had spent hours in the woods and was a highly experienced woodsman and a skilled outdoorsman. He felt more comfortable under the Carolina oak and pine trees on some backwood path in the middle of thick forest than he did on the black asphalt of any nearby town or city.

Snake may have had limited book knowledge, but he could smell the stench of a Carolina black bear or sniff out an opossum hiding from inside some fallen hollow tree. He had tracked a deer for miles on his hands and knees, and legend had it that he could even smile a turkey down from its perch sitting high in a tree. On this particular early morning, he knew something was wrong. He did not really smell anything or see anything unusual, as the moonshine operation was more than one hundred yards away. But he sensed danger in the air. He had that old Rushing moonshine feeling deep within his gut that something was really wrong.

He quickly motioned back with his hand to his trailing buddy, and he stopped fast in his tracks right at the creek bank. They paused as motionless silhouettes there in the dark. Snake slowly turned his head right and then left again, trying to pick up any strange sound in the woods. He had traveled this path for months, and it was carefully hidden from the road and hidden from any view. But on this trip, he knew that the wildlife in the woods had been bothered. The night sounds seemed different, as if they were struggling to communicate a warning to their friends in the forest. And Snake had picked up the warnings.

He slowly moved off of the log and stooped down to the path. There were prints of a boot that were foreign to him. Snake got closer to the ground and studied the prints. They were not prints from just one man, traveling along this beaten trail. The imprints were different from each other. Snake figured that there may be five or six strangers on the trail.

Odd footprints on my old footpath... not good, he thought.

Revenuers. The thought hit him like a rifle blast tearing through the shadows of his mind. *They must be revenuers... but how... but... but how could they have found the trail, let alone the hidden still?* he wondered to himself.

He had traveled now some twenty-five yards upon his knees with some of the gravel along the path slashing little punctures into the flesh of his knees through the gapping holes from his pants. But he paid no mind to these trivial inconveniences. He was completely locked onto these foreign tracks and the enemy ahead. He crawled upon the ground like a soldier preparing for battle, edging himself slowly to a hill that overlooked the valley that held one of his favorite stills.

He turned to his buddy that had been following close to Snake wondering why all the concern.

"Either it's revenuers or some of those nasty Brown brothers from the other side of the county," Snake whispered. "There must be someone up ahead. Let's be careful and see if we can get closer to our still to see just what's goin' on. I should have grabbed my shotgun and we could have gotten a jump on 'em. But...let's...move up...very...slowly. *Shhhhh!* Let's go. And we'll stay off the path because that's where they'd expect us."

With that line of attack, Snake and his buddy quietly got back upon their feet and moved off the path by at least thirty yards or so. They began to parallel the path, taking each step carefully. Stalking was something that Snake had learned as a youngster, first by playing in the woods with his friends, and then by stalking game during hunts in his early childhood. There was a strategy to walking quietly in a woods covered by a blanket of fallen leaves, branches, and twigs. Some used the heel-toe technique, though Snake liked the tip-toe method of some of the early Americans.

He looked forward and then down as he slowly placed the toes of his foot softly upon the ground. Then he shifted his weight only to find another place to set his other foot upon, keeping most all of his weight shifting from tip-toe to tip-toe. The tactic was to avoid any small twigs of any kind. Larger branches seldom broke. But a small twig, particularly those partially hidden from view by some fallen leaves, was the kiss of death. Bear, turkey, and especially the whitetail deer had carefully tuned ears for the sound of a breaking twig. But it was not just the wildlife that had become accustomed to this fearful forest "snap," but also the moonshiner and the revenuer. It meant that something or someone was approaching, and for both the moonshiner and revenuer, that meant trouble in their world.

So Snake and his friend continued closer and closer to his still location. They were moving but a few yards every minute. As they stalked closer to their ultimate location, Snake could begin to smell the strong odor of his fermenting mash every time the breeze blew their way. The sun had not yet come over the horizon to begin the day. But the early morning had broken as the bright colors of a new dawn had begun their painting of the eastern sky. Oranges, bright blues, and a reddish hue colored the sky, providing a beautiful canvas backdrop for the wild scene that was about to unfold. Snake loved this time of day. The skies were often picturesque, and the wildlife, from the blackbird to the early waking gobblers, seemed to all awaken at once as if shaken from their slumber by some instinctive inner alarm clock. The sounds of an early morning woods were always filled with the break-of-day melody of the awaken creatures.

As Snake's senses were working overtime to experience and embrace this beautiful tapestry and concert of forest life, he was abruptly shaken back to the reality of his early morning stalk when he came upon a shadowy figure walking amongst others around his favorite still. There they were, a couple of federal agents along with a handful of local county sheriffs. He was shocked to see them walking around his still as if admiring the handiwork.

Did they just stumble across it and were lucky, or did someone turn me in? he wondered.

He stopped abruptly and immediately aligned his tall slender figure with a nearby tree while motioning for his friend to do the same. He had learned that he was better hidden, whether from revenuers or wildlife, if he blended his big vertical frame alongside a tree. He stood there for some time trying to control his breathing and keep quiet. His heart was racing, and his temper, which often got him in trouble, was beginning to boil. He wanted to race right into the mix and take them on all by himself. But the lawmen were armed with shotguns, rifles, and what appeared to be a box of dynamite. It was difficult if not impossible for him, and he knew it. There was nothing he could do but stand there and wait.

He then saw firsthand what until then he had only heard about. One of the federal agents tipped over the still while another took a long-armed axe and began to chop holes in the mash barrels. Another took the condensing coil and began to chop holes in the pipes with another short-handled chopping axe. They worked and worked on the destruction of the still until the sun finally made its appearance up and over the tops of the surrounding tree line. Their objective was clear and obvious. It was the complete and total demolition of the still until all of it was destroyed and lying in the mud mixed with whatever mash had still been in the barrels. Their goal was to wreak such havoc on the physical components of the illegal operation that the moonshiners would be out of business. Though they usually accomplished their goals of destroying the stills, it usually just made the moonshiners more determined in their fight against the government. Most of them were back in business with a new still within a few days.

Such was the case with Snake and his buddy. But to see their handy work destroyed by government officials literally made Snake sick to his stomach. He just could not believe his eyes. He got madder and madder, but with some grace from above, he was able to hold it down to just below the boiling point until he saw one lawman begin to place dynamite around the already damaged still. Snake turned to his buddy and whispered, "Why, I'd kill 'em right here and now if I only had my guns. Why, I'd—"

At that moment his buddy, who had been standing much too long, lost his balance and moved his foot out from the tree to steady himself. A twig that he had inadvertently stepped on went *snap*.

In a quiet wooded area, with no sounds around, that simple snap went off like a stick of dynamite. Snake jumped, as did the agents. The feds had been so busy destroying the still that they had not noticed Snake standing just out of camp. As quick as the broken branch had screamed their way, they grabbed their rifles and shotguns while others pulled their pistols. The flying mixture of buckshot, bullets, smoke, and shot wads immediately tore through the sanctuary of the morning woodland air. Branches from all around Snake and his friend were falling from their trees as the agent's fired their weapons at the two young men.

Snake screamed out, "Run for your life, partner. Don't stop . . . run like a jackrabbit on the fly." The two were off like a couple of wild prairie chickens. Shots were being fired out time and time again as the agents ran toward the two scrambling boys. One of the agents slipped and fell into the creek, while yet another one got caught by the seat of his pants in a briar patch just this side of the creek. Most of these agents were Yankee federal agents. They could cuss and shoot and tear up a local still, but they were no match for Snake in his own woods.

Snake and his buddy ran for fifty or so yards and then split up, one running to the left and the other circling back around to the right. They had previously decided that if ever such a chase took place, they would run, split, and meet up under the rock outcropping just the other side of the highway. It was back in the woods, across from both the creek and the road. It provided just the shelter they needed to hide awhile if ever chased.

The agents continued to shoot blindly into the woods in front of them, even after losing a visual on their young suspects. Occasionally, misguided buckshot softly fell from the tree cover above just to lightly drop on or around Snake. He was huffing and puffing when he finally arrived back at the roadway crossing. He peeked out from a large ivy thicket and saw no cars and certainly no lawmen. He quickly crossed the road and continued back up to the small cave-like fissure in a large rock formation. He swung around the granite opening and jumped down into the small opening. His buddy was already sitting there with big catlike grin upon his face. It was really bittersweet—they had escaped, but they had lost their still. They had outmaneuvered the lawmen in the woods with neither a bullet hole nor a scratch to show from it.

During the race for freedom, they had heard both the gunshots and then the cussing and cursing as they had begun to outrun the agents.

"Catch them suckers, they're getting away," the agents screamed. "I know it's them moonshiners. Put a hole right though the middle of one of them," another yelled.

But try as the may, they were losing ground on the young bucks as both were in better shape and were running with a purpose—do not ever get caught. They also had a plan, and they knew they were safe if they left the '49 convertible hidden for now. They could easily make it back into the woods under the dark of night, retrieve their concealed car, and get back home. In the meantime, they had plenty of time to sit in their rock-surrounded hideout and discuss their next still and the improvements that they would build into it.

After a couple of hours of talking about their moonshine business, the two drifted off into a midday slumber just about the time the revenuers had set off the dynamite in their old moonshine camp.

Boom! Bang! Kapow! The explosion rocked the woods, reverberated through the forest and echoed right into their hideout. Both jumped to their feet and stood awhile without saying a word almost as if they were in a reverent silence for the still they just lost. After a couple of additional hours of waiting, Snake got up, and the two walked back through the woods to the hidden convertible. they ran back to the house in the silence of darkened woods and spirits. It was never easy to lose a still. To a professional moonshiner, it is about like losing a family member. Neither of them talked until Snake finally broke the silence by saying softly, as the cool night air blew through the Ford, "We'll be back..."

"Yea...you can count on that," his friend agreed.

BLUEBIRD AND THE GREEN HORNET

Moonshine cars always have a shortened life span. They usually die of engine failure from being pushed too hard one too many nights. Or they are wrecked on some too sharp turn, wrapped around a tree, or smashed into some rock formation. Still others are rolled over and over until they are no more than a pile of metal ready to be melted down and made into some other piece of machinery.

Snake loved cars, and he especially loved fast cars. As is the case with most bootleggers, he named his cars. He purchased a '49 Ford coupe and put new tires on the old thing. It was blue and resembled a fast-flying bluebird, once Snake worked the bugs out of the old engine. So he named the old coupe *Bluebird*. It lasted for a few runs, but one of his favorite early cars was the *Green Hornet*.

Snake had just built his largest still ever and really needed a fast car for the distribution of that hillbilly pop. The typical "southern shine businessman" ran the still, bottled the 'shine, and then occasionally delivered some of the liquor. Snake and the entire household took great pride in the entire process. However, Snake had always been drawn to the more glamorous side of the actual runnin' of the liquor. So he bought an old green 1955 Ford and began working on it when he was not minding the 'shine making. It ran hard and fast. Snake had been in over fifty runs when he began to notice the many bullet holes in the old Ford.

"She's a good fast baby," Snake said about the '55 Ford, "even if it is all shot up to the hilt."

"Shot up to the hilt," Snake bragged. He really liked the sound of that. A modern-day outlaw drove such a car. Many of the local law-men were found on a day after a great chase sitting in a Monroe diner and talking about the fast-runnin' *Green Hornet*.

"I about caught up with him last night," one said. Another said, "Sure, sure, call me when you catch him. I've heard that no agent has even been within twenty yards of that beast."

And of course, this is what legends and tall tales are made from—stories over coffee at a local lunch counter with federal agents discussing the legendary episodes of a 'shine-running car like the *Green Hornet*.

Though some of the stories grew with each telling, and though it may be difficult to decipher truth from fiction, the "tobacco-in-the-radiator" is a true story and is still told to this day. Jerry Rushing often ran alone, but many runs used several cars. On some runs, they all carried liquor and left together, only to separate later using several roads to arrive at the same or different destination. On other occa-sions, some of the cars were decoys, carrying no liquor load at all. In the event of a real chase, the federal revenuers might be uncertain exactly which car to chase.

Snake was becoming famous for his clean and crisp corn liquor as well as his expert driving behind the wheel of the *Green Hornet*. No officer had yet caught up with him. Many had been able to put a bullet hole into her body, but none could put her down. The best that most of the agents could boast about was to mar her body with a hole or two.

On one particular evening, Snake was running with old Jako Crooks and a few of his buddies.

One of Snake's buddies, simply referred to as Lemon, was in the *Green Hornet* with Snake. Jake had flipped a couple of his cars, and Snake had pulled up to help Jake flip his cars back over quickly before the law got there. They parked the *Green Hornet* on the side of the road, and Snake had jumped out quickly to assist his friends. This was a typical night in Snake's life with his crazy buddies.

He was always the leader in any outlaw gang. Shouting orders among his friends was expected in a panic situation.

"Hurry up...fast...the lawmen may only be a few miles behind us. Flip these babies quick...fast...push over here...pull on that bumper." Snake was an expert in flipping cars and in turning them back over. In many cases, after a little metal work, the car was ready for running again in a few weeks and maybe ready for a Saturday night race.

Once they had finished all of the flipping and Jake and his boys were ready to roll, Snake's friend asked if he could drive the *Green Hornet*.

"Please, Snake...I'll be careful. You know I'm a good driver, and I'll be careful."

"OK," Snake sighed, "but let's get going. The law may be right behind us. Hurry...let's get."

And with that, Lemon crawled into the driver's seat while Snake jumped into the passenger side.

"Start it up, baby, we've no time to waste...c'mon," Snake shouted. Lemon started up the car, gave the engine a big old rev, and shifted into first gear, tossing gravel over the road and through the farmer's cornfield across the street. The car was fine for some twenty or thirty minutes as most of the highway was over or around cornfield country on straight runs.

Lemon got the Hornet up to ninety miles an hour or so, smiled at Snake, and then, with Snake's nod of approval, he took it into triple digits. The engine hummed and the rubber tread of the tires howled a softened squeal. This was a perfect combination for any night on the road. They had to keep rolling since they had reason to believe that the law was possibly a few miles back.

All was going well until they got closer to the county's hills where the roads turned quickly back and forth to fit in amongst the topography of the land. Lemon first hit the shoulder on the right side of a turn, slipping a bit of the right side tires into the mud, throwing the Carolina mud back up and over the rear of the trunk.

"Careful, man…whatcha trying to do to my Hornet?" Snake asked. "Pull it over, and I'll take it the rest of the way."

But before Lemon could slow the Green Hornet completely to a stop, it slid to the right, hit the red mud, and began to spin 180 degrees and then back completely again. Lemon overcompensated on the wheel, and the Hornet took another dangerous 360-degree spin on the wet road and headed straight into an oncoming bridge embankment. Jerry Rushing was screaming and trying to take hold of the wheel when the front left side of the Green Hornet hit the bridge railing with an awful force.

Snake's head hit the window as his chest crashed into the hard metal dash. It was only the dash that kept Snake from catapulting from the Hornet into the creek below the bridge. He had black and blue bruises for months after. Lemon was shaken, but not hurt. He had slammed into the driver's wheel with enough force to bend it slightly into an oval shape. They sat there for a moment as if surveying the damage to their own bodies. It had been a devilish crash, though it soon became apparent that neither was severely hurt.

But the *Green Hornet* was not that lucky.

The crash had jarred the radiator, and water was spraying from a couple of holes, causing steam from the hot engine to rise high into the night air.

Snake ran quickly to the front of the Hornet and threw open the hood.

"What will we do now?" Lemon asked. "The engine will quickly overheat if we continue to run, and if we sit here, the law could catch up with us in no time."

Snake stood motionless as if surveying the situation. He was a genius at such situations. He looked at the radiator and the holes that were squirting the water upon the hood and engine.

"I've got it," Snake screamed. "Grab the cigarettes from the dash, quick."

Snake took the cigarettes and began breaking them up into little pieces and tossing the tobacco into the radiator. Lemon just watched with amazement.

"What the heck?" Lemon asked looking through his steamed-up glasses with an inquisitive look upon his face. "What the heck...?"

"Just watch," Jerry barked back. "And go sit in the passenger seat. You're finished driving for one night."

It took but a moment for Lemon to obey and to jump back into the car. Jerry jumped back into the driver's side and fired up the *Green Hornet* again. He slowly backed it off the bridge railing and turned slowly back upon the main road. Luckily the law was still behind him as the whole incident only took three to four minutes.

Snake had escaped the lawmen again. There was just no holding back this modern-day outlaw.

Jesse James would be proud of me, he thought. Funny how many times he thought this thought within his lifetime.

As Snake drove the *Green Hornet* over the bridge and back down the road, the tobacco mixed with the antifreeze solution and ran through the radiator, swelling with the water and sealing the holes, at least for the remainder of this run. Snake had done it again, and this time with the *Green Hornet*. Though it was a dangerous run, Snake had outsmarted the lawmen, and the *Green Hornet* was successful once more. It was a good run for Snake's souped-up hot rod, and it was not to be her last.

The Safety Net of God

Many of the bootleggers of the past had as short a life span as the cars they drove. Many died early at the end of a federal revenuer's gun barrel. Others died early in their runnin' car taking a sharp curve too fast. But that was not the case with Jerry Rushing. He turned, flipped, and spun more bootlegging cars than most others even owned. There were wrecks, bullets flying, and even holes in the *Green Hornet* to attest to these near-death catastrophes. Though Snake would be cut up, mangled, and hospital-bound from many of these bootlegging wrecks, he never died in them.

So I ask you, why did many find themselves before the very throne of God early in their lives, answering God for the life they lived, while others like Jerry Rushing lived to tell his story? The answer just might be found in a Lynyrd Skynyrd song entitled "Hell or Heaven." The song says that sometimes when we go through difficult times and then grow older, we may experience the hand of God on our shoulder.

Though much of little Snake's early life was a living hell, it was obvious when looking back at his death-defying experiences that the hand of God was resting right there on his shoulder, as Lynyrd Skynyrd would say. Why was the hand of God on Snake's life when it was not evident in the lives of many around him? The answer is complicated, but it is clear that God's hand was upon Snake as his life was spared time and time again. Even the Word of God says in Daniel 6:22, "My God hath sent his angel, and hath shut the lions' mouths."

God can and does intervene in our lives. He moves in response to His Word, and He answers the many prayers of His saints. God is alive and well, and He can send angels at His command, whether it is to shut the mouths of lions in an ancient lions' den or to guide a bootlegger's car around a curve with His hand upon the driver to protect him from a certain death.

God had plans for Jerry Rushing, and His angels had command over him. Jerry Rushing may have not been aware of this truth, but nonetheless, the truth of God is never shaken.

CHAPTER 4

The Birth of Traveler

THE "MODERN-DAY OUTLAW"

AS THE HAIR on their heads slowly turns white, most men sit around and brag about the women in their past or the sports hero they were on some forgotten baseball team of their youth. But this was not so with Snake. Jerry Rushing bragged about his moonshine stills and the illegal liquor that he became famous for. Beulah was his favorite still. To this day, he recalls her beauty as if talking about Miss North Carolina. She was big and long and could cook that 'shine stew like no other.

When he is not sharing some story about one of his moonshine stills of his past, he is mesmerizing a listener with his favorite topic, his bootlegging cars and the runnin' he became notorious for throughout Carolina. On such occasions, he fondly recalls his fast runnin' bootlegging cars of the former years...the '49 Ford coupe, the '49 convertible, the old *Bluebird,* or the *Green Hornet,* to name a few. Just the mention of one of his bootlegging cars conjures up all the vibrant and

77

colorful images of the past. The memories are still so vivid—certain hairpin curves taken in the rain at speeds too fast for an earthbound rocket-on-wheels, with a federal revenuer ramming the bumper all the while.

Or perhaps the recollection is of a bootleg run where several federal agents and sheriffs are working a stakeout with a roadblock while you are carrying two hundred gallons of the family sweet stuff. You see the roadblock ahead and press the gas pedal so hard you get a cramp in your right ankle. You set your chin like flint, and your forehead tightens while drops of anxious perspiration form on your brow and drip to your shirt. You brace your left hand on the wheel while your left elbow is braced against the door. Your right elbow is braced against the many cases of moonshine sitting immediately to your right.

There is no stopping now. You are the modern-day outlaw, and the chase is on. You are being stalked like a wild animal, and the federal trappers have set the trap. The hunters have all taken their place, and the ambush has been set. Their main ambition is to bring in the "Snake"—dead or alive. Their professional dream and personal aspiration is to drop the noose around the neck of the fastest bootlegger in the Carolinas.

The captain of the revenuers told them to "not take it personal," but they cannot help it. Each time they return without their prey, without "Snake the bootlegger," they experience the agony of defeat. They quietly keep the score in their mind, and Snake is ahead. In fact, the feds have not yet scored. They may have buried a bullet or two into the side of one of Snake's runnin' cars, but they have never yet brought him down.

"The man that brings him in will be a hero in these parts," their captain declared, hoping to increase the morale of the squad. The squad now has Snake in their crosshairs. They have fingers on the triggers, and they are sure they will have him soon. The roadblock is impassable, and the reports are that he is just a few miles downstream and headed their way.

But it will not be that easy . . . it never is! But let's listen to Snake, as he is coming up around the bend, no more than a mile or two from the deadly "Bonnie and Clyde"–style ambush, tell the story from his perspective:

> Strange as it may seem, as you are picking up speed, you are sensing some sort of imminent danger. But you shake your instinct because your destination is before you and there is no turning back. Your mind drifts to your own trapping skills in the forest. You are a skilled and proficient trapper and seldom does any wild forest prey evade your snare, though occasionally even a fox can sense danger or sense the likelihood of a trap and reverse his steps to avoid the inevitable. But you cannot turn back. Perhaps your determination and stubbornness prohibit you from turning back.
>
> Nevertheless, you will not turn back. The true testing time has come, and you are ready to prove yourself. Nothing stands between you and freedom but a roadblock of several federal and state police cars, several wooden blockades, and a dozen lawmen with as many firearms all locked, cocked, and ready to rock. They are all pointed your direction—you are the target of their affection. You are glad to be loved.
>
> You round the last curve and see images in the distance that appear to be what they are, revenuer cars, blockades, and many moving images in the woodline on both sides of the road. As you approach the roadway obstacles, you are able to slowly make out the shifting images. They are officers looking, pointing, and shouting your way. *Why all the excitement? It's only me,* you ponders in your mind.
>
> And then you hear the first of many shots fired. Many whiz by your fast-moving car, and a couple find their mark in the chrome fender or the front quarter panel. You continue to press forward, only occasionally entertaining the thought of danger or death. You are bearing down into hell itself, without considering the consequences of your actions. You are but one hundred yards from impact, and then only seventy-five yards. Time stands still as you glance to the left and then to the right.
>
> You are now only fifty yards away, and you can distinguish the mixed facial expressions of hate and hope upon the officer's faces. Some are taking aim where others are firing away. Still others are reloading from their last barrage. You come within thirty yards and cut a strong right on the steering wheel. The

rear of your car goes into a fearful skid while you down-shift and head up the grassy embankment directly into the line of fire from the tree line above the bank. Those left on the street fire away, many missing their mark during the excitement. Others fire into the left side of your car, exploding gallon after gallon of the illegal whiskey stacked and loaded in the back seat. You continue into the tree line, which is the only sanctuary the officers have for themselves.

Unexpectedly, the cavalry turns coward as they head back into the woods in a fast-running retreat not unlike some Yankee line being chased by the men in gray. You follow them up into the woods, carefully picking your line of travel, plowing down bush after bush and any tree with a diameter smaller than your forearm. You turn a sharp left, sideswiping one large pine, and head back down the embankment slightly on the other side of the barricade obstruction, all the time watching the surprised faces of those still firing your direction. Gallons of whiskey are still being exploded from their gunfire. Whiskey is spilling out of the holes on the side of your car. It is also splashing and spilling all over you as you speed back down the embankment on your two left tires. The right tires are more than two feet off the muddy ground below as you walk a tightrope between a successful getaway and flipping your car, landing right in the middle of them all.

And somehow, you do it again as you hit the pavement behind them leaving smoke, the smell of freshly burned rubber mixed with the aroma of your fresh batch of homemade whiskey. The lawmen still fire in your direction as if trying to hit some phantom bootleg driver. They empty their loads, only to stare in unbelief at the smoke line and wet moonshine stain left all over the highway. They continue to stare as if wondering if they ever saw the bootlegger. Did they?

They stare at each other in amazement that you drove right through them, wondering how you did it. The lawmen that had hidden back in the woods walked back to their post from the cover. Most hang their heads in shame and defeat, while others shake their heads in unbelief. As the frustrated and foiled agents begin to disassemble their blockade, you are heading down the road, laughing and shouting. You always would laugh during and after such an escapade.

Some just thought you were happy. Others seemed to think running from the law was such fun for you that a smile would erupt across your face and come out of your belly in laughter. But those that knew you best felt that it must have been your youthful and defiant rebelliousness that fueled such laughter, as you would escape their valiant attempt to snare you.

But only you knew the genuine answer to their riddle. It was the "modern-day outlaw" within you, the Jesse James mind-set, and the daring desperado that pushed you to drive so hard. And in your victory, the defiant laugh of Jesse the bandit lived on.

Childhood dreams do come true.

Not for all little boys, but they did for you, Jerry Rushing.

IN THE BEGINNING...

Snake enjoyed making the moonshine. There was something about lighting the fire next to some mountain creek on a late fall evening, stirring the mash, and watching as the newly condensed whiskey dripped into the gallon bottle. Depending on the size of the still and the length of the condensing coil, sometimes the moonshine dripped, and at other times, with a large still operation, the whiskey flowed out of the spout like poured lemonade from a crystal pitcher on a summer day.

Was it genetic, or was it a learned appreciation for this fine art of moonshining? On some evenings, just the smell of the mash delighted a man's soul as it fermented in the night. On other evenings the damp, fall fragrance of fallen leaves blended with the strong aroma of the newly made mountain juice caused his senses to dance with delight.

Though there was an inherent danger in the manufacturing of moonshine, the greatest danger for the modern-day outlaw was in the moving of the 'shine from the still to the consumer. The runner could be caught by some federal revenuer, shot in an escape attempt, or even run off the mountain and left for dead. The bootlegger needed of a fast car that could handle the wicked turns, outrun the fastest of the revenuers' chase vehicles, and had a body that could store multiple gallons of the whiskey and conceal it from view during the transporting.

By the middle of the twentieth century, the large-body Chrysler was the preferred automobile of many of the bootleggers. It was a fast car with a trunk was so large that it could hold many gallons of whiskey. Jerry Rushing loved the large-body Chrysler. Though he used Fords in his early runnin', he ultimately graduated to the Chrysler.

Snake had already made hundreds of runs when his buddy helping him at his still one night mentioned a car that he had seen on one of the local used car lots.

"It's a real hot Chevrolet," Billy said. "In fact, I think that we could pick it up for only a few hundred dollars. Whatcha think?"

"Don't know," Snake replied. "Help me with this last run of 'shine, and let's catch some sleep. Maybe we can drive by tomorrow and look at it before I make that run to Wilkes County. But I don't think I want no Chevy. I've been lookin' at those big old Chryslers that they're makin. I think that we need to change over to those monster-bodied machines. Besides, those HEMIs in the big Chryslers run down the highway like scalded dogs. Wow, they can run."

Billy continued in his relentless selling of the Chevy, "I don't know, man. This thing is fitted with chromed accessories and a 780 Stage III Holley. On the dyno, this steam launcher makes 530 horsepower at 5,000 rpm, and 540 lb/ft of torque at 3,200 rpm. Backing up the 502 is a 400-Turbo fitted with ten-inch 3,500-stall converter and an aluminum driveshaft. Can you beat that, man?"

"I don't really know about any of that stuff," Snake answered back while shifting another clean gallon jug under the 'shine spout. "But I do know that the standard Chrysler packing a HEMI and fitted with a custom double four-barrel carburetor can outhandle any other Chevy two-to-one on the road. I don't care how many horsepower or rpm or pounds of torque or whatever else you said. Now, let's finish this here run of batch, and we'll see tomorrow."

Snake still had aspirations of being the fastest and baddest bootlegger in the county. He already had a fast-growing reputation throughout all of Union County and many of the surrounding counties. To begin with, Snake had never been caught. He had made whiskey and delivered it throughout Carolina. He had been staked out, run down, blockaded on highways, and shot at, but he had never been put down or brought in.

Many revenuers knew of his reputation, and they also knew just how dangerous Snake had become. Some called him the "mean man of Monroe," where others called him evil or crazy. Snake stopped at nothing to run his whiskey. He had grown up from an innocent little moonshiner's son to a cruel and callous young man who seemed to thrive on hate and anger. If anyone got in his way or crossed his path, he would just as soon give them a brutal beating as look in their face. And many received such a beating. His job, his calling, and his profession were in the running of the moonshine. He continued to buy and soup up cars, and he leaned toward the Chryslers.

It was not that he didn't like the large, boxy Chevy of the mid-fifties. It was just that the Chrysler seemed like a longer car with a larger trunk space and a wider body that could better absorb the fast hairpin curves that stressed every inch of the frame and body. Jerry and Billy never got around to looking at that Chevy the next day. A revenuer stopped by that night and told them about a fast, hopped-up Chrysler that would be on the auction block at his office the next morning.

They had finished the last four bottles of whiskey and walked out of the woods sometime before midnight. Both were tired and ready to turn in for the night. They returned home, pulled into the gravel drive, and turned off the car engine. Between runs, they were cautious to drive slow and careful so as to not attract any attention of the revenuers or local sheriffs. It was not as if the federal agents did not know who was making what and who was running what. But they had to catch them in the act of making the whiskey or transporting the illegal juice. With only circumstantial evidence, bootleggers like Snake could continue their operation without the bother of jail time.

Shortly after they had turned off the engine and began to get out of the car, a large black revenuer's car turned into the drive, blocking their retreat back onto the road. Snake sat stoically in the car, carefully studying the shadowy outline of the driver behind him.

"Let's run for it," Billy whispered. "Hurry, he's getting out of the car now."

But Snake did not move a muscle. Like a mountain cat, crouched behind some rock outcropping, he only moved his eyes as he explored the figure that was approaching the car. Snake was armed with a shotgun on the front seat and a crow bar below the seat on both the driver and passenger side of the vehicle. There was only one officer in that car, and only one officer meant a real beating for him, if he stepped out of line. Snake was ready for battle, but he did not believe that he would have to battle on this particular night. Billy began to mumble something about running out the back and heading in different directions. He was surprised as Snake bounded from the car to give a big old handshake to the dark figure that approached them under the cloak of night.

"Hey, Snake," the officer greeted him like an old friend.

"Hey, officer, what brings a Yankee like you out on a big old Southern night to see someone like me?" Snake responded. "I thought all Yanks would be asleep, all nicely tucked in their beds at this time of night." Snake loved joking with the federal revenuers, especially those that came down from the North.

Snake continued, "Was I speeding or something? Or are you confusing me with some of those mean old nasty bootleggers from this here Monroe town?"

"Neither...but since you brought up the subject, Snake...well.
..were you out making some 'shine tonight, or did you just finish a run without my knowing about it?"

"Well, officer, I must tell you the truth. If I were making 'shine tonight, I probably wouldn't tell my closest friend, let alone you. But if I were runnin' the stuff, I would have come into town, shot out a streetlight or two just to get your attention, and then enjoyed the run. Now, you know me. What fun is it to run moonshine without some kinda chase goin' on? I just love a good old-fashioned chase, especially between a northern Yankee type and myself, just a good old boy, never meanin' no harm. Know what I mean?"

"OK...cut the funny stuff," the revenue officer responded, all the while looking behind him and to the right and left as if he himself were delivering some type of illegal whiskey. Well, he was not delivering any moonshine on this particular night, but he was in the delivery business.

"Snake, come over here," he whispered. "James Colter, the Wilkes County moonshiner, was caught last week running some of his stuff. I mean he was caught with over one hundred gallons of whiskey. They brought him in and confiscated his car. It's one of those fast 1958 Chryslers with the HEMI engine. I hear it's real fast, and you could pick it up for just a little bit."

By this time, Billy had crawled out of his side of the car a bit shaken by even seeing a federal agent so close, let alone a federal agent talking to his friend Snake.

"What time is the auction?" Snake inquired without wasting another moment.

"Ten o'clock on the button."

"I'll be there."

And with that, the officer was back in his car and starting to back down into the street when he paused and motioned for Snake to come closer to his car. He did not know Billy and did not conduct his business around strangers.

"Snake, who's that other guy in your car?"

"It's just Billy . . . pay him no attention."

The office returned a quick reply without a smile. "You know, Snake, that I don't do business around no fool I don't know. So just have that shine, four full gallons of it, under that bridge overpass, you know where, after you bid on that car . . . you hear? And don't you go taking to Billy with you on that run. Nobody—"

And as if he were reading the officer's mind, Snake continued his sentence for him, "—I know, I know, nobody knows your business. I've heard it before, man. I appreciate the tip. If I like the car and get it at the auction tomorrow, your whiskey—all four illegal, unlawful, prohibited, and criminal gallons of it—will be . . . well, you know where."

With that, the officer quietly pulled back onto the road in the darkness and disappeared into the night.

"What was that all about?" Billy asked.

"Nuttin' much . . . jes doin' business . . . jes doin' business." Snake muttered while all the time thinking about that '58 Chrysler that would appear at the auction tomorrow. And Snake had already made up his mind. If that was a 300-D, it was as good as sold.

Now, few people had any idea that many of the federal revenuers were as crooked, or more so, than the moonshiners and bootleggers themselves. They often made a small salary as compared to the cash that flowed amongst the bootleggers. It was a huge temptation to assist their partners in crime, even though they were hired and obliged to bring the illegal activity to an end. Whether it was in the purchase and distribution of the much-needed sugar, the obtaining of the gallon jugs, or in the simple distribution of information like the auction of a fast-running car, many revenuer agents took advantage of this underground trading business to pad their own pockets.

When the morning came, Snake was one of only a few men at the auction, and he knew why he was there. He was only interested in the Chrysler that had been recently confiscated from another area runner. The auction has not been widely advertised, and Snake felt confident that he could buy this one for himself. Several old trucks were auctioned off, one for fifty dollars and the other one for sixty-five dollars and some change. Several old partially wrecked Chevys and a Ford were then auctioned off and sold relatively cheap. Most men had already purchased their prize and had left the revenuer's office when the bright white Chrysler was driven up to the auctioneer. It was the most beautiful white piece of machinery Snake had ever laid eyes on. She was an absolute beauty. He had pocketed over three hundred dollars for this car if it was one of the newer models of the 300-D.

It was the 1958 Chrysler 300-D that had been hailed as one of the fastest Chryslers that ever moved off the production line. Snake was ready to throw all three hundred dollars at the auctioneer and run off with this white knight, but he stood quietly as a young man from across the yard started the bidding at fifty dollars. Snake quietly raised the bid to seventy-five dollars. Another man bid one hundred and two dollars and smiled at Snake as if he had secretly won some kind of silent battle of the wits between them.

Snake looked back at the man with his stone-cold look of hate and death that could freeze any mortal man to his boots on an August day.

"One hundred and fifty dollars," Snake loudly proclaimed as he continued to look deep within his competitor's eyes, burning death threats within his soul. He began to lift his hand for another bid as Snake continued to squint and stare from across the yard. *Go ahead and bid against me,* the stare seemed to say. *Sign your death sentence today, you fool.*

"One hundred and fifty dollars...going once."

The man looked nervously at the beautiful Chrysler and then looked back to Snake.

"One hundred and fifty dollars...going twice."

The man looked again to the car and then back to Snake while Snake silently mouthed his final death wish for the stranger: "I will kill you, man...I will kill you," he mouthed without moving a muscle except for his lips. His chin was set and the frown upon his determined face looked as if it was chiseled from stone.

Whether the man was moved by the frown, or the stare, or whether he ever made out the slight movement of Snake's lips, one will never know. But he nervously lowered his hand, broke eye contact with his adversary, and then in silence stared back down to the ground below him without ever saying a word.

"One hundred and fifty dollars...sold to the man in the big, black Stetson hat."

Snake just smiled.

A 1958 Chrysler 300-D

It was the brightest, whitest Chrysler Snake had ever laid eyes on. It was a 1958 and just stood there proudly, waiting for the auction, like a beautiful lady ready to model down the runway and show her stuff. The two rear lighted fins on the back of the long, sleek body stretched the car body out well beyond the trunk. The car had bright wide whitewalls with shiny chrome hubcaps. There was chrome side trim on both sides of the car that extended from the car door to the rear of the fins themselves. Toward the rear of the fins, and within the chrome trim, was the logo of the model number, the famous 300-D. It was nearly four inches in diameter and was mounted alongside the car in a very proud attempt to proclaim the model of this famous beast of the road.

The front of the Chrysler had a bright chrome bumper that dropped down in the center below the grille. On both sides of the grille sat large double front headlights protruding from the front of the car. Special chrome rearview mirrors were mounted on both sides of the front glass. Except for the specially mounted rear springs, the entire car was nearly original factory issue. Many folks thought that bootlegging cars were mounted and rigged with a special holding tank for the liquor. But that was not the case. Only in the movies were bootlegger's cars rigged as tankers. Real bootlegger cars were never rigged with tanks for the moonshine. It would have been too difficult for the moonshiners to load the whiskey from the still to a tanker and then to the customer.

When Snake looked into the inside of the 300-D, he was equally surprised. The upholstery was surprising good-looking for a bootlegger's car. Apparently the now jailed shinerunner had either taken good care of the car or had run whiskey for only a short time before being jailed for the illegal hauling. The interior dash sparkled, and the seats looked brand-new. Not a bad buy for only one hundred and fifty dollars. When Snake looked into the back of the car, he was not surprised to find that the bottom of the rear seat had been removed. This allowed for the loading of the whiskey directly onto the floorboard of the car. It also allowed for several additional cases of 'shine that could be stuffed behind the driver.

The factory springs of the new Chryslers were not nearly strong enough for the thousands of pounds of illegal 'shine that most haulers lugged throughout the Carolina mountains on a busy moonlit night. Without custom springs the car rode too low, giving away the hidden 'shine to any experienced revenuer with just a simple look at the back end of the car. It bottomed out and scraped the fenders against the rear tires. Therefore, the springs were always changed out for heavier-duty steel springs.

Snake crawled under his newly bought car and smiled a big smile when he saw the large custom springs under the rear end. This one had already been rigged with special springs like the heavy springs of some tractor-trailer. *Boy, I could run a curve at over one hundred thirty miles per hour without the front end moving,* he thought to himself. *In fact, I could push it faster than that with fifty cases in the car. I jes bet the back end would stick good and not even bounce. Man, I jes gotta get this loaded and on the road. I bet this babe will ride right flat and on the faster corners, jes dig in,* he decided.

With the heavy-duty springs in this new car, Jerry knew he could load it to the hilt, and it would still sit good and level, which was important to a professional bootlegger. While Snake admired the upgraded handiwork of the underside of his new car, he had caught the attention of one of the local officers.

"So," the officer said as he too bent over to see what Snake was admiring, "just what are you going to do with this car, Mr. Rushing? Looks like a big fast car to me for some backwoods trapper."

Jerry pulled himself out from under the car with that famous big smile already growing upon his face. He slowly got up from the ground and picked up his big, black Stetson hat that had been resting on the hood of the new car. He placed it slowly on his head and pulled it just so over his left eye, so that it so it cast a shadow on his forehead. He knew that he looked tougher that way. He then looked square into the face of that revenuer, and with a cocky and arrogant smile he replied, "Why, sir, I've got some trips to make next week, and I need to make them fast. And I just think that this here's car is jes the ticket. Ya know?"

"Not thinking about bootlegging some of that illegal stuff from the backwoods, are ya?"

"Well, why would ya think such a thing of me, now officer? Do I look like the kinda guy that would run that 'shine stuff?" Snake smiled an ornery smile and then continued, "But if I do decide to do it, do you want to be invited to the party?" He laughed one of those big deep belly laughs as if he was just daring that officer to try to catch him someday.

As the agent turned around and headed back to the office, Snake yelled just one more time, not willing to let the confrontation go, "Hey, guy, if I do run some tonight, I'll run through the town square and burn some donuts, and that'll be the sign for ya that I'm on the road again."

As the officer turned to leave, knowing that he had lost the verbal battle of wits with the Union County boy, Jerry pulled open the rear trunk. It was the biggest trunk he had ever seen. He just stood and imagined how much whiskey he could load. It was deep, wide, and stretched from one massive rear quarter-panel to the other. The fins, which protruded out the back and sides of the rear end, gave the trunk space more volume than most cars. Jerry closed the trunk lid and walked around to the front of the car.

It looked like Christmas at the auction yard, and Jerry looked like a little boy admiring the new present that he had just opened. The paint job was exquisite and the inside was like new. He remembered that he had not yet looked into that engine compartment to inspect the new HEMI. When he raised the hood, he was awestruck as his eyes gazed upon that large engine topped with twin four-barrel carburetors. Most bootlegging cars were a combination of big, fast factory cars with a change or two made by garage mechanics that specialized in custom souped-up engines and suspension systems. *These boys certainly knew what they were doin'*, Snake thought. *Wow, what an engine!*

By the time that he had bid on this new white Chrysler, Jerry Rushing had graduated into the big stuff. He was running whiskey at least seven times a week. It was like a real job, working full time each day of the week and each week of the month, with his regular runs.

"Well, I just feel like a regular milk man," he used to say. "Load me up and let me run. If you're thirsty, your liquid refreshment is on its way!"

On some occasions, he looked like a milkman as he loaded up his delivery vehicle and pulled out only to drive from house to house, delivering the banned 'shine to client after client until the wee hours of the morning.

"'Preciate it," some yelled as they paid for their jugs of whiskey while others just whispered, "Thanks, big hat man...you're the greatest." Still others just took the whiskey, pushed the cash into his hands, and then quickly disappeared back into the night. Jerry's business was growing, and that meant more 'shine. More 'shine meant more time on the road, and with a larger capacity car like this new Chrysler, he could haul more on each run. He was no more the little runner, making little whiskey runs for his daddy. He was now becoming the modern-day outlaw of his dreams, and he was both respected and feared. People knew that you never crossed the Rushing boy. If you did, you might not live to tell about it. With this souped-up new Chyrsler, he was ready to become the legend he had dreamed about.

And a legend he became.

CUSTOMIZING THE 300-D

There were many large sporty sedans on the market, but Chrysler was proud of the HEMI engine and was advertising the 300-D as the car of the future. Walter Chrysler, the president of Chrysler Corporation, had resigned as an executive of General Motors Corporation in 1920. He had started by designing the "Chrysler Six," which was one of the first high-compression six-cylinder engines available in an affordable car. Walter Chrysler and the Chrysler Corporation began concentrating on their product innovation by designing faster models in the mid-twenties and thirties. Their first models tested out with a top speed that was twice the speed of Ford's Model T. Ultimately Chrysler introduced the Plymouth and the upscale DeSoto, and even surpassed Ford in sales for the first time prior to Walter Chrysler's death in 1940.

During World War II, Chrysler produced army vehicles, army tanks, antiaircraft guns, and airplane engines for the B-29, as well as their famous car line. Chrysler was now specializing in fast hardcore equipment. In the 1950s, Chrysler was criticized for the design of very large boxy cars while GM and Ford was launching a more sleek-looking style. But to the bootlegger, the large boxy style of the 300-D meant more cases of moonshine per run. Chrysler paid the criticism of their body styles little attention, as they were too busy producing the fast 300-Ds. Some buyers were busy racing them in the fast-growing sport of stock car racing. The new 300-D could travel at speeds over 140 miles per hour and could easily outrun the more traditional vehicles of the federal agents. With the help of a local car mechanic, the bootlegger could modify the factory Chrysler to hit speeds over 180 miles per hour.

Every bootlegger either had a friend that worked on cars, or he had a close association with an auto mechanic that could provide him the typical upgrades and modifications. Certain changes in the car could make the difference between successfully running bootleg whiskey or being caught with a free trip to the local slammer. Jerry had such a mechanic. Buck had been a friend since childhood.

"Hey, Buck," Jerry yelled. "Come out here and see this thing. Is this not the most beautiful car you have ever laid your eyes on?"

"Wow, Snake. Where in the world did you find such a fine piece of machinery? She's a real beaut."

"You'll never believe it," Snake answered back as he leaned over Buck and whispered his reply as if it were a closely held secret. "Would you believe at a revenuer's auction?"

"Woo-boy . . . I bet she'll run like a scared mountaincat in a forest fire."

As Buck inspected the engine and the springs, he asked Snake, "So just whatcha want to do with this baby? She looks ready to run to me."

"Well, let's work on that engine a bit and get all the horsepower we can out of that baby. I wanna get her up to at least 180 miles an hour on a straightaway. Can ya do it?"

"Sure. In fact, I can have that ready in a day or so. Anything else?"

"Well," Snake answered, "let's go in the garage and get a cold one. I'll explain to ya a great idea I wanna try on this one."

They retired into the shade of the garage, and Snake began to explain a couple of major modifications that he wanted to make on this 300-D. First, he told Buck to install some toggle switches on the dash. One toggle switch cut off all of the taillights, including the reverse lights. This way, he could back into a building without being seen. The other toggle switch cut off the brake lights, leaving the other rear lights lit. Using this switch, you first took several fast curves with your foot on the brake. This set up the federal agents to actually drive off of your brake lights. When you braked, they braked as well. Once this pattern was set up, you threw the switch and hit a fast curve with your foot on the brake. However, with the toggle switch thrown, the brake lights did not come on, and the revenuer hit the curve at full speed completely unaware of the approaching turn. They realized it too late, and over the hill they went.

Buck thought both ideas were great and within a week he had the engine tuned and timed and ready for a test drive. He had also installed the toggle switches on the 300-D, and Snake could hardly wait to try them out on a real whiskey run. They both jumped into the new Chrysler and started down the road. Snake and Buck watched as the speedometer quickly climbed to 100 miles per hour, then 125, and up to 140. The windows were down, and Snake had to pull his Stetson down tighter on his head just to keep it from flying out the window.

"Push it Snake. She'll go faster... I promise ya," Buck screamed over the loud rushing noise of the wind.

Snake really needed no encouragement as he pushed the pedal down to the floor, all the while watching the horizon of the road with one eye and watching through the rearview mirror with the other. The car seemed to just hum down the roadway as it climbed to 150, then on to 160. As the Chrysler climbed over the 170 mark, Snake let out with a yell as he pulled the car quickly to the left and then back to the right as he cut a donut in the center of the road, leaving his heated rubber signature in a circular pattern all over the roadway. This circular rubber mark ultimately became Snake's signature through the county and beyond.

"Just perfect, and I mean perfect," Snake said as he and Buck pulled back into the garage. Snake jumped out and turned to Buck. "And now for the finishing touches. I need you to make me one more major modification that will help me when those revenuers get too close to my back end.

"I need you to install an oil tank in the trunk and then run tubes from the tank to the bottom of the rear bumpers. Install a switch under dash that will allow me to run the oil from the holding tank to the tubes to release an oil slick in front of those filthy agents. Get too close to old Rushing, and you'll pay for it..."

Buck's eyes grew with each description of the "oil-slickin' machine," as he called it. He often repeated Snake's comments back to him in an affirming way. He had always admired Snake and was honored to play even a small part in this illegal business of moonshining. It sort of made him feel like an outlaw. "Woo-boy... Snake. If they get too close to old Rushing, they'll pay for it, won't they?" Buck parroted back to his idol.

"Yea...they'll pay," Snake replied with an evil smile on his face. "They'll pay."

Snake really loved the danger and the challenge of running moonshine. With the addition of his most recent purchase, he had the edge in running against the plain factory-issue revenuer cars. His hatred, which had always simmered right under the surface, fueled his war with the law. His running of the illegal liquor was simply an outlet for the hatred that he felt for most any authority figure. He did not really wish harm on any particular federal agent. But let any one of them try to stop his running, and as far as he was concerned, they were destined for death. He ran like an injured cougar on the run and earned the nickname Wild Buck. He had no fear of death and did not even consider it an option. He was quickly closing in on his ambition to become the fastest bootlegger in the entire state of Carolina when he purchased this '58 Chrysler. He was becoming the biggest bootlegger of the unlawful 'shine in the entire area. The federal agents were bent on closing him down and shutting off his supply of whiskey. He was becoming a legend in the South, and many other younger moonrunners were patterning their lives after the wild Rushing boy. If revenuers could shut Rushing down and put him behind bars, it would serve as a notice on many other bootleggers in the Carolinas.

The race was on, and Rushing was getting hotter and hotter with each passing day. He drove down a particular road or highway, and within a couple of days that area was swarming with federal agents trying to sniff out the wild man of the South. If he had simply gone fishing down on a river, within a day or so the entire river was crawling with agents looking for any signs of him. The whiskey was flowing, and most of the time the agents were a day or two behind his running.

He was even known for bringing whiskey back into Union County. Occasionally the federal agents found some of the local stills and destroyed them using dynamite. The availability of whiskey dried up for a season until the moonshiners rebuilt their backwoods production facility in another woods near another stream.

So the businessman in old Rushing simply evaluated the low supply situation and made runs out of town to Wilkes County for additional gallons of shine. If Wilkes County was low on juice, Snake might travel all the way to some operator in Tennessee to acquire the whiskey. One way or the other, Snake moved the whiskey from producer to the user, and the users were growing with each run Snake made. The "Big Hat Man" and his favorite car were quickly becoming icons throughout the South.

But where did the name *Traveler* come from?

WHY THE NAME *TRAVELER*?

To better understand why a third-generation southern moonshiner and bootlegger named his favorite whiskey-running car *Traveler*, one first must understand the culture of the late nineteenth and early twentieth centuries. The country had just been through the bloodbath of the Civil War, and though the Union was no longer divided geographically or politically, the division between the North and the South was still deeply embedded in the people, especially southerners. The southerners would always be southerners, and some still embraced the label of Confederates. Their love for the southern way of life and their hatred of the evil Yanks were inbred. The southern sentiment was seldom a first-generation feeling, as the Civil War was now more past than present. The southern feelings were generational as family members passed down the mind-set and southern pride for many years after the war.

The events leading up to the conflict between the states started on December 20, 1860, when South Carolina voted to secede from the Union. During the next couple of months, Mississippi, Florida, Alabama, Georgia, Louisiana, and Texas followed with a complete secession. It was not until later in the spring of 1861 that Arkansas, Tennessee, Virginia, and Snake's own North Carolina followed in seceding from the Union. A convention of the seceding states was held in February 1861, and a constitution was ratified that closely resembled the federal Constitution. Most people to this day do not understand that the Confederate constitution strictly prohibited the African slave trade.

Though the constitutional and political organization of the Confederacy was nearly identical with the Union's, the war greatly emphasized the differences between the two groups. The North's population was more than 22 million, compared to the South with a population of only 9 million. The North had more than 900 factories with sales of over $115 million. The South had only 150 factories, and over 90 percent were textile factories serving the cotton industry with sales of only $8 million. It was be surprising to many that, though the South had many slaves, the North had mroe than 500,000 slaves at the time of the secession.

The South had no powder mills and few good iron works. Only one plant was equipped to turn out large field guns, the Tredegar Iron Works in Richmond, Virginia. The southern states found themselves fighting a war against overwhelming odds. Though the South was lacking in factories and general financial assets, they made up for it with the passion, pride, and zeal that was instilled in every southerners. The self-esteem and sense of southern dignity was inherent in the very soul of the Confederate general Robert E. Lee.

Robert Edward Lee is considered to be one of the greatest generals of all time. He was opposed to secession and slavery. However, his loyalty to his native birthplace of Virginia and his great love of the South drove him to lead the southern army in the War between the States. He had freed all of his slaves, which he had inherited, long before the start of the war. He had always admired George Washington. On several occasions Lee had shared that he felt that he was leaving the Union as Washington had left the British Empire. He had even referred to the Civil War as the second war of independence. Abraham Lincoln had offered Lee the field command of the entire United States Army. But Lee could not fight against his native state. He expressed his hopes when he said, "I will never be called upon to draw my sword."

But as history has recorded it, Lee was called into action and headed up the Confederate army in the war against the northern states. It was during this time that Lee called into action one of the most beautiful horses of all time. During the Civil War, most leaders rode great horses into battle. This was the case with Lee, as he rode a great horse of tremendous stature. The horse was a large white horse with a dark mane and tail. General Lee could be seen in battle from a great distance as the horse galloped and pranced, getting General Lee into position as if it too had a sense of the great southern pride for which it fought. It was a very muscular horse with marvelous strength in its legs, giving it an advantage in running. It was one of the fastest horses in the war and quickly became known for its bravery in battle and its speed. General Lee loved this horse and named it *Traveler*.

After the northern forces cut off and surrounded Lee's troops at the Appomattox Courthouse in Virginia, Lee surrounded to Ulysses S. Grant on April 9, 1865. One of the greatest visual displays of Confederate dignity was Lee's last ride down the lines of his troops on his horse *Traveler*.

It was upon *Traveler* that General Lee addressed his troops:

> We have fought through the war together. I have done my best for you, and my heart is too full to say more.

Traveler moved slowly through the crowd in a sense of holy reverence as his rider, the leader of the entire southern army, bowed in defeat on that spring day. It was a difficult time for Lee, and he said that he would have rather died a thousand deaths than to face the events of that afternoon. Only his best friend, *Traveler*, made it easier. Traveler slowly trotted, occasionally looking back at his friend and master, as if to console him in a way that only a general on a horse like *Traveler* understood.

Lee became the president of Washington and Lee University in Lexington, Virginia, and died there on October 12, 1870 of heart problems. He was buried in the Washington and Lee Chapel where *Traveler* was also buried. Lee and *Traveler* were captured in a beautiful painting by Douglas Miley, which shows General Lee sitting high and proud upon his white horse named *Traveler*.

Now Jerry Rushing was about as southern as one could get. He was born and raised in North Carolina and was proud to be a southerner. This pride of native culture was not really taught, but rather was handed down from every granddad to every dad and then to every dad's son. They did not always know why they were proud, but they knew they were. Though they knew that they had lost the war, they had stood up for their honor. They had fought for the pride of the South and felt that it had been the only noble, "southern thang" to do. Snake felt the pride, but just thought of himself and his kin as southern folk. Back then, they did not really care about the "Yanks."

But instilled within him and the culture of the time was the general concept that you just did not mess with those Yankees. This alone built up a certain pride amongst the southern folks. As Snake used to say, "I was born, nursed, and bred southern, and somewhere, I was taught to hate Yankees though I don't really know if I've ever met one." As Jerry grew up, there were really few Yankees down in the South. In fact, Snake had never really met a true Yankee, because most northerners had not made it down to his part of the backwoods.

But he did know about his southern heritage, and he did know that General Robert E. Lee headed up the Confederate army. Most importantly, he knew that Lee's horse was one of the fastest horses the general had ever seen or ridden. So once he came to own the fast, bright-white 1958 Chrysler 300-D, it was only right for him to name it for the fastest white horse of all time, *Traveler*.

Once Buck, Jerry's personal car mechanic, finished the engine, installed the extra light switches on the dash, and fixed the oil tank and hoses, he met Jerry for a final inspection of his beautiful piece of work.

"Whatcha think, partner?' Buck asked as Jerry walked around the white Chrysler admiring Buck's handiwork.

"Looks real good, Buck. It looks really good."

"Whatcha gonna name her, Snake? Have you thought of a good name yet?"

Snake took a close look at the car, walked up to the engine, and began to daydream of future battles against federal agents and revenuer officers. Then he thought of a name for his recent purchase.

"I just hate those revenuer agents...those Yankees, coming down here into my part of the South, telling me how to live my life. Northern Yankees..." he repeated. "It will be a battle just like the War between the States."

With that thought still vivid in his memory, Snake turned to Buck and replied to his question, "Her name will be *Traveler*, just like General Lee's fast white horse."

"Her name will be *Traveler*," Snake repeated, "and we will go into battle shortly, and I'll ride her like no other."

THE REAL BATTLE

Snake could barely wait until he could ride *Traveler* into battle. He thrived on the excitement and the adrenaline rush of the whiskey-running war between himself and the federal agents. *Traveler* was a perfect companion in the combat that took place at over 140 miles per hour while being loaded down with over a ton of that illegal moonshine. He just knew that she would ride fine.

But there was a greater battle that Snake was involved in, and this battle was as real as the moonshine skirmish that took place nearly every night between midnight and the early rising sun. Snake knew all about the whiskey war. He knew his adversaries, he knew the battleground, and he certainly knew how to fight to stay alive. But Jerry Rushing of Union County knew nothing of the invisible battle that waged war daily against his very soul.

The Scriptures say the following about this invisible battle:

> For though we walk in the flesh, we do not war after the flesh:
> (For the weapons of our warfare are not carnal, but mighty
> through God to the pulling down of strong holds.)
> —2 CORINTHIANS 10:3–4

In this scripture, the apostle Paul is talking about a war that is not fought with our flesh (that is, our earthly bodies). The weapons used to fight this battle are not of this physical world. The weapons are spiritual and powerful weapons from God to destroy the enemy's (the devil's) strongholds. But these spiritual weapons are only available to the man who acknowledges Jesus Christ as his personal Savior. Though this modern-day outlaw, this Jesse James that was terrorizing lawmen from one county to the other, knew nothing about this devilish battle for his soul, he was nonetheless intimately involved in this battle, and he was losing the war.

The real enemy in the invisible war for his soul was the devil. He had infiltrated Jerry's life through generational sin. The sin of disobeying God, even of ignoring God and His Word, was simply passed on from each generation. Snake did not decide what family to be born into as he entered the world. No one does. He was a Rushing, and Rushings hated the law, made moonshine, conducted bootlegging as a business, and wreaked havoc on every lawman that crossed their path. They were filled with hate and were rebels at heart. God wants to change rebellious hearts and soften them to the point that He can work His will. But Jerry's heart was cold and hard. He could beat a man within inches of his life and then look at the near-dying man and laugh at him.

"You should not have messed with this Rushing," he screamed at his enemy as he lay bleeding from battle. Jerry was a warrior, and war was what he did best. But it was sad for the Rushing bootlegger, for he really knew nothing of the real war for his soul.

Paul wrote again in the Bible that we do not wrestle (or battle) against physical foes: our major enemy is of the spiritual dimension of this world. He says that we fight against rulers of the dark and against spiritual enemies and wickedness in spiritual places that we know not of. Consider this scripture:

> For we wrestle not against flesh and blood, but against princi-palities, against powers, against the rulers of the darkness of this world, against spiritual wickedness in high places. Wherefore take unto you the whole armour of God, that ye may be able to withstand in the evil day, and having done all, to stand.
> —Ephesians 6:12–13

Though we are battling this great enemy in this invisible war, the writer of Ephesians encourages us that we can go into battle with the complete armor of God so that we can withstand the assaults of the enemy. There is no need to fall to the evil adversary as God will assist us in our battle. But God is there for us only if we turn to Him and acknowledge Him as the God that loved us and died for us so that we might overcome the enemy of our soul.

As Snake prepared *Traveler* for his earthly battle, he was totally unaware of the spiritual battle that was taking place for his soul. The devil had deposited enough hate in Snake's heart for almost every sin imaginable.

The devil had been with Snake from his earliest days. The enemy of his soul controlled his heart and almost every waking thought. Though the Union County bootlegger had already been in many spiritual battles for his life and soul, the greatest spiritual battles were ahead of him. Some of the battles were for the continued hardening of his heart, and other battles were for his actual physical existence. Snake was about to enter into some spiritual skirmishes that would attempt to claim his very life and send him to an everlasting life in hell itself.

Except for the hatred and evil within his heart, Snake was a good man who worked hard and cared for those close to him. But the devil didn't care. Snake was entering into a spiritual battle in which he could lose his life, yet he was not even aware of the impending storm.

But the storm clouds were gathering.

CHAPTER 5

Traveler Never
Let Him Down

RUNNIN' FAST AND HOT

THAT WHITE CHRYSLER 300-D ran as fast and hot as Snake had hoped. In fact, *Traveler* so outperformed the revenuer's vehicles in horsepower and handling that Snake would often just slow down on a moonlit run so that the agents could catch up with him again, only to lose them on the next series of turns. Where most cars would speed up on the straightaways and slow on the curves, Snake would speed up on the curves and push the 300-D as hard as he could push it.

With a load of whiskey and a low center of gravity, the car performed great. The springs were very strong, and, with a load of two thousand pounds, the tires bit into the road, even allowing for acceleration around hairpin curves. Without the extra load and the custom springs, this type of driving would be impossible.

Liquor was often transported in simple one-gallon plastic jugs. The gallon jugs were loaded in cardboard boxes, six to a case. The cases were packed in the backseat floorboard, the trunk space, the front passenger side seat, the front floorboard, and occasionally stacked right up to the front dash of the car. The moonshiners could stack the cases individually as each case weighed in at approximately fifty pounds.

One night, Snake was running some of the sugar whiskey from Wheatsboro. One of the local Wheatsboro boys asked Jerry, "So how much do you want to haul tonight, Snake? How full do you want *Traveler* loaded?'

Snake pulled a pad from his front pocked and surveyed the names on his delivery list. "The boys are right thirsty down in Union County. I also have some folks in Wilkes County. Several stills have been blown up by those nasty federal officers, and folks are just lying low. So..." he thought for a while, "Load me up to the hilt; let's see just how much of this 'shine you can get in her."

"Well, if you have to run hard back to Monroe, can *Traveler* here take the stress and strain of all the weight? We'll load her to the top if ya really think she can take it. But if you're asking me, I jes don't think she'll take it."

Jerry just stared at his list and, without moving his head, adjusted his black Stetson and mumbled out the words quietly, "I done said to load her to the hilt...no need to repeat it again is there?"

"Is there?" Snake asked again, moving closer to the car to make another count himself. He knew better than to pay for whiskey based on some moonshiner's count of cases or jugs. He had been cheated before, but never cheated more than once. Jerry was a fast learner.

Without hesitation, the moonshiners, one big burly guy and a short tiny bald man, began to hustle around the barn and quickly stacked the extra plastic bottles into the last cases they had available. They knew of Snake's reputation and did not really want to experience his fury firsthand. Quickly they packed the trunk and moved to the rear seat. After packing the rear seat to slightly below the window line, they turned to the front seat and packed the seat and the floorboard so tight that they barely left enough space for Jerry to crawl into the car.

"Fifty-three, fifty-four, fifty-five cases in all," the little short moonshiner counted off. "Wow," he somewhat smirked out loud, "these here cases weigh over fifty pounds each. This will never work. Lotta weight for any bootlegger to carry over these mountains. That must be...ah, let's see...fifty-five cases and...uh...they weigh fifty pounds each...uh, the total weight would be...at least... well...uh...well...a lot of weight. Are ya sure—"

"Close to three thousand pounds," Jerry interrupted. "And yes, I'm sure. Do you want to ride on the hood tied to the front bumper just to see how she'll ride?"

"No, sir," the little man replied. Funny how the short little moonshiner immediately found his manners. He too had heard of the wild reputation of the Rushing bootlegger and thought it best to just say "No, sir" to the man in the black hat and back out of the conversation while he could.

Snake paid for the load and pulled back out into the night to begin his run. He had carefully mapped out his trip back home and had hopes that the run would be a simple one. He had been on several long runs each day for over a week now, and he was tired. Fortunately, this run back to Union County was a simple one as no federal agents were stationed that night along Snake's selected highways. He sat back, lowered his windows, and just enjoyed the ride. Even if he were not being chased, he liked riding a bit faster than usual and watching old *Traveler* grab the road on the tightest of turns.

"I just love to run that whiskey, loaded full on a moonlit night," Snake bragged to his friends. "I love coming down that road and hitting the bumps and listening to the 'glug, glug, glug' from those liquor jugs. I'm in love with the sound of that whiskey sloshing around in those jugs mixed with the aroma of that illegal alcohol." Occasionally the whiskey dripped from a jug onto the cardboard case. Once the wind started running through the car, the aroma quickly filled the air. It was like heaven for this moonshiner.

The maintenance of *Traveler* was minimal. The engine needed new plugs from time to time, and Snake's mechanic kept the engine tuned and timed perfectly. That Chrysler HEMI engine just purred running down the highway. The only problem that he ever experienced with *Traveler* was with the rims. He ran *Traveler* for over seven years, and over that period of time he broke at least eight rims. He drove *Traveler* as hard as General Lee drove his own horse. He drove fast and hard into the curves, and then punched it for additional speed.

The speed, combined with the sharpness of the curve and the weight that *Traveler* was carrying, stressed the frame, body, and wheels on the Chrysler nearly beyond capacity. On several occasions, forces from the curve put so much pressure on the rims that they bent and eventually fractured. The mechanic changed the tires and installed new rims, and *Traveler* was up and ready to run again. During one year, Jerry put over 116,000 miles on *Traveler* with no major service except a rim or two. He loved that workhorse as much as General Robert E. Lee loved his *Traveler*. There were many memorable runs with that sleek white steed, and Snake loved holding the reins and running her hard. He especially liked the chase when some revenuer pulled out from hiding in hot pursuit of the Big Hat Man.

"Bring it on!" he often said. "Set your federal hounds a-huntin', and I'll give them a run they'll never forget."

TRAVELER'S LEGENDARY RUNS

On one such occasion, the federal revenuer agents became aware of one of Jerry's runs in *Traveler*. He never knew whether they were tipped off by an undercover agent or a by one of his friends for a few bucks. Occasionally an agent sitting in his car planted next to a major highway caught a visual on *Traveler* as it headed down the road and they called in the report to the main office. At any rate, *Traveler* had been loaded down with over thirty cases of the white lightning and was facing a two-to-three hour bootlegging run, depending on whether or not he ran into trouble.

It was after 10:00 p.m. with a light summer mist falling. The highways were damp and a bit slick from the light rain. However, there was little standing water on the road. *Traveler* was loaded with about 1,500 pounds of 'shine and rode tight on the road in spite of any rain. Jerry had just pulled out on a major highway when he saw the dark black unmarked car pull out behind him. He pushed *Traveler* and increased his speed, only to see the unmarked car pull up faster behind him. When he slowed *Traveler* to approximately the speed limit, the car again slowed down. Sometimes the revenuers were quite silly in their tactics. It was obvious that the car was following *Traveler*, but it was also quite apparent that the chase car had no intentions of trying to pull him over anytime soon.

Whenever this happened, Jerry knew that either the agent was calling in for additional chase cars to assist in this potential capture or he was calling in for a roadblock ahead.

Though Snake did not know the revenuer's intentions, the officer had already radioed the station regarding his recent find.

"Car 74 to base unit...74 to base unit. Come in, base unit."

"This is base unit Alpha, go ahead 74."

The officer continued his pursuit of *Traveler* as he called back.

"I think I've got a visual on a moonrunner. There's a big white Chrysler that's headed north on Highway 603."

"Did you get a visual on the load? Over."

"No, sir, I sure did not. It passed my stakeout going pretty fast, and I did not get any look inside the vehicle. But I am behind him two hundred yards or so, and it looks a little low to the ground. My guess is that it just might be loaded with lots of that there moonshine. Permission to continue pursuit."

The officer at the base unit quickly called to his commanding officer, Sergeant Wilder. "I've got unit 74 on Highway 603 headed north behind a '58 Chrysler that just might be running whiskey. He is requesting permission to continue pursuit. What do I tell him?"

Sergeant Wilder jumped from his desk, almost spilling his coffee in his sprint to the small communications room that he had set up in the local sheriff's office.

"Ask him if the driver is wearing a big black hat. And also..." he scratched his head as he stretched his recollection regarding the stories he had heard about a big white Chrysler when it hit him, "...ask 74 if he thinks that it is one of those big 300-Ds."

With that the officer on the base unit called back for a better ID on the car. Officer Wilder jumped and slammed his hands on the desk when he heard car 74's response.

"Unit 74 to base unit. Tell Sergeant Wilder that I did get a pretty good look at the side, and it does have fins. I think that I saw the

300-D emblem on the side of the rear quarter panel. Oh, and by the way, the driver is wearing a funny big cowboy hat. Not seen anything quite like it up north."

That was really all Sergeant Wilder needed when he first ordered unit 74 to apprehend the suspect for an inspection of his car. Then after another thought or two, he grabbed the microphone from the base unit officer and shouted loudly, "Hold on, unit 74. I think that I know the driver of the car you're following. He's a local Monroe guy who's really dangerous. He has several tricks up his sleeve, and I don't want you to even try to apprehend the suspect."

The officer in pursuit quickly called back regarding the warning.

"He may be tough, sir, but I've brought in a many rough bootleggers in the past couple of years. This guy doesn't scare me a bit."

"Don't be silly, 74. I know better," the sergeant continued. "If it's who I think it is, he is one of the meanest and most dangerous runner of these whole parts. His entire family for generations has made the stuff, and now he is the runner, and one of the best. If we shut him down, we'll dry up most all of Union County. I think his name is Jerry Elijah Rushing. Hold back and follow him loosely until we get a plan."

The officer of unit 74 immediately slowed down and swallowed deeply. Though he did not make any comment except for the word, "Copy," a certain fear and horror gripped him. *Jerry Rushing,* he thought. *I have heard that name.* Recently he heard about one of his agent buddies that went over a hill chasing that Rushing character. In the midst of the chase, he ran off of the road and rolled his car six or seven times in a cornfield before it came to a stop. He had broken both arms and suffered some internal injuries and was still in the hospital. He had heard the story, and rumor had it that he had been in a chase with this guy and the officer had lost control of his car and had nearly been killed. Maybe he would just follow at a close distance.

Snake continued on his trip up north, always keeping a watchful eye on his friend that trailed at a safe distance behind him. The light rain had stopped, and the moon, a quarter-moon sliver, had appeared slightly over the treetops to his right. He was ready for a chase, but felt that perhaps the officer's intention was just to keep an eye on old

Traveler until some roadblock was set on down the road. He watched each intersection and was especially careful at each bridge overpass as most roadblocks took advantage of a bridge to seal off the roadway.

Back at the station, Sergeant Wilder was busy organizing a road-block. He was trying to get several tractor-trailers to set up well north on US 603 in the northbound lane. This completely sealed off the road making it impossible for this bootlegger to escape. He had read the records of previous capture attempts and knew that Rushing had run through most of the wooden roadblocks of the past. He had even wrecked his "running car" into the officers' vehicles of other road-block attempts and disappeared into the woods on foot.

Sergeant Wilder was barking orders as if this were a war and the enemy's capture was close at hand. He was smelling victory and could see tomorrow's headlines in his imagination, Sergeant Michael Wilder Captures the Notorious Jerry Rushing.

He was ready to move. "Unit 74...are you still in pursuit?"

"Ten-four," the officer replied.

"Does he suspect anything?" the radio barked back.

"He may, but I am holding back."

"Well," Sergeant Wilder continued, "we've already set up a tight roadblock fifteen miles north of your current location. If the white Chrysler stays on course, you'll hit it within ten minutes or so."

"What's the roadblock, sir?"

"Three tractor-trailers, and the entire northbound lane will be cut off. There will be no options but to stop or hit it. We are running the rigs completely across the highway, up the shoulder, and to the wood line. We've got this sucker finally! Do you copy?"

"Ten-four, Sergeant. I will stay on course."

As *Traveler* and the Big Hat Man continued on course, the tractor-trailers were driven onto the highway from a truck stop further up the highway. Though Sergeant Wilder wanted to be at the scene, there was no possible way for him to catch up with the action. He had to settle for listening to his car radio and running this battle from behind the scenes. He pulled his car out onto the roadway, and turned on his flashing lights and siren, hoping to head to the scene where he would eventually cuff the county's most notorious desperado. Rushing was a bandit on the loose, and the entrapment had been set, with over a dozen officers ready for the ambush.

Old Snake had been in tight spots before, and he could sense that another challenge was ahead of him—it was an instinctual sixth sense of danger that had always been a part of him. The adrenaline had already started its trip through his veins. Snake was always ready for the fight. He loved a fight, and the words *quit* and *surrender* were just not part of his vocabulary, let alone his thinking. So with a sense of an impending danger, Snake did what he always did. He began to chat to *Traveler* no differently than General Lee must have talked to his own horse. "Let's go, baby...it's you and me against those dirty feds, and you've never failed me yet."

With that, Snake pushed the pedal down farther and watched the needle of the speedometer jump up to over one hundred miles per hour. The officer behind him was having trouble keeping up, and Rushing tightened his seatbelt, expecting the worse. The factory '58 Chrysler did not come with seatbelts. In fact, no cars in the mid-fifties came with factory seatbelts. But accidents and rollovers were part of a typical bootlegger's life behind the wheel, and *Traveler* was fitted with a special seat belt constraint that Jerry had been taken from a airplane.

Snake was looking well down the road when he first saw the large boxy shadow on his side of the highway. The headlights of the oncoming cars on the other side of the median were casting a shadow of these mysterious objects well down the road in Jerry's direction. They must be only a half mile or so up the road, and he continued to pick up speed. His throat began to tighten and his knuckles turned white from his fingers tightening their grip on the steering wheel. He was fully confident in both his ability to maneuver through tight spots and in *Traveler's* ability to respond to his lightning-quick steering.

Within what seemed like seconds, *Traveler* approached the shadowy objects, and Jerry was able to tell that they were massive tractor-trailers that had completely blocked off the highway. Though he had but a second to determine his next move, the entire situation seemed like a slow-motion movie. He glanced at the three trailers to see if there was any way to maneuver between the rigs—there was none.

He decided that he could ride the shoulder and run up the embankment. He had tried this trick on numerous occasions. But there was no room as one of the trailers was stretched far over the shoulder and up the steep embankment.

There were three options. His mind was racing.

Number one—he could stop and give up. NO OPTION!

Number two—he could plow right into the tractor-trailer rigs and perhaps kill himself and an agent or two. NO OPTION! He was not afraid to die, but he did not want to die tonight.

Number three—he could turn into the median, pull into the dangerous oncoming traffic, and take his chances. He only had a second to decide as *Traveler* continued to accelerate toward certain disaster. At the very last moment, he made his decision—to the shock and amazement of every officer at the roadblock.

Snake quickly whipped the steering wheel of the 300-D toward the median, crossing the muddy grassy highway separator, throwing grass and mud twenty feet into the air. He headed right toward a large Ford pickup that was southbound on US 603 and pointed in his direction. He then turned the wheel a sharp left, leaving thirty yards of burning rubber all over the road as he barely missed the oncoming truck. He was headed northbound in the southbound lane of US 603, dodging oncoming traffic and still traveling at speeds over 110 miles per hour.

The officer running car 74 slammed on his brakes just before he hit the median. He could not believe his eyes. He called back to his sergeant, "Sergeant Wilder, Sergeant Wilder, do you copy?"

"I'm with you. Did you stop old Rushing?" the sergeant asked.

"Don't you worry about it, sergeant. He crossed the median at more than 110 miles per hour, and he's hitting a bunch of southbound traffic. He's liable to wreck anytime—wait…a minute…it's a strange thing, but—"

His message seemed to trail off into the darkness, and there was nothing but silence on his end of the radio.

Snake and his trusty Chrysler stallion had defeated death again. He must have dodged ten or eleven cars as he drove right through them, cutting left and then right again. Together Snake and *Traveler* used the entire highway from the left shoulder to the far right near the grassy median, which he had just crossed. Two cars locked bumpers, and at least a couple of cars ran completely off the highway and disappeared out into the night. But Snake and *Traveler* continued northbound on that southbound lane until they came to the first intersection where *Traveler* turned her nose toward a more secluded backwoods highway and then ultimately vanished into the night air, still on time for the midnight delivery.

The poor officer from unit 74, as well as a dozen or so other lawmen, just looked down that highway for some time wondering just how that Big Hat Man in the giant white Chrysler made it past them again.

Sergeant Wilder continued northbound on Highway 603 yelling into his radio, "Unit 74...come in. Right now. What's happening? Come back! I said come back."

As he pulled up to the massive eighteen-wheelers sitting right in the center of that big highway, he did not have to ask what happened. He read it on each face of his officers as he surveyed the tire tracks in the median and rubber tire marks that were freshly burned into the pavement on the southbound lane.

"That had to be Jerry Elijah Rushing," he muttered to himself. "It just had to be."

And it was the one and only Union County born-and-bred Jerry Elijah Rushing.

On many occasions like this median-crossing escape, the actual getaway was the result of Jerry's guts, daring, and downright nerve mixed with some fairly fancy driving ability. Because he had been driving moonshine since he was barely a teenager, he had grown accustomed to sitting behind a fast-running car. He could outmaneuver most any other moonrunner in Carolina. There was an increasing number of federal revenuer agents that were becoming exasperated with his fancy driving and his method of slipping through their every trap. Though many of his escapes from the revenuers were because of his gutsy driving, many times he used mechanical trickery on old *Traveler* to avoid the law.

Such was the case one fall night when he had loaded up *Traveler* with thirty-five cases of moonshine. The trunk and backseat were full. He had pulled back into the barn of one of the nearby Wilkes County boys that made some pretty good sugar whiskey. They were known for stretching their liquor by the use of additives. Nevertheless, Snake was anxious to make the run for them down south of Monroe right over the South Carolina line into Lancaster County. Now he was not only hauling the illegal homemade alcohol, but he was crossing state lines with it. In any case, getting caught with the unlawful stuff was a federal offense with the verdict always being a quick trip to federal prison. But Snake feared no prison, because in his mind he never intended to get caught.

Many felt that Snake was just overly cocky and arrogant. And to a certain degree, he was. But it was more than just being fool-ishly conceited. In reality, he was extremely confident. Snake had played out these scenes time and time again in his mind when he was young, and he had seen himself as the most pursued outlaw of the entire South. By now his reputation was growing with both federal lawmen and the local moonshiners. The revenuers dreamed of this prize catch and made up schemes to capture him. The backwoods moonshiners knew that when Snake and *Traveler* were running their whiskey, there was a greater chance for the whiskey to find its home. Only if the 'shine was successfully delivered did the moonshiners get paid for their efforts. More than once or twice did a moonshiner lose hundreds of dollars by their runner getting busted. When this hap-pened, the jugs of whiskey and the car were both confiscated by the authorities. Snake was now in high demand, and this often meant a higher dollar on his deliveries.

When he put on that big Stetson hat and climbed into *Traveler*, he was ready for battle. Defeat in battle was not an option. Only an unmistakable and full-blown victory was acceptable. He and *Traveler* triumphed over every foe. And tonight was no exception. He was ready for the run and slowly counted the cases as they completed the loading of the newly made liquor. However, this night he felt an uneasy feeling about the run to the South Carolina state line. He strolled around *Traveler* a couple of times in a futile attempt to walk off the anxious emotion he was feeling. The revenuers had been on his tail and had been only a day or two behind his every action and run. Somehow they got some information on his whereabouts, and he would be especially careful on this night's run.

Prior to the loading of the whiskey in his trunk, Snake had loaded another precious commodity into the trunk area of his Chrysler. He had loaded eight gallons of used automobile oil into the holding tank in the back of his trunk. Buck, his favorite mechanic, had rigged the tank with flexible hoses to the backside of the rear bumpers and had promised to keep the used oil for his friend. Snake had not yet tried out this new contraption, but he was anxious to do such. The idea was to allow the revenuer's car to get close to your back end during the chase and then, on a curve, hit the switch on the dash that flooded the road with oil. If it worked as planned, the revenuers would slide right off the road, losing control of the vehicle when they hit the oil slick at high speed. Maybe tonight would be the night to use of this new oil slicker.

In any event, Snake was ready.

He took another look at his map and the location of the delivery drop, shook hands with his moonshining buddies, adjusted his Stetson, and climbed into *Traveler's* saddle.

Snake looked out the window and addressed the oldest of the bunch, "You guys get another bunch of cases for that Charlotte run you talked about next week, and I'll be back to haul it for ya."

"We'll have it fer ya by the end'a next week. You stop by, and we'll load ya up again." The moonshiner paused for a moment or two and continued, "Ya don't think that you'll have any trouble tonight, do ya? Them agents have been real hot to trot over the last few days. They been askin' around a lot and all."

Snake smiled his ornery grin and just answered their question with a question.

"You boys ever hear of me gettin' caught by those filthy federal agents?" He paused for a moment and watched as they all shook their heads back and forth, almost feeling guilty that they had asked this "moonrunnin' legend" such a question.

Snake furrowed his brow and stared right back into the midst of them.

"I didn't think so. I'll have no problem tonight. *Traveler* will run like the wind."

That settled, he fired up *Traveler* and saluted the boys standing in the barn as he slowly pulled out into the field heading toward the highway at the end of the pasture. The boys in the barn looked silly standing in the shadows and saluting their whiskey runner illuminated only by a dim forty-watt light bulb. They always kept the lights down, as they never knew when a revenuer might drive down the road and pull into a local farm for some snooping around. Snake pulled out without his lights, watching the edge of the field as he worked old *Traveler* through the edge of the woodline and out to the highway. He slowly pulled out onto the gravel shoulder of the road and momentarily paused as he looked both right and left. All four windows were down—he loved the cool evening breeze that blew in the fall.

Leaves were starting to fall, and some of them on the road were still damp from the rain the day before. He had to be careful, because wet leaves on a sharp corner turn at over one hundred miles per hour could be as dangerous as the oil slick that he was prepared to use. He put his head out the window and listened for a whisper of a hidden revenuer. He surveyed the adjacent woods for any sign of flashlights or even the end of a lit cigarette. He was the prey, and he had to think as the prey. A small spark of a cigarette had given away the hidden location of many a revenuer hiding in seclusion. Once Jerry felt that all was clear, he looked back at the boys in the barn that were still standing there waiting for the final departure of their comrade in crime.

Snake slowly moved his fingers toward the light switch, turned the lights on, and steered *Traveler* onto the road. He had mapped out his trip taking advantage of most of the back roads, trying to stay off most of the major highways. Snake loved the open road. He loved running when the sky was dark and clear and when most in Carolina had long since turned in for the night. He operated his business efficiently and thought of himself as a professional businessman. Well, actually he thought of himself as a cross between a businessman, Jesse James, and a modern-day Robin Hood. He ran whiskey for money, it took money to run his moonshine business, and it took all the income he made to keep himself in cars and to take care of his family.

But now he was on the road again and *Traveler's* engine was running smoothly. He accelerated up to fifty, sixty, and then beyond seventy miles per hour. He wanted to make this run as fast as possible without running the risk of attracting unnecessary attention due to excessive speed. He had made that mistake before. He was ready to turn the speed up on his trusty Chrysler, if needed, but only if needed. His mind went back to when he was but a little boy and dreamed about such an outlaw life. He loved his job of running better than anything else that he could imagine doing. He continued his drive, but as he crossed over the state line, he had that funny feeling again. He slowed *Traveler* a bit as he scanned the tree line on both sides of the road. It was there that most whiskey agents hid out, just waiting for a passing car that seemed to be running too low to the ground. He rounded one long winding curve and then another when a pair of headlights seemed to show up out of nowhere behind him.

Was that car always behind him and just now catching up to his Chrysler, or did the pair of headlights just pull out onto the roadway from some hidden stakeout? Snake's heart rate begin to rise, and he immediately began to sit up straighter in his seat. From that vantage point, he could see both the road in the front and watch the approaching car from the rearview mirror.

Is that one of those blasted federal agents or just a car traveling in my direction? he thought to himself. He continued for three to four miles when he just had a hunch that the headlights behind him must be from a revenue officer's car.

Well, if it ain't, it'll soon be lost in the wind. But if it is, it'll try to run with me, he decided. *And if I wait too long and it is a revenuer, they will have time to set up another roadblock, and I don't want to run one of those tonight.*

With that final thought, Snake took a long, deep breath and pushed the gas pedal all the way to the floorboard below. The HEMI whined as the double four-barrel carburetors sucked great gulps of gasoline quickly into the engine's combustion chambers. The car jumped into passing gear and rapidly accelerated to over one hundred miles per hour. Snake kept one eye on those two bright lights behind him. At first, the lights seemed to drift further back down the highway, and

Snake thought that there was no reason for concern. Then all of a sudden the lights seemed to come to life, and they quickly began to gain on the 300-D as they slowly got larger and larger in Snake's rearview mirror.

"It's those feds!" he screamed out loud, as if he was trying to warn himself. "We've got ourselves a race tonight, *Traveler*. Let's go."

Jerry pulled his Stetson down tighter upon his head as he mentally prepared for the clash ahead. The highway had become very windy as the road ran parallel to one of the local creeks and was curving right, left, and then right again. It had more curves than a rattlesnake on a hot afternoon. As he pushed *Traveler*, the tires began to squeal on each curve. The weight of the whiskey provided the grounding the car needed on those wicked curves. On some of the curves, Snake again pushed on the gas pedal and actually increased his speed on the curve itself. But with every curve and with each accelerated push, the pursuing vehicle continued to stay within fifty yards or so of *Traveler*.

Not a bad chase car, Jerry thought to himself. *But can he handle the oil?*

The oil…should he dare to dump the oil? The federal agent was closing in, and Snake felt he had no option but to try his new oil-slick contraption. He pulled a hard right again at the next curve and then back to the left, only occasionally catching a reflection of the moon above on the smooth water of the nearby creek.

I live for times like these, he thought, as he reached his right hand for the toggle switch on the dash. He watched the lights in the mirror as the chase car tracked his every move.

I will wait for the sharpest turn and let old agent whoever drive right up to me before I drop the stuff. He will not expect a thing, he planned.

Just then he whipped the car around a fast left-turning curve and immediately, almost by instinct, hit the toggle switch, which poured several gallons of the slimy oil all over the roadway. The reaction time was only a second or two as the agent's car hit that oil slick while he was trying to maneuver the fast-approaching left turn…only his car was not turning. Jerry stared in the mirror at the two lights that he had watched for over an hour now as they shot out of his mirror and off of the road like some ill-aimed rocket headed up in the air and right over the trees. Snake stomped on his brakes and watched as the dark Buick ripped right through several large pine trees, taking branches and needles with it as it went. Within seconds, the Buick had traveled several hundred feet, through trees and space, only to crash right into the rocky bed of the creek below. It flipped over and over until it finally came to rest in an area of water deep enough to begin running into the driver's side window.

Snake sat for a moment or two and had a fleeting thought of walking down to the creek to see if that old fellow was all right. But it was just fleeting and left as fast as it came.

"Besides," he bragged to his friends later, "there could have been other agents on the way as he had chased me for a long time and could have radioed back for help."

Then Snake began to tell the stories that he had become so famous for.

"You should have seen that old boy when he hit that oil in the road. He did not know what hit him. He shot off that high embankment like a rocket, and he must have flipped over nine times. It was great. You shoulda seen it. Like a rocket...just like a rocket. That oil tank and spreader is the ticket...I'm telling ya."

The reputation of Jerry Elijah Rushing continued to spread among the federal agents.

"Just be careful," the man that had been behind the wheel of the Buick told his comrades from his hospital bed. "Don't follow him too close. We surveyed that road all over, and we don't know where that oil came from. It couldn't have already been there because it didn't affect his driving at all...unless...unless, he has an oil dump on the white Chrysler. You know what? I bet he does."

"We've gotta stop that guy," his friend replied. "He's calling his Chrysler *Traveler*. All the moonshine boys know it. I guess that was somebody's horse in some war. Crazy."

And crazy it was. That Union County boy had grown up to be a crazy runner of the southern 'shine. He stopped at nothing and for nobody.

There was not a federal agent that could hold a candle against Snake's knack of wild driving when he was behind the wheel of

Traveler. He had become accustomed to the stakeouts of the revenuers. Their tactic was to wait along a well-traveled moonrunning road and jump any car that looked like it was loaded with something in the windows or riding too low. Essentially, Snake was hunted like a wild animal and pursued like a dangerous gangster. He was riotous and unruly and seemed to actually enjoy the attention and notoriety bestowed upon him.

"Why last month, I was jumped thirteen times in old *Traveler*," he bragged to one of his friends. "Thirteen times in one month I outran those crazy feds. They need faster cars, 'cause they ain't even giving me a good running in the old things they're driving. Just wasting their time." In Snake's storytelling fashion, he could continue with his opinions or continue with the telling of the stories of some recent run. It was not that they weren't true; it was just that he enjoyed bragging about all of his accomplishments and loved to blend one story right into the next one. Snake was really just full of himself and loved telling about it. And the funny thing was, most all his friends, kinfolk, and others loved to hear about his outrageous escapades.

The law was always jumping him, so there was no end to the stories. Sometimes the confrontation was a nasty one, and other times it was merely a simple race whereby the HEMI just flat outran the law. One night Snake and a buddy named Skeeter had picked up a large load of liquor from Concord, North Carolina. Concord was located about thirty-six miles north of Monroe. They had picked up some supplies in Concord and then picked up the moonshine from a local corn farmer just a few miles outside of town. The farmer had made some high-quality corn liquor, and he had a reputation for making some real strong high-proof stuff. It brought top dollar on the market. The farmer had not always been in the moonshine business, but he could make more money per bushel of corn manufacturing liquor than he could make at selling the corn at the market. So he and his family had opened their new business and ran the still back behind the cornfield in the woods that had a nice stream for the condensing operation.

Snake and Skeeter had helped load several cases in the backseat and then put a few in the trunk. They were always very concerned in balancing the load of whiskey throughout the big Chrysler. They headed back on US 601 at about seventy miles per hour. Jerry had put his hat in the backseat on top of several cases of the whiskey, and Skeeter had his feet on a case of liquor that they had loaded on the floorboard just in front of him. They were busy laughing and joking along the southbound lane of 601 when an officer in a police car pulled up right along side of *Traveler*. They had not seen him come up from behind the car. Perhaps he had been following them for some-time, or he might have jumped out from some hiding location. Better yet, maybe he just pulled on the highway headed south and by pure happenstance pulled along the most notorious runner south of the Mason-Dixon line.

Skeeter first saw the officer before he had turned his lights on.

"Don't look now Jerry, but there's a big old blue shirt lawman driving right there by your left elbow."

Before Jerry could even laugh at what he thought was just a stupid joke, the lights came on and the siren blared inside the open window.

"What the—" Snake yelled in disgust. "Turn that darn thing off."

"Pull over immediately! This is the police. You are both under arrest if that's moonshine in that back seat!" The loudspeaker seemed to announce the officer's intentions to Jerry, Skeeter, and half of Cabarrus County, just north of Union County.

Jerry looked at Skeeter with a strange perplexed expression on his face.

"He said what?" Jerry asked.

"He said something about moonshine. We better pull over before he shoots somebody," Skeeter replied. Skeeter was always a bit scared about getting in trouble and was somewhat nervous about ever getting shot. "Don't want to get shot here . . . I mean today . . . here, if you know what I mean?"

"Sure, Skeeter. I don't want to get shot either, so—"

Jerry looked over at the officer, grinned that ornery grin, and then his expression grew into a large crazy smile as he waved to the angry officer that kept his microphone up to his mouth screaming,

"PULL OVER! THIS IS THE LAW. I SAID PULL OVER. THIS IS THE LAW."

With a simple, "Gotta go," to the officer, and a nod and a wink to Skeeter, Jerry just scalded that thing and took off. One moment, *Traveler* was running neck to neck with that old police car, the next moment *Traveler* had bolted down the highway, leaving the officer holding his microphone and staring into space.

"Look at those headlights, Skeeter. You can just see them headlights sinkin' back behind us. I'm 'bout embarrassed for that man, Skeeter, down right embarrassed!"

Within a minute or so, Jerry and Skeeter were well down US 601, and they never looked back again. Once Jerry hit 120 miles per hour, he just continued to cruise at that speed until they crossed the Union County line.

"Was that really necessary?" Skeeter asked. "You took off driving so fast, I 'bout messed my pants."

"Well," Jerry answered back, "you didn't get shot at, did ya?"

They laughed about the look on that old officer's face when Jerry just smiled, waved, and stomped on that old Chrysler. The officer just did not know who he was messing with, and so he continued to sit out on US 601 for the next several weeks. However, he never got another opportunity to run down this moonrunner. Jerry and *Traveler* sat low for the next few days, especially in Cabarrus County.

On another occasion, Skeeter and Snake had driven up north to Stanly County to pick up some whiskey for a major run. They had traveled up highway NC 200 from Monroe to an area right outside of Locust, North Carolina.

"Locust," Skeeter laughed. "Now who would name a town after locusts? How 'bout spider or mosquito or even termite? Ya, termite." He and Jerry laughed.

They were friends, and Jerry enjoyed his company on some of the longer runs. A bootlegger had to be careful of his friends. Some were friends just long enough to try to turn you in for some type of prize money. Jerry often warned his contacts that they could turn him in, and they might collect the reward money, but they would never be able to spend it. He said no more and did not even attempt to explain the warning with its implications. It was just understood what he meant. Many a man had crossed Jerry Rushing and had suffered the consequences. Sometimes they met the end of his handgun barrel, while others were introduced to his trusty twelve-gauge shotgun. Occasionally, one came in contact with the crowbar Snake kept right under the front seat of *Traveler*. Still others just got acquainted with the right and left fist located on the six-foot-four-inch frame of the Big Hat Man. This was one moonrunner that always made an indelible impression on all he met, especially all that tried to cross him. One way or the other, it did not matter as Jerry kept an eye on all of his friends, sometimes being real suspicious of the best of them.

Snake and Skeeter continued on NC 200 until they arrived in the town of Locust. There they found NC 24 and turned right to head east out of the little town. They had discussed eating at some diner in Locust, but were running late on their pickup. They drove exactly two miles when they saw the gravel drive to the right, exactly as the map had shown it. Down the gravel drive approximately one mile was an old shack on the left.

Down the gravel road they drove, watching the woods carefully on both sides of the car. After approximately one mile, they saw four or five shabbily dressed men and a couple of boys. As was Snake's custom, he drove right by the shack, carefully surveying the entire situation. This always gave him a better assessment of the place. He then turned around and headed back to the pickup station. In this way he was also headed back out of the drive in the event of any trouble.

He jumped out the car and walked briskly up to the strangers.

"I'm Snake. Let's get this stuff loaded. I've gotta get right back on the road." He knew that he was most vulnerable during loading and unloading of the whiskey. There was little time to talk.

"Whatcha waitin' for. Load this baby up!" With that order, the boys quickly began to load the cases from the shack to the back end of the car. Snake grabbed a bottle and poured some into a glass jar he had inside his Chrysler. By checking the beads around the top of the poured whiskey, one could check the proof and make certain that you were hauling the good stuff. Snake also unscrewed several of the jugs just to get a sniff of the strong shine. Most knew not to double-cross this bootlegger, but he always liked to check his load to be sure. Nothing was worse than hauling water except maybe being hauled in by some lucky revenuer.

Once the loading was complete, Snake settled up with Main Man. He never knew his real name. He just guessed that he was the main man in the operation and over time he just became known as Main Man.

Snake and Skeeter leapt back into the car, fastened their custom seatbelts, and headed back out to the highway. They were well on their way out of Stanly County flying south on NC 200 when they saw the grass fly up and all over the side of the highway. Two revenuers had been sitting hidden behind a small embankment and had pulled out real fast, spinning their tires through the grass, the weeds, and into the dark red Carolina clay. Surprise was always the major battle strategy for the whiskey chasers. Snake was certainly surprised to see agents on this stretch of highway. There were several turns and curves making it difficult for most bootleggers to navigate. But the curves and bends were a real asset for Jerry's type of driving, especially with *Traveler* and his modified brake lights.

Snake picked up speed, hitting the curves at over 120 miles per hour. He touched his foot on the brake pedal at each turn. He knew that the only way the federal agent's car could keep up with him was to ride his lights. Each time the Chrysler's brake lights lit up, the revenuer knew that a sharp curve was ahead, and he too hit his brakes. It was surprising how fast curves appear when you are traveling at speeds over 100 miles per hour. Jerry sped up, then touched the brakes, and then sped up again. About the time he was certain that the officers were getting accustomed to riding his lights, he turned to Skeeter and whispered, "Watch this."

He reached up to the toggle switch on the dash that disconnected his brake lights. The standard taillights continued to burn, but the brake lights did not come on. He then hit the following curve at brakeneck speed and lightly hit the brakes to keep control of the car. However, without the brake lights flashing, the agents were completely unaware of the upcoming curve and ran it at full speed. Jerry had gotten the revenuers just where he had wanted them and had really wound *Traveler* up. The feds could not have been traveling faster. They hit that curve accelerating and just kept on going...straight, that is.

Jerry's car made it safely around that last curve, but the agents' headlights looked just like you had tossed a flashlight out over the embankment and into the cornfield. They went over the hill, flipped once, then twice, and flew out into the cornfield. Jerry stomped on the brakes and swung *Traveler* around quickly just to watch the demolition and light show. The only tell-tale sign that a police car was totally out of control in that field was the two bright lights flipping over and over and over again.

"We just live for days like this," Snake howled. "I love it...I just love it. Those brake lights work just like a charm."

Within an hour, Snake and Skeeter were back in Union County making their rounds and telling their story to all that would hear it.

Bullets Fly While Traveler Runs

It was a black, moonless night, and the night air seemed thick like a sauna. Though the sun had set hours ago, the heat lingered in the air. Jerry had taken *Traveler* to Buck earlier in the afternoon for a quick spark plug change and a tune-up. He had to be ready for tonight's run. He would be carrying nearly fifty cases of whiskey and would travel northeast to Rockwell, North Carolina to pick it up. It would be an expensive and heavy load, and he would arrive in Rockwell, before midnight. He had heard through the grapevine that some agents were headed toward Rockwell and the place could be crawling within a couple of hours. He needed to get loaded up quick and head south fast.

Nights with a new moon are especially black and dreary. Snake preferred the nights where the moon shone brightly in the sky. He could run the highways or run a trap line with no lights except the moon. But tonight was different. The night was dark, and Snake seemed to sense some type of danger in the air. Once again he knew that he was the prey and that traps were set again this night throughout Union County as well as many of the surrounding counties.

He moved the white Chrysler slowly off the highway and pulled cautiously down the long drive that led to the rear of the farm where he was picking up this heavy load. The moonshiner had stacked it neatly on his back screen porch and covered it with a large tarp just to keep the cases out of site. Snake just wanted to get the whiskey loaded, make the run, and call it a night. However, the night was still young, and he had miles of highway to travel. Few words were shared as the cases of sugar whiskey were loaded in *Traveler*. Snake walked around the car nervously.

Typically, these runs were no different for Jerry than a run of an average milkman. But tonight seemed different.

Is it the heat and humidity, or do I sense danger? Snake wondered to himself. He had pulled his big Stetson off his sweaty head several times now and wiped his forehead with his large white handkerchief. Even the men loading the cases of whiskey noticed a certain nervousness in Snake. But they dared not mention anything, as they had worked with him in the past and on at least one occasion he had given them an attitude adjustment when things got out of hand.

One still had a large crook in his nose from running straight into Snake's trusty crowbar one night. So they just quietly finished the loading and retreated back to the farmhouse for their nightly game of poker. It was safer that way. They knew the Rushing boy from down south was dangerous and downright evil. Snake took a big breath and again adjusted his big black hat. Should he hide out for the night and run another night, or was he just feeling the stress of running through one of Carolina's hottest summers? August could get very uncomfortable, and the heat from the last week had been a real test of character. On more than one occasion in this heat Snake had almost busted open a man's face just for looking at him oddly while walking down the street.

Well, he decided he would not tarry, but make the run on this moonless night. He pulled out onto the highway and headed south toward Monroe. But he still had a strange feeling within him that he was the hunted animal and the hunters had already entered the woods armed and dangerous. His head on the wall was what every revenuer wanted. He had been embarrassing them for too long, and now they wanted him—dead or alive. The stakes were higher, and though he was not frightened, he did sense danger. The hunters were most likely already planted in the woods along some country highway with rifles in hand, waiting for the prey to pass by their shooting lane. If he should pass by, the shots would likely be fired.

His heart rate had increased significantly, and perspiration poured out from inside that big hat. He took it off in order to cool himself and laid it on the passenger seat beside him. The highway was fairly straight, so the oil slick or the brake light trick were ineffective on this road. Though it had few curves, it was a bit hilly, and *Traveler* raced up one hill only to coast back down on the other side. It was not until *Traveler* came up upon one of the highest hills on that road headed home that he saw the flicker of small lights in the distance. His senses had been right. The hunters were gathered for the hunt party with cars and guns pointed his way. They were poised, expecting their prey to come right down the highway upon them. Except for a small flashlight or a tiny light from the inside of one of the cars when the door was opened, they were almost invisible in the darkness of the new moon. They should never have had even the tiniest lights on; it was all Jerry needed. He now knew exactly where they were lying.

He did not want to retreat back north because of some reports of possible stakeouts that could take place that night in or around Rockwell. So he decided exactly what he would do. He would attack them, using their own tactics of surprise and shock. He ran ahead fast for a few hundred yards with his headlights on bright. He then turned a fast u-turn and headed back north, almost certain they saw his turn. He knew he was too fast and too far away for any of them to chase him. After he was out of sight, he turned off all of his lights and switched off his toggle switches. He then cut another fast u-turn and headed south again. He secretly drove right up on them in the darkest of nights and then turned on his lights and blew right through them.

He was ready to face the hunter and turn the tides. Perhaps this night the hunter would become the hunted. Snake silently headed right into the midst of them, driving toward the ambush and facing the danger directly. He slowly gained ground on the hunters. Though they had been well armed and each had been stationed at their posts, the surprise of seeing a fast car cut a u-turn and speed off took them by surprise.

"I wonder if that car was running moonshine. If so, do you think he may have seen our cars?" one agent asked another.

"Don't know really. All lights were supposed to be off, and there were no cigarettes. This is the blackest night we've had in ages," another replied.

"Well," the commanding officer replied with a disgusted snort, "if it was a bootlegger, he's gone now. Radio up to those boys up north and tell them to set another roadblock outside of Rockwell. If they're lucky, it might be a runner, and if they're real lucky, it might be that Union County boy with that fast Chrysler. I'd love to crash his party one day."

Snake was probably no further than a hundred yards or so when he began to make out the cars and the men that were walking around. They had already set down their rifles, and some had even sat back down in their patrol cars to radio in the office. Snake decided he would continue to run slowly and undetected in the dark near the shoulder of the road. He would run right up upon them without lights until the first agent made him out. At that time he would do what he had to do.

He was about forty-five yards from the agents when the first one started screaming, "Incoming, incoming!"

Many were totally confused. *Incoming what?* they wondered.

Snake turned on his bright double headlights that the Chrysler was famous for and burned rubber for the entire distance, picking up speed like a race car at a drag race. There was confusion and noise everywhere. Angry men were grabbing their guns and firing blindly into the four big bright lights that were coming their way. Some were running for cover while others jumped into their cars in spite of the fact there was no place to hide. The hunter's advantage was lost by the craftiness of the prey they were hunting. The hunted was now attacking the hunter, and the hunter was on the run.

Though it only took a few seconds for *Traveler* to be right upon them, it had seemed like an eternity. Bewilderment filled the hot night air as this missile headed down right toward them as if it had been launched out of nowhere. The midnight darkness was inter-rupted by flashlights and car lights illuminating the sky and by the red-orange blasts from several revolvers and shotguns. *Traveler* was at full speed when Snake pulled right into the midst of them. The roar from *Traveler* mixed with the screams of angry and shocked federal agents pierced the quietness of the midnight hour.

Snake's handling prowess of *Traveler* made maneuvering through the scattered men and cars relatively easy, even at speeds over 120 miles per hour. He was able to get through them without killing an agent and without wrecking any of the patrol cars. *Traveler* had come through the battle unscarred and was now running at a high speed away from the officers. However, the battle was not yet over. Gunshots continued to fill the air as the agents now took a sharp aim and shot toward the direction of that fast Chrysler. The shots were only aimed in the general direction of *Traveler* since all tail-lights were off. *Traveler* had about escaped their firing when she was first hit in the right rear quarter panel. Snake heard the bullet tear through the steel and then take out several gallon jars of the recently packed illegal whiskey. He could smell that sweet smell as it leaked through the trunk.

Guns continued to blast into the night air. Snake could see in his rearview mirror what looked like a complete Union cavalry lining up and taking fire at him.

"Come on, *Traveler*…let's get out of here," he screamed as if coach-ing the white Chrysler might help its performance.

Bang, bang, bang! It was almost as if Snake could here those spin-ning projectiles flying right past his open window. *Bang, bam!*

Another shot hit the car as a bullet creased the rear deck, ripping through the backseat and lodging itself in the roof only inches from the driver's head. Snake's eyes grew larger as he pushed his 300-D faster than it had ever run.

Bang, clink—clink—clink. One more misguided bullet found its home in the hubcap and blew it right off of the wheel. By that time Snake was well out of range, though angry officers continued to fire their weapons, reload, and fire again. Most of them knew that their bullets never reached that white horse. But somehow, they felt better while they vented some of their fury and frustration by firing into the night sky.

Snake rushed on down the road without even slowing down. He was in Monroe by 2:00 a.m., unloaded by 3:00, and back to his friend's garage before morning. Not only was Buck a great mechanic and kept *Traveler* running, but he was also a great auto body man. The bullet holes needed to be worked and patched before daybreak. They needed to be so perfect that even the trained eye of a federal revenuer agent could not detect a previous hole in the body. If the agents felt that they had hit Jerry's car, they would be after him the very next morning. If he were caught in a police roadblock within a week or two, even without a load but with bullet holes, he could be arrested until they could piece the facts all together. In any respect, the bodywork needed to be compete and thoroughly painted before anyone had the opportunity to see *Traveler* again. Buck was an expert in this type of undercover work. He even put in additives so the new paint dried without a real gloss and blended into the older paint.

So the sun came up, and it was still a hot humid August day. Snake woke up from the corner of the garage and yawned. The gunshot that lodged adjacent to his head in the roof panel was too close. But it was all in a day's work—or night's.

"Been working all night, Buck?' Jerry asked.

"All night," Buck mumbled.

"Look good?" Jerry asked.

"Come and see," Buck mumbled again. He was too tired to put much energy into his responses. He had just finished buffing the dried paint job.

"Wow," Snake exclaimed. "Looking good!"

"Running tonight again?" Buck asked without looking up.

"Yep."

"Be careful...will ya?" Buck asked with anxiousness in his voice from the gunshots and all.

"Yep," Snake replied. "Nothing brings down old Snake...you know that."

The Other White Horse

Snake loved *Traveler* probably as much as General Robert E. Lee loved his *Traveler*. Animals have always held a special place in the hearts of men. Who hasn't seen a picture of Lee sitting proudly upon *Traveler*, or Stonewall Jackson sitting atop of *Little Sorrel* as his horse proudly pranced in the military parades of the Virginia Military Institute? But there is another Commander in Chief that rode a simple colt, the foal of a donkey, in a parade many years ago.

The Bible tells us in all four Gospels that Jesus rode on a colt into Jerusalem during what we today call Palm Sunday. He was entering Jerusalem, and the crowds all gathered around Him. Matthew 21:7–11 says:

> And brought the ass, and the colt, and put on them their clothes, and they set him thereon. And a very great multitude spread their garments in the way; others cut down branches from the trees, and strawed them in the way. And the multitudes that went before, and that followed, cried, saying, Hosanna to the Son of David: Blessed is he that cometh in the name of the Lord; Hosanna in the highest. And when he was come into Jerusalem, all the city was moved, saying, Who is this? And the multitude said, This is Jesus the prophet of Nazareth of Galilee.

Jesus was entering Jerusalem for the last time. It was the season of the Passover, and He was entering the holy city as the final and perfect Lamb that ultimately was sentenced to death for crimes He never committed. He had never sinned, so He became the unblemished Lamb that shed His perfect blood for you, for me, and even for Jerry Elijah Rushing. He was God's Son and had come to Earth to take away the sins of the entire world. John 3:16 tells us that, "For God so loved the world, that he gave his only begotten Son, that whosoever believeth in him should not perish, but have everlasting life." Jesus died for our sins and took the punishment that we deserved for our sins upon Him.

As Jesus entered the city, the crowd gathered and even began to acknowledge Him for the first time, shouting, "Hosanna to the Son of David." There was electricity in the air, and the city was stirred as Jesus rode in on the simple colt. He was a loving, humble, meek, and mild Savior who loved the sinful men of the world. No doubt He waved to the crowd. He felt sorry for the nation of Israel and sad for their lack of understanding in who He was. He may have smiled at the older ladies or winked at the little children that ran along the parade. He really loves children. But He hates sin. That is why He came into the world to take away our sins. We still have time to accept Him as our Savior. But a time is coming when we will no longer have that option available to us.

The Bible talks of judgment and the day when Jesus, our Lord and Savior, will come back to Earth for the second time. Only this time He is not coming as a baby in a stable. This time He is not coming back riding a small colt. The Bible is clear about this in the Book of Revelation when it says that the Lord is coming back as a warrior riding a "white horse."

Read the following scripture:

> And I saw heaven opened, and behold a white horse; and he that sat upon him was called Faithful and True, and in righteousness he doth judge and make war. His eyes were as a flame of fire, and on his head were many crowns; and he had a name written, that no man knew, but he himself. And he was clothed with a vesture dipped in blood: and his name is called The Word of God. And the armies which were in heaven followed him upon white horses, clothed in fine linen, white and clean. And out of his mouth goeth a sharp sword, that with it he should smite the nations: and he shall rule them with a rod of iron: and he treadeth the winepress of the fierceness and wrath of Almighty God. And he hath on his vesture and on his thigh a name written, KING OF KINGS, AND LORD OF LORDS.
>
> —REVELATION 19:11–16

General Robert E. Lee had his white horse. Moonrunner Jerry E. Rushing had his white horse. Our King of kings and Lord of lords will ride back to us on a white horse. He will be coming in judgment. He is called faithful and true, His robe is dipped in blood, and out of His mouth comes a sharp sword. It will be too late for the moonshiner, too late for the bootlegger, and too late for any man to ask for mercy. In fact, verse 11 says that He now comes and will judge: "in righteousness he doth judge and make war."

The scripture above even tells us that the entire army of heaven now follows Him, and all of heaven's warriors are riding white horses.

Snake loved his white horse, *Traveler*. But that old Chrysler 300-D could not compare with heaven's own white horse ready for battle and with the ultimate Commander in Chief, Jesus Christ.

Why not accept Him today, while there is yet time?

Jesus loves you personally, died for you, and is moving in your heart right now.

If you wait until one day when you see the great white horse, it will be too late for you.

Judgment will be at hand, and you will be lost to an eternity of hell. Why not now?

CHAPTER 6

Run That Whiskey, Boy!

THE LEGEND RUNS THE SHINE

S NAKE HAD ONLY dreamed of becoming a modern-day outlaw when he was a little tot, but he eventually became the legend that he had imagined. His reputation as a bootlegger had grown from the little town of Monroe to Union County to the entire area of the Carolinas. He was also well known for his temperament and character. Many in the town called him a character. Others in the town said he had character; it was just that the character traits were in the line of cruel and callous. He was full of hatred and just seemed to enjoy taking his hate out on anyone that crossed his path at any time.

He often told his friends, "My dream in life is to always stay one step in front of the law. The way I figure it is that the law will always be after me for somethin'... either makin' the 'shine or runnin' it hard. That's OK though, cause I'll always be just one step ahead of them, or maybe two. They'll never get their old noose around this neck. I'm just too bad."

And bad he was.

Somewhere in the development years between that little forty-five- pound boy named Snake and that full-bodied muscular man, known as Big Hat Man, something changed. The little boy that liked to smile, run in the woods, and catch tadpoles in the stream slowly but surely grew mean and then malicious. The law knew just how spiteful and cruel the Rushing boy had become. He would start a fight just to have a reason to punch a man, and then he would punch the man just to see a man bleed. In Jerry's later years, he befriended the great country legend Johnny Cash. One of Johnny's songs was a favorite of Snake. His favorite verse went something like this, "I shot a man in Reno, just to watch him die." Snake often thought, *Now, I wonder just how that would feel. Just shoot a man right between his eyes with my old .45, and then just stand there and watch him die. Might try it someday. I just might really try it.*

He had a reputation of being totally unpredictable and erratic in his behavior. Many of the local lawmen did not really want to mess with him. They knew he was dangerous and stopped at nothing to win his personal war. What war? The war he had daily in his mind against all lawmen and against any authority at all. This was a terrible hate that continued to grow within him and that manifested itself in horrifying impulsive and volatile behavior. The local sheriffs much preferred stopping old ladies that slowed without stopping at one of Monroe's stoplights rather than tangle with this boy. Some knew from stories and others from experience that he was likely to shoot at them or take them on such a chase that they might never return. On many occasions, they avoided a chase with Rushing if they could.

Jerry felt that if they were ever to catch him running whiskey, they would either earn it or they would die trying. He would not come easy. He was always bragging to his friends, "By golly, they'll never catch me. And if they ever do, you can bet they will have to *earn* old Rushing here. If I ever go down, I'll go down with both fists flying and with all guns firing. Kill or be killed is my motto." As long as a buddy or friend listened to him, Jerry continued with his wild stories and threats against any lawman that dared to stand up to him.

Few ever dared.

The closest they might ever come was in a late night whiskey-running contest with Jerry way out in front of the crowd. Once they heard about his smoking tricks or his oil-slicking stunts, they would run him but keep their distance for safety. Sometimes he even slowed down to allow the lawmen to get closer, making it more of a challenge for the both of them.

"What's a runnin' race without some risk of getting' yourself caught?" he often bragged.

He loved the long runs as well as the short delivery runs right around Monroe. On many occasions, he made a long run outside the county and occasionally outside the state. Runs to Tennessee or Kentucky were typical, especially if the federal agents were clamping down tight on Union County. When they came into the county in hordes, it was a simple thing to sit tight for a season. The local folks stopped the moonshine business for a while and gave their stills a rest. Then when things got a bit dry, they made an all-night run to another state to get the liquor that folks just could not live without.

Though he loved the long runs in the middle of the night, he equally loved the local delivery market. There was a poor neighborhood just outside of town that was inhabited primarily by a very large black population. In the midst of that neighborhood lived a blind man that just loved Jerry's white lightning. Every so often, Jerry loaded up his liquor running car and headed to that poor side of town. He loaded cases in the trunk, the backseat, and occasionally on the passenger side on the floorboard. It did not really matter how much or how little he loaded as he always came back home empty with his pockets full of their cash. They just loved that hillbilly pop.

During the winter deliveries, it was as if he were Santa and it was Christmas day, only it was during the wee hours of the morning sometime after midnight. Some paid over half of their week's wages for a case of the illegal stuff. Others scraped together all the change they could find in their tiny shack just to buy a gallon of the mountain dew. The old blind man always had his money ready, though Jerry often wondered where a black blind man got such cash to buy his liquor.

Curtis Lowe had been blind as long as he could remember. His grandpa had said that he lost his sight sometime around the age of five when he got lye in his eyes during some soap making. But old Curtis could really never remember seeing the light of day. So whether it was a midnight Christmas run or a bright sunny day, it mattered not to old Curtis. His eyes could not tell the difference. But he loved that moonshine. He passed the word along to Snake that the folks in the neighborhood were running low. Through friends of the family that Snake saw in town, he passed back a message of about when he would make the distribution run. He never told them exactly when or where.

Snake new his game well and was extremely street smart. He knew that a moonrunner could really trust no one. He recognized that if the money was good enough, any of his buyers would turn him in for cash, only to find another runner to buy from on another day. There was loyalty with many of the moonshiners and runners as they took a real pride in their individual manufacturing and distributing process. But the typical buyers, especially in this neighborhood, only understood the game of survival. It was a rough and tumble way to live, and Jerry trusted none of them, not even Curtis Lowe. Curtis set his nephew out on the rugged front stoop of his one-room shack. The three steps were rough hewn out of a soft pine, and termites had feasted on them for years. His nephew sat there night after night and waited for the man with the big hat to pull slowly down the street. Jerry often made a pass or two before actually stopping and passing out his goods.

Jerry does not actually remember how it started, but it was his tradition to always stop and deliver the blind man's whiskey first. Once he thought that it might have been he was feeling sorry for the old blind guy. But he quickly dismissed that thought, as he wanted no part of being a sissy kind of guy that had any type of feelings, let alone sorry feelings. *Well, I'd kill him as fast as I'd kill any other man,* he often thought, *especially if the old man ever got in my way.*

Snake had already become a legend in that neighborhood as he was becoming a legend in all of Union County. Most everyone accepted this fact and knew all about him and his illustrious exploits. He even knew it and was proud of it. Jerry Elijah Rushing had become a real-life out-law legend. Most dictionaries define a legend as one who achieves leg-endary fame typically bestowed through unverified wild tales handed down over many years until those stories actually became romanticized myths of modern culture. And no one better fit that description than Rushing himself.

"Hey, Uncle Coootus…Uncle Coootus. It's dat man wida big hat. Uncle Cootus…come quick." The little nephew boy had been sitting on those old rotten steps for several nights when the Big Hat Man finally drove up the drive. Jerry slowly turned off the engine and car-ried a big case of some fresh brew up to Curtis's shack.

Old man Lowe slowly made his way to the door, feeling his way down the steps and arriving right in the face of Jerry.

"Is dat you, Big Hat Man?" the blind man asked.

"Yep," Rushing replied. He was a man of few words. Jerry was on a business delivery trip, and he always watched his backside, as one could never be to certain in this neighborhood.

"How much ya bring me dis time, Big Hat Man?"

"One big case of the best tastin' stuff this side of the Mississippi!" Jerry said. He did not exactly know why, but he loved the respect that these poor folks gave him. And he really liked the name, Big Hat Man. He was the hero of these parts. Not many could rise above the law and survive. In the Big Hat Man, they saw hope for tomorrow. If he could buck the system and get by with it, perhaps they someday could also rise above the poverty and filth in which they lived.

Being blind, Curtis Lowe had already had a friend count out the money needed for a full case.

"Here's da cash, Big Hat Man. Can ya just put it here inside da door. Don't ja set it on these old steps…why…" Curtis laughed out loud, "if da steps broke thru and the 'shine jugs busted and my cat-daddy poured out on the ground, I'd cry me a river. O'dat be bad."

"Yep," Jerry said again as he hoisted the case of 'shine up over the steps and then took the man's money. Jerry always counted the money fast and stuck it into one of his pant pockets.

Jerry turned to grab another case of whiskey for the old man's neighbor as Curtis returned to his shack singing, "Da Big Hat Man come again…he just come again." For being blind and half drunk most of his life, Jerry was surprised that the old man was most always singing some crazy song to a made-up tune.

Jerry quickly delivered all of that whiskey within an hour or two and was ready to run. There were nearly two hundred poor black households, all wanting liquor. Perhaps they needed the unlawful medication to drown out the sorrows of their own downtrodden lives. He ran from house to house, handing out cases or single jugs and then as quickly stuffing the money down deep into his pockets. He finished the night with money sticking out of every pocket in his pants and shirt. Knowing that he could be an easy hit and target with all that cash, he was excited to get back into his running car and hit the highway. He never brought any 'shine back home when he visited blind Curtis Lowe and his neighborhood friends.

It really did not matter when or where Jerry ran whiskey. He just loved the excitement of running it. He loved the night air and the sound of the whiskey sloshing back and forth in the clean gallon jugs. He also loved the aroma of the white lightning as it mixed with the smell of the rubber off his tires. It was the runner's way of life. If fact, Jerry loved running so much that he taught an old mule to run the stuff.

One of the most difficult aspects of the moonshine business was getting the raw material, which was corn or sugar, from the road to the still and then getting the whiskey from the still and loaded into the car or truck. Some years earlier, Jerry had an idea and he and a buddy, Goshen, had bought this old mule from a farmer in Union County. He had just bought a load of sugar and packed his Bluebird plum full of it.

"Whatcha think," he asked Goshen, "about teaching this old mule to run our stuff from the truck to the still? I know you can't teach a dog new tricks, but what about this old mule?"

Goshen just scratched his head, "How in the world would we teach this dumb old mule any tricks at all?"

"Well, we have all this sugar. Let's go back to the barn and load up the old beast and bring her down to where we've got old Bertha cooking the shine." Now remember, Bertha was his big submarine still.

So Goshen and Snake backtracked to one of their old barns, hitched up a trailer to Bluebird, and loaded up the mule for the ride back to the creek. Goshen was still trying to figure all of this out when he asked Snake, "Now just how will we teach this old thing to work for us?"

"Well, I think that you and I will take turns walking it down the trail from the car to the still and then back again, loaded with a couple bags of sugar on each run. Then we'll see if it can remember the trail by walking it herself. It would sure take a load off of our work if it can be trained."

With that, Snake loaded the mule up with sugar and started down the long wooded path back to the creek and then up the creek a ways. There stood Beulah cooking some of the best 'shine in Union County. Snake unloaded the sugar and used some sacks and leather roping to tie some finished bottles of 'shine to the mule's back and slowly walked it back to *Bluebird*. There sat Goshen sipping on a hot soda that had been sitting under the front seat of Snake's running car. "Boy, this thing's must be bad . . . it tastes rotten," Goshen complained.

"Well, jump up and toss that thing into the woods. That's been under the seat caught in those springs since I bought this baby. Now, hurry up, Goshen, and load some more bags of sugar on this mule and walk it back down the trail and then back again."

Snake sat down on the trailer, always keeping a watchful eye on his surroundings. He was like a wildcat on the run. His enemy had pursued him for years now, and he knew their tactics. They loved to come in shooting and surprise their prey. But Snake was as aware of his surroundings as an old buck sneaking through the woods. Snake often said, "How does an old buck get to be an old buck? Simple . . . by being smarter than all the other dead bucks." Then he laughed one on his big old belly laughs and continued, "And just how do you figure old Snake here has lasted this long? Simple . . . by being smarter than all the other dumb moonrunners behind prison bars."

Snake moved through the woods and the highways like a jungle cat moves through the tropical forest. He never rested and he never relaxeed. His senses had become sharpened and his traveled woods and roads were his jungle. He knew every jungle turn and the curve of each road and highway. They were his turf, and he was one with it. He also knew each mighty tree, each fallen tree, and every bend of each creek in his personal jungle woods where he traveled. Survival depended upon it.

Nearly an hour had passed when Goshen reappeared on the footpath leading the old mule with another load of that sweet whiskey fluid. "Where the heck have you been?" Snake barked. "I was about to come down there and work you over, man. What's the deal?"

Well, Goshen knew better than to get Snake upset, but he also knew better than not answer him. "Sorry, boss. I jes worked up a real sweat and thirst by the time I got down to old Beulah, and I just could not help but take a swig or two..."

He had not even completed his sentence when Snake was on his feet and in his face.

"What have I told you about drinking my profits, man? Well, I have half the notion to just beat it outta ya right here and now. If I was not in the middle of trying to train this old mule. So, since you're already liquored up, load another batch of this here sugar on the beast and take another trip."

Without any sign of complaint, Goshen loaded up another load of sugar and started down the path again. This continued with the old mule for most of the afternoon until Snake was ready to test his running buddy. He had run whiskey for most all of his life. Maybe, just maybe, if this mule had any sense at all, it could become one of Snake's whiskey runners as well. So Jerry loaded the mule with another load of sugar and told Goshen to hold that old mule for ten minutes or so in order for Snake to make it down the path and sit at the still. Then Goshen was to release the mule on the path and give it a gentle slap and push in the right direction. Goshen stared at his watch until the last minute, and then walked the mule to the path, slapped its butt, and pushed it down the trodden path.

"Go on, you dumb old mule. You're probably just gonna get lost in these woods and we'll lose that sugar... now get." As legend has it, that old mule arrived right at that still in less than ten minutes with every bag of sugar intact.

Snake jumped up, excited, and pulled the sugar off its back and hugged its neck. Funny for such a mean and uncaring man to be seen in the middle of some dense woods hugging the neck of an old mule. Without showing too much affection for this old beast, Snake loaded up the whiskey and again pointed the mule in the opposite direction. Jerry waited a minute or two and began to stalk the animal from a safe distance. It slowed at the ditches and walked carefully up the wet banks as if it knew the treasure it was carrying. And in another ten minutes or so, it came out of the woodline right at the hood of Blue-bird. Jerry came running out of the woods, nearly causing old Goshen to have a heart attack right there.

"What are you doing, Snake? I about passed out thinking that you running out of the woods was one of those old revenuers."

Snake just laughed and pushed Goshen back down onto the trailer floor where he had been lying.

"We got ourselves a work horse here, old buddy."

"It's not a horse, Snake. It's a stupid mule."

Snake just laughed again. "OK. So we've got ourselves a stupid work mule, if you've ever heard of such a thing."

Snake continued to use this mule for years as one of his favorite running buddies. He transported that old mule from still location to still location, and it only took a few trips for the mule to catch onto the path and off it ran solo. On several occasions when the revenuers caught up with one of Snake's old stills, Snake was fast enough to get away. However, the old mule just stood there as the agents ran in and destroyed all parts of the operation. Then they confiscated the mule and auctioned it off at the next county auction. Snake had invested too many hours into the training of that old mule to see it go. He always managed to have someone at those auctions, working undercover, to bid on that old mule and bring it back to his stills.

So Jerry Rushing always stayed one step in front of the law whether he was running on some all-night trip to Tennessee and back or some short delivery run to some poor old shanty town. He had become the legend that he had only dreamed about. As he continued to outrun every lawman in the county, the legend continued to grow. Folks sat in town bars and in fellowship dinners at the local church gossiping about the Monroe boy that had gone bad. "He runs all over the South," some said. Others added to the story, "Why, I've heard that he has killed several agents, running them off the mountainside spraying down the cop cars with some type of oil gun that's hidden in the trunk." Others thought the mere mention of his name was sinful enough to evoke God's wrath upon them, and they just kept silent. One boy at a local drugstore was overheard sharing, "Why I've heard that he has trained hundreds of packing mules to carry his gear, his stills, and supplies deep into the mountains where the devil dares not to travel."

"Legends and wild stories...just legends," the druggist replied, filling the boy's order while paying little attention to the boy's deepening frowns.

"I don't think so, mister," the boy whispered to himself with a grin.

The boy's thoughts carried him back to the stories he had heard about the famous Monroe moonrunner.

"Maybe one day I will be a modern-day outlaw, too. I could be a legend." With that, the little boy grabbed his mother's prescription and headed back out the door.

"Silly kids with those silly stories," the druggist laughed to his stock boy.

So what does a druggist know?

THE MORE NOTORIOUS RUNS

A hard-working moonrunner like Snake easily put more than one hundred thousand miles on his car within a year of running. Most of those miles were hard-driving miles loaded with illegal shine. This type of rough and brutal driving wore a car out fast. As soon as Snake wore out one car, he bought another and was back on the road within days.

One of his car purchases was a big, black 1958 Chrysler that ran curves loaded at over 120 miles per hour. He had a set of four-to five-inch-thick hardened steel springs installed on the rear of that Chrysler. He believed that the mechanic made them out of old railroad springs from a boxcar. Those thick steel springs made the car so stout that it would not give at all on those fast corners, even loaded down with fifty cases of the shine. Because it was big, black, and long with those characteristic big fins located on both sides of the trunk, Snake named the car *Batmobile*. He loved to ride it into some of the shantytowns around Monroe where he often ran liquor to the poor folks living in those one-room shacks. He liked to hear all those half-naked little kids run down the street yelling, "It's da *Batmobile*; look at dat *Batmobile* comin' down da street." The kids ran and yelled until Snake pulled back out of the neighborhood and floored it down the street just to peel off a bit of rubber for the sake of the young ones watching.

He ran that *Batmobile* one year for more than 125,000 miles. Hundreds of the runs were quick and fast Union County runs, while others were from one side of North Carolina to the far side of Tennessee and back. Local lawmen, county sheriffs, and numerous federal agents chased him in that streamlined black Chrysler. They were determined to stop at nothing to bring in that *Batmobile* and its wild-man driver. But though many got close, they could not keep up with the power of Snake's bat-car, though he did have some close calls.

On one such occasion, Snake was making a run fully loaded with a fresh batch of corn liquor from Union County to Wilkes County. He was running alone with no one riding shotgun and with no decoy drivers. It was a relatively short run, and he expected to have the delivery complete and unloaded prior to midnight and be back home early. He had been on the road for only a short time when he felt the handling of the *Batmobile* become slow and sluggish. He did not need any trouble at a time like this when he was fully loaded with so much unlawful stuff. But he knew what this type of handling meant. He slowly looked for a place on the shoulder to pull off and check his car. It was exactly what he thought, a flat rear tire.

"A nearly flat rubber piece of junk…don't need this now," he mumbled to himself as he walked around the car. *A spare, do I have a spare?* he wondered. And about that time he kicked the gravel from the shoulder nearly across the street. "Sure I have a spare…right next to those twenty cases of liquor we loaded earlier tonight."

That meant he had to pull to the side of road, fix the flat quickly, and hit the road again. Snake thought fast. He pulled the *Batmobile* slowly back onto the roadway and looked for an opening in the woods that would at least get him off of the major street. He drove for only a few hundred yards when he saw a small opening in the pines on the left-hand side of the road. He quickly surveyed the woods and pulled between two giant Frazier firs whose low-lying branches would provide some cover for his emergency nighttime operation. The dark black color of the *Batmobile* would help in the camouflaging of the hidden automobile. He got out of the car, closed the door, and moved to the trunk. He had already removed the small lights inside the car, inside the engine compartment, and in the trunk for such a time as this. Any tiny light that shattered the darkness in the middle of the night was just enough to reveal your whereabouts to a watchful revenuer's eye.

On more than one occasion, a pair of lights came running down the road, causing Snake to duck quickly behind his hidden car and freeze his position in the night air. Once the lights had passed, Snake would pause for a moment or two and then begin unloading again. He worked up quite a sweat as he labored there alone.

Finally he was able to withdrawal the spare tire, jack up the Chrysler, and then change his flat. Seldom did he work so hard during a short midnight run. But within thirty minutes or so, Snake was again loaded and ready to run. He first walked out to the street and silently scrutinized the landscape for any sign of life or light. When all looked clear, he walked back into the tree forest and fired the *Batmobile* up. He looked like Batman without his sidekick as he pulled quickly out onto the highway and was instantly lost in the darkness of the evening. Like most of their other outlaw relatives, moonrunners liked to run their operation in the cloak of darkness. And Jerry was no exception.

He did not arrive the old man's place to unload until well after one in the morning. He had been delivering cases of white lightning for many years now, and the old man had just continued to get older and older. His hair was as white as snow and his scratchy dirty beard ran down his chin and was tucked into his bib overalls. Snake was always paid well for his hauling, but he knew the man by the only name he had always called him, and that was just Old Man. He passed the drive as he often did and then ran past the place again. One could not be too careful with all the federal agents that were dispatched to slow the whiskey flow into and out of the Carolina area. He then pulled into the drive and continued until he came to the old man's concrete block building where they stowed the stash. There he met the crew that unloaded the whiskey as fast as they get it out of the car. The old man with the cash came running out of the building as excited as Snake had ever seen him, and he was stuttering with his customary lisp.

"Ya won't believe it, Big Hat Man...dey came an sat all 'round this road. They went in da woods and then parked down da street in da woods. They had this whoooole place staked out." The old man's voice was shaking so that Snake could not really make out what he was trying to say. It made Snake nervous, so he just stood in the doorway scrutinizing the boys that were unloading and the driveway he had just entered.

Snake got out of the *Batmobile* quickly and ran into the door of the building as the old man stood in front of him shaking like he was having a seizure.

"Calm down, Old Man...what in heaven's name are you trying to say? If this is a shake-down, I'll kill ya on the spot, and I mean here and now." Snake took the old man's arm and held him firmly but gently against the rotten doorframe. The old man was both young enough and dumb enough to try to double-cross him but too old to rough up too much. "So tell me, what's going down?"

"Well," the old man steadied himself against the doorframe and against the frame of big Snake, "Just five minutes 'go, da feds pulled out. I mean dat I was scared as an alley cat on fire. Dey were crawlin' all over the farm and in da woods an' ever' where. Dey showed up at sundown around 6:30 and stayed till after midnight, leaving just a few minutes back. I jes knew dat you were comin' at midnight and dey would catch ya. And I could not get cha. I was soooo scared dat I thought I was gonna throw up."

"Well...what do you know?" Snake shrugged, "If I'd been on time, I'd be in jail right now."

The old man was still shaking and looking at Snake through eyes as big as saucers. "Where'd you been, Snake? You're always on time. I jes know de'd catch ya tonight. I was prayin' you'd not come right in da middle of dem."

Snake had no time for explaining the whole story to Old Man, so he counted the man's payment and bid him farewell as he jumped back into the *Batmobile* and ran at eighty-five miles per hour back out the drive< spitting gravel all through the cornfield and back toward the old block building. The old man and his friends just stood there, still in shock as they watched the Big Hat Man disappear back into the night as fast as he had appeared.

As Snake raced back down the highway to home, he could not help but ponder for a moment the old man's statement about a prayer, "I was prayin' you'd not come right in da middle of dem."

But Snake pondered that only for an instant. Then his mind raced on like the Batmobile he was running, focusing on his future runs and his other whiskey dealings.

Not only did Jerry Rushing run whiskey for a living, but he also ran the actual supplies for the moonshine. These often needed to be purchased on the black market and then swiftly delivered, undetected, to the moonshining operation. For example, sugar was actually rationed. In the event that you purchased more than two five-pound bags of sugar, you had to sign for them at the store. On many occasions, the federal revenuers checked the local stores for the sales of sugar. They checked the ordering slips and the purchases against the actual inventory. In the event that there was a discrepancy, someone would have to answer for it. Therefore, Snake often bought his sugar from some underground salesperson, or sometimes he purchased it from an actual dishonest federal revenuer that was making money on sugar, whiskey, or gallon plastic jugs on the side.

On one such occasion, Snake had purchased hundreds of pounds of sugar from a supplier outside of his county. This man happened to be a church deacon that ran a grocery store. They always believed that he acquired it underground from some private southern source. Because he was a deacon in his church and an upright citizen in the community, they tried to keep it quiet and load it up behind the store at night. Snake was required to load it up right after midnight and haul it back to Union County before sunrise. If one was caught with that much sugar, it was as serious an offense as if you were hauling a full load of liquor. Sugar was especially hard to haul in a car because it was so heavy and bulky.

But it was safer hauling bags of sugar in a car than a truck. Revenuers suspected hauling bales of sugar in a farm truck rather than a car, but they did not expect such a thing in an old coupe. So Snake used his 1949 blue Ford coupe he named *Bluebird* to haul sugar in. He could load over thirty-six bales of sugar in that monster, but they had to be stacked in there exact and precise like eggs in a carton. Sugar weighed sixty pounds per bale, so *Bluebird* could haul well over a full ton of sugar in one load. She had been outfitted with gigantic steel springs like most of Snake's running cars.

Snake pulled *Bluebird* up quietly behind the grocery store and turned off the engine. His deacon friend was standing there in the dark, slowly puffing on a big old cigar and watching smoke rings disappear into the frigid night air. Winter was behind them as it was the first week of March, and spring was peaking over the Appalachians. But the nights seemed to hold onto the winter frost, and Snake could see his breath as he approached the grocery store owner. It was Sunday, and the time was slightly after midnight.

"Good morning, Deacon," Snake greeted his friend.

"Good morning," the deacon replied.

"Good church service today, Deacon?" Snake asked with an ornery grin on his face. Imagine working such an illegal and illicit deal with the most respected deacon in the town's largest church.

"Great service today, Snake. You should have been there," the deacon chided back.

"Oh ya... so how much sugar ya got for me tonight? I really need a full load."

"Never to disappoint you, Snake. I've got more than that old '49 coupe can carry."

"Don't think so, Deacon. This Bluebird can carry over a ton of that white stuff. Let's get loading."

So the deacon's boys began to assist Snake with the careful and methodical loading of the sugar bags.

"Thirty-two, thirty-three, thirty-four... well, I'd never believed it unless I saw it with my own two eyes," the deacon exclaimed, now biting on the end of the old cigar. "You've loaded thirty-four bales of this stuff in this old Ford. Why, you've only left me with two bales. You did about take it all."

Not to be stood up, Snake grabbed another bag and loaded it right on top of the seat adjacent to him and tossed the last bag onto the passenger side, resting on several other bags and sitting partially on the dash.

"Nope," Snake said with another of his ornery grins. "I said I could haul it all, and I think that you're about out." With that, the Big Hat Man smiled, paid the deacon storeowner in cash, and pointed to his cigar as he walked out the door.

"You know that those can be real hazardous to your health, don't ya? Especially for a deacon."

The old deacon laughed and shook the big moonrunner's hand, thanking him for his business. Snake jumped in the front seat, turned *Bluebird* around in the rear lot, and headed out front of the store without his headlights. When all seemed clear, he pulled back out onto the street and headed for the highway, finally turning on his lights to see the way. He had several miles to run on an old country road before he got to the highway. The road was referred to as Black Snake Road. It had more twists and turns than a big old black snake on a summer day. Snake stepped on it and took off on that old twisty road. The load of the sugar held the car to the ground, and the massive, custom rear springs kept the car from rubbing bottom. He was anxious to get the sugar back to the still, and he had a ways to run.

The cool night air was blowing right through *Bluebird* and was a bit chilly. Snake rolled up the windows and turned his AM radio dial to the nearest country station and cranked up the sound. The speakers were not the best, and Hank Williams was cracking and a'popping but playing all the while. About the time he had sat back and started to enjoy the ride, a lawman in a hidden car pulled out of a deserted drive right behind him. Snake liked the *Bluebird*, but it was not as fast as some of his other cars, and the lawman was really eating him up with that little Ford coupe. Try as he might, he just could not shake the lawman's fast car. He turned left and then back right on the winding road, and the bright lights of the cop car were still blinding him through the rearview mirror. More than once Snake thought the best thing to do was to look for a grassy embankment and to jump from the loaded car and make a way through the woods.

There's a grassy spot, he thought. *I'll jump here.* But Snake was not the kind to give up on any challenge. So he decided to run a bit longer and see just what he could really do in the old *Bluebird*. He quickly came upon a sharp curve in the road that could only be taken safely in a typical car at speeds of thirty-five to forty miles per hour. He quickly glanced down at his speedometer, and he was pinging slightly over one hundred miles per hour. He seldom really thought about death, but this time was different. *I'm gone this time,* he thought.

His only hope was that there was no gravel on the curve and that the two tons of sugar with his heavy springs would stick him on that curve like a tick on a hound dog. Before he could really analyze the situation, the curve was upon him. Snake never looked back and never took his eyes off the road. Except for the dim headlights of the *Bluebird*, the road was pitch black and the wood line on both sides of the roadway nearly undetectable. His foot did not move off of the accelerator as he hit the curve at one hundred miles per hour. The car squealed and squeaked as it was sitting so low with the sugar. But it stuck to the road as if you had just glued it there. He began to hear the body cracking on the car, and steel began to actually buckle. Though the time to execute the curve was only four to five seconds, it seemed to take a lifetime. The body was cracking from the force of taking the curve so fast and sticking to the pavement. Any ordinary car could not have absorbed the force and would have run right off into the woods. *Bluebird's* frame, suspension, and wheels were not bulging, but the body could not take the excess forces.

The body twisted and warped so much on that curve that the doors actually sprang open and slammed outwards, bending the hinges. If Snake did not have his seatbelt fastened, he would have simply catapulted right out of those open doors. The force almost cut Snake in two as the seatbelt cut into his abdominal cavity. The force of the turn at high speeds combined with the weight of the shifting sugar pressing against the body nearly separated the body of that old Ford coupe from the frame and suspension. Snake pulled out of that curve about one hundred yards in front of the lawman as the police car slowed to snail's pace maneuvering the same turn.

As Snake raced down the road, he continued to outpace the officer. When he had only ten to fifteen miles to go to the still, he began one of his famous tricks. He knew the layout of the land and roadway systems in Carolina better than most anyone. So he began to take side roads, driveways, backsides of cornfields, and any other means of travel to lose the officer. He finally lost the agent completely and was yet able to arrive at the still during the dark early morning hours. The federal agent returned to his office with amazement at how an old coupe could maneuver such a turn at high speeds without wrecking and escape his pursuit. But by then, Snake had unloaded the sugar at the still and was investigating the damage to *Bluebird's* body. "Didn't get me tonight," he whispered in the night air to himself. Of such, are legends made.

In addition to *Traveler*, perhaps the only other moonrunning car of Snake's that attained legendary status throughout Carolina was the *Gray Ghost*.

The *Gray Ghost* was another 1958 gray Chrysler. The color was something between a silvery white and a shiny gray. It only had one carburetor, but it could still run at least 130 miles per hour, while most of the law vehicles on the road were lucky to run an even 100 miles per hour. It was one of Snake's favorite bootlegging cars, almost a legend of its own. When Snake made his moonshine runs to many of the poor black neighborhoods throughout Union County and the surrounding counties, those boys sat out on the front porch waiting for the *Gray Ghost* and the Big Hat Man.

They began calling it the *Gray Ghost* because one minute, they would just be sitting there waiting on the liquor man to show up, and the next minute, it was parked right there amongst them in their shanty town. The *Gray Ghost* would just come gliding into their neighborhood unsuspected at night. It was as if it were a ghost appearing in the midst and then, in the next instant, disappearing again. Snake never told them exactly when he was coming and which way he was coming from. "Just look for me," he told a friend to tell their friends. Sometimes the *Gray Ghost* pulled up to their poor segregated neck of the woods, appeared for a moment, and then instantly disappeared as Snake detected either some lawman or other strange activity in the area. They could never set up the Big Hat Man in the *Gray Ghost*.

Though all bootlegging runs had some degree of danger associated with it, others were less dangerous than others. His favorite whiskey run, which was somewhat less treacherous than the midnight chases, was his monthly run to an old black Sunday school teacher named Sally. Jerry Rushing and his wife had but one child, Darlene. When most children should have been playing with other neighborhood children or growing up at home doing 'little girl' things, Darlene was occasionally busy helping her father in the whiskey business. She loved to make the run over to Sister Sally's house. Darlene must have been no older than four years of age, but she was proud to sit in the front seat of the *Gray Ghost* as it pulled into Sally's part of town.

Sister Sally was famous for her Sunday school teaching at her church, and as a hobby she loved fishing for catfish. Each time the *Gray Ghost* pulled up in front of her house, she was either sitting on the porch working on her Sunday school lesson or skinning a big tub full of catfish. She loved to fish the rivers near Wadesboro, just east of Monroe.

Snake and Darlene cruised right up to Sally's shanty, and the Big Hat Man climbed out of the car like royalty arriving for a celebration.

"It's da *Gray Ghost*...it's da *Gray Ghost*," Sally screamed as it came to a halt under a big oak tree in her front yard. "I jes love da *Gray Ghost*."

"Hey, Sally," he shouted. "How's my Sally doing?"

"Oh my...Big Hat Man," she said, addressing him with the dignity and respect that any well-cherished bootlegger thought he deserved. "I'm jes working up this here Sunday school lesson...ya got me anything, Big Man?"

"Oh yeaaaah," Snake drawled out in his typical southern fashion. "I gotcha fifteen to twenty cases tonight, Sally. And this is got to be the best run yet. You're gonna love it, Sally."

"Big Hat Man," she replied tenderly, "I love just about anything you ever brought to me."

Snake just smiled while Darlene hung on to both his pinky finger and every word Sister Sally was saying to her daddy. She just loved her daddy.

"Big Hat Man...you's just in time. Let's unload right out here. Man, we're having a camp meeting down at church, and, Lord, they're just gobbling this stuff up, and I'm about out. I'm telling ya, as long as it's in the Lord's will, I will keep it there for them to gobble."

So Snake, Darlene, and Sally worked together to unload that whiskey while Sally explained her next Sunday school lesson to the Big Hat Man, who usually only pretended to listen.

"Not so...wow...ya don't say," he replied softly to her comments.

Snake did love to hear about Sally's church escapades. It was funny to him how she sold the whiskey right in the church parking lot. Sally loaded up her car and drove to the church right in the middle of the camp meeting. She just sat there in her car and sold the illegal whiskey right out of her trunk. They would be praying, preaching, and drinking that liquor—and not necessarily in that order. Snake's old neighbor used to attend that little black church. He was a white man named Sam Drice. He was usually drunk on some of Snake's homemade brew. During the camp meetings, old Sam just walked right in to the church and claimed that God wanted him to preach.

He yelled out, "Da Lord has called me to preach to the white man and the black man."

"Preach on, brother...do what God's called ya to do," others screamed back. He got up in that little church and preached. Then he said that he had to go outside to spit. But when he went outside, he took another swig of that forbidden fruit and then went back inside and started preaching again. Well, this happened several times during one service. Sam preached, went outside to spit, secretly taking a swig, only to return, preach, and take another trip outside to his jug again. The more he spit, the louder he would preach, until after one last trip to the outdoors. Sam Drice came in swaggering back up to the pulpit, tripped, and passed out right there on the praying bench.

One old black man sitting on the front row was heard to say, "Seems like Mr. Drice just spit one too many times."

Snake and a couple of buddies once saw old man Drice's truck down by the river. Snake, being the ornery type, drove Drice's old truck to the top of the mountain overlooking the river, and knocked it out of gear and just let it go. Down to the river it went, hitting tree after tree, on one occasion sitting right up on its nose. It finally found its way to the rushing water and floated right out of that county.

The next time the Big Hat Man drifted into the shantytown to deliver more 'shine to Sister Sally, she asked him, "Big Hat Man, did you have anything to do with Brother Drice's old truck floating in the river?"

"Now, Sally, you know me better than that. I'm a certified bootlegger, not a truck wrecker. It'd take a real mean man to do somethin' like that, now would not it?"

A real mean man, Snake thought to himself. *Why would I do something like that?* he silently pondered again.

'Cause I'm a real mean man, he silently answered the question to himself.

Some whiskey runs were not as memorable as the runs in the *Gray Ghost* to Sister Sally's shack, but they were certainly more dangerous. Snake was running whiskey in an old Ford one night when several lawmen joined in the chase. They were on their radios calling each other, trying to cut off Snake's path of retreat. The revenuers had gotten word that he was running with a big load, and they were well primed and ready to bring him in. Several cars were involved in the chase, and they ran Snake for over two hours. He cut down old logging roads, went through cornfields, and ran on fire trails in the nearby forests. He backtracked on the highways and sometimes turned 180 degrees to surprise them, passing their cars at over 100 miles per hour before they even realized what had happened. They were well on his trail, and he could not shake them. Had he been driving *Traveler,* he could have easily dropped an oil slick or tried the old brake trick, but this car was before *Traveler's* time.

He found out later that the federal agents had called in three times requesting permission to "shoot to kill" Snake and end this cat-and-mouse chase in Union County once and for all. However great was their desire to approve the request, the commanding officers could not give the OK. Finally, they decided to set up a fast roadblock on the highway on which he was traveling. He came up and over the hill too late to stop when his eyes say the boarded up right lane of his road. The center of the highway contained a deep ditch full of water, and the pursuit cop vehicles were right on his tail. He really had no option but to run the roadblock, and that is exactly what he did. He busted through the wood roadblocks, exploding the wood in every direction. He tore right into barrels that they had set up, and then his right fender caught an officer's bumper, spinning him in several 360-degree turns before his car came to a stop against the right highway guardrail. The officer's radiator was busted, and hot water and steam poured out in every direction.

Snake looked back, and several police cars were tight on his trail. He jumped through the window and took off running up the embankment of the road as fast as his legs carried him. His big Stetson hat blew off in the run, and though Snake loved that hat, he knew there was not time to stop for it. Men were screaming and shots were being fired all around him. He was not sure if they were warning shots or shots intended to kill. But he did not intend to stop and ask. Snake was a big man, but he could run. He had plenty of practice running as he had several stills that had been raided by the lawmen, and during each raid, Snake made off on foot.

"Stop or we'll shoot!" they screamed. "You're a dead man now. Stop…we're warning ya. We're gonna shoot if you don't stop."

Snake was still running, but inside he was somewhat smiling at the irony of the thing. "Stop or we're gonna shoot." He thought, *You're already shooting.* So he kept running.

When he could run no longer, he happened upon a big bunch of honeysuckle plants. They were big and thick and covered the hill like a blanket. Snake took advantage of the situation and quickly jumped right into the middle of the honeysuckle and army-crawled as far as he could into the thick cover. When he heard the men's cursing and screaming get closer to his location, he stopped crawling and laid flat upon the ground. His breathing was labored from the running and the chase. His right knee was aching, perhaps from hitting the steel bottom of the dash when he crashed into the blockade. Nevertheless, they had not caught him yet, and he was trying to keep every muscle still. He could hear them walking all around the honeysuckle and the surrounding hill. Their flashlights were shining radically all around the roadway and the embankment.

"Lord in heaven...we got 'em. Just where we've got 'em...I don't know," one officer screamed.

"Over here," another yelled. "Did he cross this little water-filled creek between the lanes?"

"Don't know," a commanding office barked. "Take a couple of men over there into the woods on the other side of the water, and I'll take a few up into these woods. We've got 'em...we've just gotta find 'em."

They looked for Snake a good couple of hours all over and around that highway until the wrecker arrived and hauled the whiskey runner's car back to the station. As they unsuccessfully continued their search and became more aggravated, they cursed him for his elusiveness. Then in their frustration, they even turned on their fellow officers, cussing at themselves in the darkness of the night for their failure. It was quite a sight as Snake just lay still in the cover of the honeysuckle bushes smiling his silly grin. He knew quite well that he had cheated the law again and foiled their attempts to capture the legendary Big Hat Man.

Somewhere in the night, after the shooting, the flashlights and the cursing, Snake fell asleep under the safe cover of the sweet-smelling honeysuckle. In fact, he had a great night sleep as he felt as at home in the woods, under the stars as he did on a warm mattress under a clean cotton sheet. Sometime right before sunrise, he awoke to a gentle "whooing" of a nearby owl. He rubbed his eyes, thought for just a moment how lucky he was, and then crawled back out from under the cover. He headed home, staying under the cover of the nearby woodlands and inside the camouflage of a summer corn crop that easily hid him from the view of any nearby road.

Over the next couple of weeks he bragged to his town buddies about this honeysuckle incident. Just a couple of weeks later, Snake was sitting near downtown Monroe over at the newsstand in one of his fast cars with a buddy named Jon.

"Can ya believe just how stupid those cops were? They were standing there right above me, swearing and cussing and getting real mad. I just loved it, though I was real sorry to lose that car and that good batch of skull cracker....but that's the moonshine business."

"Yea, Snake," Jon replied. "Those cops are real stupid, not as smart as you, Snake. Why, just look at that stupid officer sitting over there. He's been watching us all night sitting here as if we're doing somedun wrong or somedun."

"Watch me start up this car, and see if he starts up his car, Jon," Snake said.

Snake turned on his key and revved up the engine, only to watch and hear the officer start up his engine as well. Snake turned his car off, obviously followed by the officer turning his car off as well.

"Looks like he's lookin' for a race, Snake...give 'em one...c'mon, let's give 'em a ride for his life." Snake was a sucker for a dare, and with a wink of his eye, he fired up his car and revved his engine a couple of times to give sufficient warning to the officer. And then with a smile on his face he warned Jon, "Hang on, buddy...you asked for it, and here it is."

And with that, Snake ran his car backwards right out into the street at over fifty miles per hour, and then shoved it right down to low gear and took off like a stock car at a race track. He did a burnout, leaving several feet of burning black rubber as his signature piece right out from the heart of town. He blew out of Monroe at over one hundred miles per hour with the officer trailing close behind him. The officer was new on the force and had been bragging around town that his car would bring Snake's episodes to a fast end. Snake drove right down to High Hill Bridge; he knew from experience just how fast he could take that final turn before the bridge. But he was counting on the new officer's inexperience with this territory to work in his advantage. This was Snake's terrain and forest, and the officer was about to find this out.

Though it was still early in the evening, the night was dark. There was cloud cover and no moon shining in the sky. On several occasions, he had taken that curve at ninety-three miles per hour. Most people could not handle a curve like that at a bridge going seventy miles per hour. He got close to that curve and hit the toggle switch for his brake lights so he could touch the brakes on the curve without giving the officer any indication of the need for braking. Snake hit the curve at ninety-three miles per hour, slightly touching his brakes to navigate the bend safely. He could see the officer coming up way too fast.

The dispatcher heard the excitement from his side of the radio in the county office. Officer Hailer screamed over the radio transmitter, "I've got that sucker in my lights. He's mine, over."

His last transmission went something like this, "I am still on his tail...coming around a curve to High Hill Bridge..."—*bang, crash, boom.*

Then the transmission expired. Snake watched through his rearview mirror as the officer had been riding Snake's brake lights and then missed the curve, crashing right into the bridge and causing sparks and pieces of metal to explode high into the air and fall into the river below.

Though Snake did not hear it, the next dispatch over the Monroe police radio went something like this, "Officers in the vicinity of High Hill Bridge, please proceed directly to that area. An officer has wrecked his car into the bridge. Request the assistance of an ambulance *ASAP*. God, I hope he's not hurt. Over."

Snake and Jon laughed all the way home.

"Another totaled police car...and I mean trashed and totaled...completely trashed. Did ya see him hit the bridge, Jon? I mean, did you see it?"

"Yea, Snake...I mean, you're the greatest. Someday, they'll tell stories about ya, Snake, ya think?" Jon asked.

"Someday," Snake just smiled. "Someday."

Sometimes Runnin' on Foot

Most of the time, running and bootlegging was with fast-riding, souped-up automobiles. But there were times when Snake had no option but to run on foot to avoid the law. Most of the federal agents focused both on finding and destroying the stills of the moonshiners while stopping the flow of liquor by catching the bootleggers. Snake would often hide his car a good distance from the actual location of a new still. One spring afternoon, Snake had just started setting up the still near a stream in some backwoods of Union County. They had carefully scouted out the area and had entered in such a way that regular revenuers from the road never suspected their travel path back to the stream. He had hidden his car off the road inside the woods some quarter mile from their still.

As they worked on the still, Snake was aware of a low-flying plane that seemed to fly around and around their neck of the woods. It bothered him as he watched it circle time and time again.

Jerry was usually not one to worry, but on this particular day he seemed troubled, "Guys...maybe we should break down and start over some other time. That there plane has circled this area too many times. I think we're gonna get caught."

"Oh, come on, Snake," one of his buddies replied. "Under these big magnolias, he'll never get a sight of us. We've no fire here for him to see any smoke. He's just looking."

Well, Snake had just knocked the cap off of the still and was starting to set it down when he looked around and saw some five men with double-barrel shotguns jumping the creek and headed in their direction. One of the agents lost his footing in the creek and fell right into the water, his gun blasting into the morning air....*bang!*

With that, Snake and the boys at the still took off running as if their lives depended upon it. And they did. The agents were shooting and hollering and running, stopping only to reload so they could run and shoot again. Tree limbs from the surrounding magnolias were falling all around Snake and his buddies as the buckshot hit the trees, missing their prey. Snake had run through the woods toward his car, but was shocked to see an agent sitting behind the car with another police car blocking his escape.

Snake made an instant decision to abandon his car right there and take off across the field. He and another buddy ran across a field, through a barn, and right out into the yard of an old country house. And standing right there in the middle of the yard was the preacher's wife looking at him, half scared to death. Snake had pulled his shirt off and she was looking at all of his tattoos as he ran past her soaking wet.

"Howdy, ma'am," Snake said, trying to look normal as he raced crazily past her house. Frightened, she bolted to her front door, leaving Snake to run through the garden in his flight. She ran right to her phone and called the sheriff's department and reported an escaped convict at her house.

They consoled her and told her that they had just flushed a whiskey still and the fellow with all those tattoos was a real kingpin of the moonshine business. They thought they had cornered him and finally caught him. Little did they know.

As Snake and his buddies continued to race toward freedom, one of his buddies ran into two women in a garden picking peas. He was looking behind him as they ran back out of the woods and crashed right into the ladies picking peas and tossing them into a pea sack that hung from their shoulders. He crashed into the first lady, knocking her from one row of peas to another. He looked like a bumbling fool as he fell four or five times just trying to get out of that garden. He fell into the tomato rows, tripping and knocking over several luscious plants. Jumping to his feet, he raced from the garden with tomato juice and seeds from his head to his toe. Finally they cut across another area of woods and lost the agents in the dense forest before returning home.

Snake had won the foot race, but he had lost his hat, his still, and his car. So whatever happened to his hat, his still, and his car? The agents took his white cowboy hat as a souvenir and hung it up in the sheriff's office. One day when Jerry was downtown in Monroe, he found himself eye to eye with one of the local deputies. Several people were hanging around, so the deputy thought he would give them a kind of show.

The deputy turned to Jerry and said in a loud voice so the town folks could hear him, "Jerry, why don't you come into my office and get that hat of yours? It's hanging up on our wall. Looks real good here, and I thought you'd like it back. So where did you lose that good-lookin' hat?"

Snake just smiled, "Why, I don't remember where I lost that expensive Stetson, but I'm glad you like it. Maybe, just maybe, I will come in and take back that hat. I do appreciate the offer."

And Snake just laughed. He knew better than to go into their office. They knew it was his hat and they knew the still was his, but back they hadn't caught him in the act yet.

But what happened to the still? The agents sold it for scrap to the junkyard just like it was. The owner of the junkyard hid it in his barn until he could call Snake. He then sold it back to Snake, and he put it back in the whiskey business again. In fact, that particular copper still was sold to the junkyard and then sold back to Snake for the moonshine business three or four times before the agents finally realized what was happening. Then they took steps to destroy it completely.

But what happened to Snake's car? The agents took it to the sheriff's office and locked it up for auction. But a simple-minded federal agent would not undo Jerry Rushing. Jerry phoned the sheriff's office and reported that his car had been stolen.

"Stolen," the sheriff said over the phone. "And where did you park it last?" He asked this question as if it would trick Jerry, thinking that he would say that he left it uptown.

"Well," Jerry began to spin his tale. "I met my wife, and she was going to a funeral and she wanted me to go with her. I was working out on some farm. So I parked my car down there in the woods so nobody would steal nothing and went off with her to the funeral. When I came back late this afternoon, it was gone."

The sheriff knew that he was in a verbal battle of wits. "Well, Mr. Rushing, come back up here and get your car. I've got it right here locked up. By the way, you boys left out pretty fast today." Jerry knew what he was trying to do and just played dumb.

"Well, officer, I don't know what you are talking about. My wife drove quite slowly to the funeral, sir. Is there a problem?" Jerry did not admit a thing, and finally the sheriff said he could have his car. They had no way of arresting him since they had not caught him directly in the act. Jerry sent his wife and his mama up to the sheriff's office to pick up the car. They paid the wrecker bill and got the car, and the sheriff kept the hat.

THE ETERNAL RACE TO RUN

Jerry Elijah Rushing spent most of his life running—running whiskey, running from the law, and most importantly and sadly, running from God. See, God had a wonderful plan for Jerry Rushing's life. He had an eternal purpose and an eternal race for him to run in life. And God's perfect plan for Jerry's life was not contained in running from the law.

Paul wrote in 1 Corinthians 9:24:

> Know ye not that they which run in a race run all, but one receiveth the prize? So run, that ye may obtain.

God sent His only begotten Son to die for Jerry's sins, to die in his place for all of his sins. And the gift of accepting Jesus, God's Son, as his personal Savior was eternal life.

That is the prize. We are to run in this earthly race to acquire the prize, which is eternal life through Jesus Christ, God's Son. We get this prize simply by asking Jesus to come into our messed-up life and to take control of our situation. When we ask, Jesus will forgive us of our sins, and we then are given this prize…eternal life.

But Jerry Rushing was not running this eternal race. He was so caught up in his personal races and running that he had no time for God's purpose or love in his early years.

Are you tired of running? Are you running for God's eternal blessing and eternal life, or are you tired and worn out by running your own race of worldly cares, sin, and temptations?

Paul also tells us that he considers any worldly fixation as nothing compared to running the race for Jesus Christ. This is recorded in Acts 20:24:

> But none of these things move me, neither count I my life dear unto myself, so that I might finish my course with joy, and the ministry, which I have received of the Lord Jesus, to testify the gospel of the grace of God.

God has a race for each of us. God has a task for us to complete while we are here on earth. Have you ever asked God about the tasks you are to complete for Him? Are you running your own selfish race and wondering why life is empty and dead?

Are you sick and tired of being sick and tired?

Jerry Elijah Rushing finally got that way.

Why not try God?

Stop running from Him and try running to Him. Paul felt that his life meant nothing unless he finished the race that God gave him. If your life seems like nothing, perhaps you are running the wrong race. Ask God to change your life today.

Sooner or later, each one of us will face our eternal future. Do you believe in heaven and hell? The Bible teaches the plain and simple truth that heaven and hell exist. One day, you will find the truth out, or the truth will find you out. Why wait until it is too late? Accept Jesus today, and ask Him to come into your life, forgive you of your sins, and change your life for eternity. If you do, God will come into your heart and you will experience being born again into His kingdom. It you don't today and slip into eternity, you will find out too late as you will be led by the devil and his demons into the pits of hell.

It's not too late now... right now. Why not?

While Paul was getting old, he wrote to Timothy:

> I have fought a good fight, I have finished my course, I have kept the faith: Henceforth there is laid up for me a crown of righteousness, which the Lord, the righteous judge, shall give me at that day: and not to me only, but unto all them also that love his appearing.
>
> —2 Timothy 4:7–8

Can you say that you have fought the good fight? Paul could! He kept the faith, he ran the race, and he finished it for God.

Why not stop running your own sinful, sorrowful, and selfish race that ends with a regretful finale in a burning hell? Why not run the race with God and win the eternal prize, which is the salvation of your soul, and spend eternity in heaven?

You can decide today.

Stop running!

Jerry Elijah Rushing ultimately did!

Jerry with Mom
and Dad

Jerry as a
child

Jerry drinking moonshine

Jerry stacking sugar for another
batch of Rushing 'shine

Jerry at
still

Jerry the
bow shooter

The original Boar's Nest

Jerry's fur trading

The old jail on
Jerry's property

Traveler restored

Jerry and Daisy at the 2005 Duke Fest

Jerry with Traveler, 2004

Jerry in his favorite black hat

Jerry with a " Jesus
smile " on his face

Jerry with Ben Jones
(Cooter) at Dukes of Hazzard
Convention, 2004

Author and son, Gabriel, with
their best friend

Author and son, Gabriel, hunting
with the "Real Duke"

What prayer can do for
a marriage ... Jerry
with wife, Dean

CHAPTER 7

Filled With Hate and Flirting With Disaster

A LIFESTYLE OF DANGER

THE LIFE SPAN of the typical bootlegger or moonshiner between the 1930s and the 1960s was only thirty to forty years. The bootlegger often died a tragic death on the road driving a fast car too fast around a curve. Or occasionally he died at the end of a gun barrel while being chased by a lawman trying to make a name for himself. Most federal revenuer agents hated moonrunners. The federal agents had slower governmental-issued automobiles that did not stand up to the bootlegger's hot souped-up cars. They also did not quite have the driving skills and car-maneuvering abilities that the local runners had acquired. Therefore, they were often embarrassed and humiliated by the bootleggers that most always sent them home empty-handed.

The moonshiner's demise, however, did not come from running fast cars. The typical death of a moonshiner often happened in one of two ways. Frequently a maker of the southern Appalachian sugar whiskey died from overindulgence in the very product in he they specialized. Sometimes this was from just drinking too much and then dying from a health-associated failure. In other instances, he suffered an alcohol-related accident or drank some poisonous concoction that just did not come out right. Still others were known to die from fights linked to the occasional warring of moonshine families and other rival producers of the white lightning.

The entire culture of the moonshine and bootleg way of life embraced an evil danger that had countless associated risks. It was inherent in their everyday life and touched all who embraced the culture. Seldom did anyone enter into this dark life of whiskey making and liquor running who did not suffer some of the consequences for their actions. This lifestyle left horrible scars upon the lives of all of the participants and their families. All suffered who entered there, including Jerry Rushing. The third generation of moonshiners, his family suffered the same woes as other whiskey-making folks. And this misery was passed down from generation to generation. This story, in part, is documented in a song that Jerry Rushing wrote himself about the whiskey-hauling business.

Danger was part of the lure of the bootlegger lifestyle, and Jerry E. Rushing loved the danger that surrounded each day of his life. Early in his career, Jerry was driving an older Chrysler and delivering a large load of moonshine. Part of the danger of this business was that most everyone was on the take, meaning enough cash could buy most moonshiners and lawmen alike. Snake was always looking over his shoulder, as he trusted no one. Most of the time, he told no one when he was running, where he was running from, and what road he was coming up.

But on one particular run, Snake had let one of his buddies know what road he was running up and approximately what time to expect him. He had wondered at the time if he should have just kept quiet, but he felt that this fellow could be trusted. So as Snake made his late-night delivery run, he kept in the back of his mind that one man knew his plans.

All went well until he came within a couple miles of his final destination. As he ran the Chrysler toward the unloading spot, he kept the speed up between seventy and eighty-five miles per hour. Then as he made a fast turn around a sharp curve, he heard a bullet shot ring out in the night air. It struck home right behind the front driver's side tire. Snake quickly pressed the gas pedal to the floorboard, and the tires squealed from the pressure of the turn and the weight of the shine. Snake was not certain where the shots were coming from, but he was sure whoever it was must be shooting at his tires to hijack his load. He immediately thought of his buddy who must have squealed about this run. *He will pay for squealing on me,* Snake thought. *I hope he made enough money to pay for a couple of weeks in the intensive care unit...he will need it.*

His rambling thoughts of hate were only interrupted with the continuing blasts from the nearby wood line. The revenuer agents were in the woods; he could see the fire blasts from their rifles.

Bang, bang, bang—crack. Many more shots rang out, some of them finding their home in the thick metal of that old Chrysler body. Some ripped into the front quarter panel while others bored holes through the door and embedded themselves deep in the upholstery of the front seat where Snake sat. He ran through a curve at more than 85 miles per hour and then hurriedly accelerated upwards to over 120 miles per hour, leaving the poor marksmen shooting blindly into the dark night air as he escaped their grasps once again. They had set up an ambush, hoping to stop the runner with their gun power. Once Snake broke through, they knew they had no chance to catch him as he was just too fast.

Now he was wondering just what to do. Should he abort the mission or pull into his unloading spot, pretending that nothing happened? He decided to boldly drive right into their hands. He was to unload behind his buyer's house in an old garage that was now only used to load or unload whiskey. Most of the house and garage were hidden from view by the cornfield in the front yard. He quietly pulled up in front of the cornfield and watched for a while. Then, without any lights, he pulled the Chrysler into the long drive and proceeded around to the back of the little farmhouse. There they were, sitting on the back porch in the dark, drinking, smoking, and generally celebrating something. Snake pulled parallel with the porch and tipped his big black Stetson. He then backed into the garage, giving him the opportunity to escape in a moment's notice if something went wrong. The boys, led by their ringleader, Spider, came out of the screen porch, puffing on their cigarettes and carefully watching the bootleg driver. Snake could see the surprise on their faces—they really did not expect him to make it through the ambush. They seemed skittish and nervous as they greeted him.

"How 'boutcha Snake? Glad to see you made it," Spider greeted him with a certain nervous twitch in his right eye.

"I am, too," Snake responded, slowly getting out of the old Chrysler. "Didn't have no doubts about it...did ya, Spider?"

"No sir, I mean, no sireey. Snake...you're da man. Always have been and always will be."

"Got my money, Spider?"

"Absolutely, Snake. Why wouldn't I?"

Snake did not respond but stared deep within Spider's right eye, causing the twitch to increase rapidly. Snake was full of hate and was ready to bounce upon Spider and crush him in a moment. He loved making men shake.

Spider turned to his men and gave them orders to unload quickly. "Stack that stuff up against the back wall, next to that sugar lightning. Hurry, I'm sure Snake has places to go."

Snake just stood there and intently watched their every move. "No, I'm fine, Spider. Actually, I have no place to go after this. Take your time."

Snake knew he had been set up by his buddy, and now he knew that Spider must have known about it as well. As Snake walked deeper into the barn, he was shocked to see a shadowy figure appear from the darkness of one of the unlit stalls. That shadow had a sheriff's uniform on, and Snake broke for the car, thinking that he had been really busted.

"Wait a minute...hold on there," Spider screamed. "That there's Don, and he's OK."

"What do you mean, he's OK?" Jerry replied with one hand on his door and the other on the crowbar he kept next to the front seat.

"Old Don here's on my payroll. He gives us some protection and some inside information, when we need it, in exchange for cash and, of course, some of this here's famous Rushing whiskey."

Snake did not like the looks or feel of this run. First he was nearly killed in an ambush, and then there's a sheriff at the unloading. It just did not feel good. He was anxious to finish the unloading and then hit the highway again. His only real friends he could trust were the lonesome road, his trusty Chrysler, and the cool breeze of the midnight air. He felt comfortable around these friends but few others. Spider paid Snake and thanked him for the load. Snake pushed the cash deep within his two front pockets and then stood there for a minute staring at Spider, Sheriff Don, and Spider's men. The silence was nearly deadening. Snake did not move. He just shifted his eyes from one to the other, looking them up and back down again. Should he whip up on all of them, or just scare them real good and leave?

Finally, Spider could take the silent stares no longer. "What's the matter, Snake? You're lookin' real mad or something. You don't have a problem with us now, do ya?"

Snake just continued to stare them down as he made his way to his parked car. He slowly and purposely climbed into the car without saying a word and without breaking his gaze. He knew that they knew of the ambush. Now they thought that Snake just might know they knew. Neither said a word as the tension mounted between them. Snake fired up the Chrysler, nodded at the crooked sheriff, and floored it out of the barn, throwing dirt and straw mixed with some stinking manure all over the cases of moonshine he just delivered. He ran the Chrysler around the house two or three times tearing up what little grass they had in their lawn. He cut circle after circle, spitting up the sod in big bunches. He then sped right up to the open barn door, slamming on his breaks and sliding to a halt.

"Never again...boys," Snake chided them as they stood there open-mouthed, staring at the wild man's escapade. "Ever cross me again, boys...ever hear of you hearing about a doublecross without you warning me...well..." Snake adjusted his Stetson and looked out from underneath it, "I'll boil ya in my whiskey mash and make a special Spider Shine."

Snake ran another couple of laps around the place before pulling into the cornfield and cutting a few of his legendary figure eights, leaving broken and twisted cornstalks all behind him.

He was known for his burnouts and his figure eights. On many occasions, he drove to the town square of Monroe, just to wind it up and cut two or three circles, burning rubber all the while right in the middle of town. The local lawmen chased him clear out of Monroe without ever getting close enough to catch him and bring him back in. Sometimes he so quickly outran them that it was barely any fun at all. He then turned around, spinning a "180" in the middle of the road, and ran right back at them. The lawmen in pursuit were shocked to see him returning and turned around and chased him back into Monroe and back out again, still unable to bring Snake down.

If the lawmen were not trying to ambush him, he was in town terrorizing the locals with his dangerous antics. One of Snake's favorite stunts was to drive into Monroe and start shooting out the stoplights. He pulled up to a light, aimed his shotgun at the overhead lights, and blew them right off the electrical lines. He loved the smell of that gunpowder and the excitement of shooting from a fast moving car. He was a dangerous and perilous man who prided himself on his outlaw status. As a little boy, there was little, if any, admiration or affirmation showed by his father. He was merely a Rushing and often took the brunt of his father's drunken rages. Acceptance might have changed his lot in life. All boys need a parent's love and affirmation, but he experienced no acceptance as a little boy. Without that love and accetance, a little boy will grow up looking for the affirmation from another, and that is exactly what Snake did. His acceptance came as he became known as a real modern-day outlaw. The recognition did not come from his parents but from the local renegade and criminal culture that was drawn to this crazy man from Monroe.

It was as if he lived for acceptance from his criminal buddies. Within the culture of the outlaw, Snake was the "Godfather" of sorts. He was the desperado who did anything to anybody to prove his worth. He was evil and malicious in his dealings, as the anger within him came bursting through, exploding onto anyone in his way. He loved danger and embraced it. Often Snake created havoc for people just to see them frightened. He went on terrifying binges just for fun.

As he grew in the liquor business, he became an increasingly hard and brutal man. He ultimately did not care for life or limb, and he cared for nobody. If anyone crossed him, he threatened them just as he did Spider and his boys, or he taught them a lesson in fright. He thrilled in terrorizing with drive-by shootings. He was notorious for driving by a rival's home and firing his machine gun right into the side of their house. He often shot out every window in the house while the children and parents ran for their life from the exploding glass. Or he took his twelve-gauge shotgun and shot through their windows, attempting to blow out all of their interior house lights. Nobody ever wanted to cross Snake. In fact, most everyone stayed away from him for likely cause.

If he did not shoot out their house lights and windows, he followed them out of town and then opened fire on their car. He shot out their rear lights and then followed them until they were thoroughly terrorized and panic-stricken. He often bragged about these episodes, saying to his criminal buddies, "I am hell-bent on creating havoc, and there's nobody that's gonna stop me now. I guess I'm just hell-bent on being hell-bent." He grew up in a hellish home and was living out the outlaw life he had dreamed about as a little boy. Now grown and a dangerous menace to all of Union County, he viewed himself as a contemporary Robin Hood or Jesse James, claiming his right to fame as they had years ago.

Snake increasingly became evil as the hate within him grew. Many times the hate and anger intensified out of control, and erupted on the mere innocent. There was many a man who had walked the town square of Monroe, only to find themselves backed up to a tree or backed up to one of the local buildings with the Big Hat Man staring them in the face. At times it was the way they looked at him or the way they simply looked his way. Every now and then, it was nothing at all. The man was just in the wrong place at the wrong time. Snake spontaneously jumped on someone and cold-cocked him into tomorrow. He jumped a stranger right in the city square of Monroe, popped him a few times in the face, and then left him for dead snoring on the sidewalk. He kicked him a couple of times for good measure, screamed some obscenities at the crowd of onlookers, and then jumped back into his car. He was out of Monroe before the lawmen could even be contacted. These dangerous incidents grew both in frequency and in ferocity as Snake's lifestyle of danger spiraled out of control. He was slipping out of control, and he knew it.

OOZING WITH HATE

Hate is a strong word, and it is even a stronger emotion. The dictionary defines hate as an intense emotional hostility and aversion in an individual, usually derived from fear, anger, or a sense of injury. Though Jerry Rushing could not have so articulately defined this emotion that he felt, he knew that it was filling his life and overflowing into every aspect of his being. The sense of hate was ruling and ruining his life. He had an intense hatred toward the federal revenuers, toward the local sheriffs, and toward anyone in authority. In fact, his hatred began to spill out onto anyone that happened to come in contact with him at the wrong time. Such was the case with a boy known only as Ruckus who lived somewhere outside of Monroe in Union County.

It was sometime after Thanksgiving in late November when Snake and a couple of his buddies decided to take a ride into town. The night was still young, and they were looking for some fun. There was little happening with Snake unless he was cooking up some moonshine or running it from town to town. When he was not in full production and not bootlegging some of the illegal stuff, he was often off hunting or trapping. But without the hunting, moonshining, and bootlegging, it was hard for a young man to occupy his time. Snake often got bored, and such boredom frequently led to trouble.

Snake and his buddies pulled into a local beer joint just to make the scene. Snake was still young, having not yet turned twenty, but often hung out with an older bunch. They parked their old truck on the side of the little run-down joint and proceeded to the front door when they noticed a bonfire on the other side of the little shack. Eight or nine fellows were drinking beer and warming themselves around the fire.

"Hey, Snake," one of his friends hollered out. "Let's check out that fire."

"What the heck…why not? We've got all night." So Snake and his buddies moseyed up to the hot flames of the bonfire.

"Howdy, guys," Snake said as he warmed his hands over the fire. "What's happening?"

The fellows just drank their beer and stared into the fire, pretending that they heard no one speaking. Snake took an instant dislike to the biggest one of the boys and decided to address him. "So what's your problem, partner? Cat got your tongue?"

A little fellow standing next to the ringleader turned to Snake and gently whispered, "You really should not talk to Ruckus like that. He really doesn't like nobody to talk to him, ya know?"

Snake furrowed his brow. "What the heck do I care? Speak up, Ruckus…what's your problem?"

The big, tall one named Ruckus looked up under a ragged and torn ball cap and frowned. "Don't ever talk to me like that, or I whoop ya into tomorrow and you'll not know what hit ya."

"Whoo, man," Snake shot back. "Don't even think about bringing it on with me, ya hear?"

Ruckus turned and mumbled something as he reached into his pocket. "I told ya once…now I'm gonna hurt ya bad." And with that, Ruckus pulled out a long hunting knive and pointed it at Snake as he slowly made his way around the fire. His buddies watched with wide-opened eyes cheering him on.

"Cut him, Ruckus," one screamed. "Slice 'em big time and teach that cowboy a real lesson," another yelled.

"You're mine, cowboy," Ruckus sneered. He had cut many a man over the years, and most feared him. The knife was long and sharp and was shaped like a bowie knife. It was polished and oiled, and it brilliantly reflected the jumping flames of the nearby fire. "I'm gonna whoop ya real bad, boy….come here for your beating."

And before he could make it halfway around the bonfire, Snake shocked Ruckus and his buddies as much as he stunned his friends. Snake had been standing there with both hands in his jacket. His right hand quickly pulled out an old .32 gun that he had been secretly carrying. He had dreamed of being a real live outlaw, and just carrying the thing made him feel big and bad. Snake had been carrying that .32 gun for several weeks now, but had told no one about it. He hadn't had a reason to draw the thing. But now it was out, tempers were flaring, and the hatred quickly manifested itself with gun blasts. *Bang, bang, bang.* Three shots immediately rang out and filled the night air with bullets and with horrendous terror. Boys began to scatter screaming, "Oh my God, he's gotta gun—he's gotta gun."

Some began to run while others seemed to be frozen in terror. Snake's friends were not certain what to do. It was a real outlaw gunfight, and Snake was standing right there pulling the trigger over and over, shooting into that rowdy bonfire crowd. Ruckus dropped the knife as he too was scrambling on the ground to escape this wild man that was shooting in every direction.

Snake's buddies began to scream in utter fright, "Run, Snake, run. Get to the car fast; we've gotta run." They had not been in an actual gun battle before and were all headed to the car door.

Men from the beer joint had heard the shots and the screaming and began to rush to the door. It was utter pandemonium as screams and shrieks pierced the night's darkness. Snake began to run, and then, as if the hatred that had grown within him was actually in control of his bodily functions, he stopped. He turned and laughed a devilish laugh at the crowd still running for their lives. However, by now Ruckus and his friends were nowhere to be seen.

Then Snake, in a deliberate demonstration of defiance, slowly strolled back to the waiting car of his screaming comrades and jumped into the front seat as they burned rubber all the way down the road. They hit speeds of over 120 miles per hour pulling out of Monroe that night. The fellows were shouting and screaming at what a show Snake had put on.

"Man, Snake, you're the man. Did you see them boys run?"

"You showed 'em, Snake. You're da boss-man!"

Still another basked in their outlaw glory, "Did you see that Ruckus' face when ya pulled out that gun...where'd ya get that thing?"

Snake just smiled trying to hold himself down as the adrenaline continued to pump through his whole body. *Well, I am a real live outlaw...just like Jesse James,* he thought. They never did really find out what happened to Ruckus and his friends. But Snake didn't care.

He got in his way, and in Snake's world, that meant paying the consequences. They did hang low for a few weeks trying not to draw any real unnecessary attention their way.

This was one of the many stories that Snake loved to tell time and time again.

"Guys, I just guess I shocked those old boys. He'll never mess with old Snake again," he bragged.

This was just one of numerous times the growing hatred exploded, leaving his rivals fleeing for their lives or just lying and bleeding on the cold ground. The hateful explosions and outbursts did not always result in a shooting. In fact, Snake rarely used a handgun. He did not need to. He was a strong and robust man that stood well over six feet tall with arms like a mighty oak. He could crush a man with his bare hands and often enjoyed personally inflicting pain onto the face of his foe with his fists alone.

On one occasion, Snake began the brawl with his bare fists and finished it with a ball bat. They were standing around the schoolyard early one evening. Snake and a few buddies were just hanging out and passing an otherwise warm and humid summer night. The sun was just starting to fall behind the distant horizon when another group of young fellows meandered into the schoolyard where Snake and his buddies were standing.

One of the fellows yelled out to Snake, "How about a good old-fashioned whippin'?"

Snake, always ready for a fight, screamed back, "I don't think so."

The trash talking went on for a few minutes until the mischievous quarrelling was broken up by the squeal of tires and a car that was running into the school parking lot at a high rate of speed. They all looked up to see the driver of the car slam on his brakes and come to a screeching halt. Immediately, one of the boys in the front seat jumped out of the seat with a shotgun in his hand. To this day, Snake is not sure what the fellow's intention really was. Was he prepared to use it on Snake or one of his friends? Was he just showing off a new gun purchase? No one in the crowd had any idea at all. Some screamed and others stood there in amazement. Still others ran back a bit to gain their composure before deciding just what to do. But Snake was different. While others seemed to be a bit frightened over this young man shaking a shotgun in the air, Snake was super-charged by the challenge.

He immediately jumped into action and hit the fellow so hard on his eye that it knocked him right back into the car top. Snake leaped right on the boy, grabbing the shotgun with one hand and vigorously beating him with the other. *Pop, pop, slam, pop.* He popped his face four or five times before the boy collapsed right back into the front seat. As the boy fell back into the seat and then collapsed right back out of the car at Snake's feet, Jerry realized for the first time that he had beat the boy so severely that his eyeball had popped out of its socket. The boy sat crumbled onto the dirt with his right eye hanging nearly halfway down his cheek. It was held in place only by a few eye muscles that were attached to the back of the eyeball.

Though Snake still felt no compassion for the kid, he did take a moment to stare at that eyeball just hanging there like a kite on a string. He had never seen anything quite like that before, and to tell you the truth, he felt a bit proud of this odd achievement. But that is just how hate works. It is an awful disease that spreads until it explodes like an infected boil that spits and splatters once pressure is applied to it.

As the boy lay unconscious at the base of Snake's feet with one eyeball blowing in the wind, his buddy came out of the backseat with a ball bat. His intentions were to teach Snake a lesson or two. He grabbed a bat and screamed, "You're a dead man—flat out dead...you're mine."

With that threat barely out of his mouth and with his body just climbing out of the car, Snake jumped in his face and planted his fist right square onto the boy's nose, busting it wide open. Blood splattered all over Snake and all over the boy as he fell backward into the rear seat along with his bat. No stranger to danger and one to always be on the offensive in a brawl, Snake jumped into the backseat of the car after the boy. Filled with a fiery rage, Snake beat the boy severely. After he finished pounding on the boy's face, he grabbed the bat and began to beat the boy unmercifully, breaking several of the boy's ribs.

The boy struggled to get out of harm's way, finally climbing out the driver's side window. He ran all the way to his girlfriend's house. Snake found out later that the boy was in such shock that he ran right through the front screen door, ripping it off the hinges as he screamed for help. Months later Snake was in another brawl and sent several fellows to the hospital as he beat them brutally. It was after that fight that a boy from the crowd strolled up to Snake, "Boy, you can fight like a crazy wild bear, ya know that?"

"Say what?" Snake replied, wondering what this guy meant and why he was taking up for Snake. "What are you talking about, boy?"

The boy continued, "I know that you can fight...because...one night you beat the tar out of me."

Snake looked at the kid with a puzzled look, "Don't know what you're talkin' 'bout."

"Sure ya do....I'm the one ya beat with that ball bat that night out in the school yard...remember?"

Snake chuckled, "You were with the guy that I hit so hard that it popped his eyeball right out of the socket?"

"Yep, that was me."

They talked and laughed about it for a time. "Well, Snake...ya could have killed me with that bat and all. Basically ya just busted some of my ribs. Still hurts when I laugh."

"Well, don't laugh, stupid," Snake chuckled back. They continued to chat, and Snake was surprised he found out that the old boy was family. His daddy was related to the Rushings, and the boy was Snake's cousin.

"Imagine that...I was beating up on my own cousin. I guess I should feel real sorry or something."

"Do ya?" the cousin replied with a grin.

"Nope," Snake replied, "can't say as I do."

Snake never felt sorry for any of his victims. He had a right to do as he wished, and he exercised that right whenever anyone got in his way. On the other hand, the victims that experienced the most severe wrath of Snake were those that crossed him in some way, especially those that lied to him. Though Snake was evil, full of hate, and possessed a raging temper, he never lied. He felt that a man's word was all he had. Snake did not lie to anybody for any reason. Therefore, whenever he caught someone lying to him, he could barely contain his temper and often went off into a tantrum.

Though Snake did not go to church, he expected that a pastor walked in accordance with his self-proclaimed biblical standards. But this was not the case with one of Snake's neighbors, Reverend Bobby Joe Kinnard. Most of neighbors referred to Reverend Kinnard as BJ, for Bobby Joe. He was a well-liked pastor of a local Baptist church and was famous for his chicken-fry dinners. The church advertised their chicken fry, and people came for miles just to eat his homemade barbecue. BJ began cooking on Saturday afternoon and continued right through the night. He preached outside on Sunday morning with a portable pulpit sitting right next to his large charcoal pits. He would preach, stop and flip some half-chickens, and then start preaching again. Well this preacher got himself into a bunch of trouble when he lied to Snake one day.

BJ just loved to ride his horse. He often took long rides in the hills and mountains of Carolina. Back in those days, seldom did one really pay attention to any boundaries, and there were few fences that separated one man's property from another. The preacher was a nearby neighbor of the Rushings and occasionally rode his horse through a large neck of woods that belonged to them. Snake had run a large quantity of moonshine, and the revenuers were leaning on many in Union County. In times like these, they hid their illegal whiskey and laid low for a while until the heat of the law passed. On this occasion, Snake and his buddies had hidden a large stash of moonshine in a deep wood line and had camouflaged it with branches and leaves.

Snake had noticed that BJ was making more trips than usual through the woods on his horse and had a sneaking suspicion that perhaps the preacher had come across his stash. It was very unusual for anyone to go through this particular area of woods due to its out-of-the-way location. So, Snake being the direct man he was, simply waited until he saw BJ on his horse again and asked the preacher about the moonshine.

As BJ rode by one day, Snake called out, "Hey, preacher man. How's ya doin'?"

"Good Mr. Rushing. Wonderful day that God has made, isn't it?"

"Sure, preacher man. So, I've got a question for ya." Snake continued. "I know that you found my liquor back there in those woods, didn't ya?"

The preacher seemed a bit fidgety on his brown horse. "Liquor... liquor? Where would there be liquor?"

"Now come on, preacher man. I know that ya know about my whiskey. Now come clean. I'm talking about that big stash hidden over there." Snake pointed his finger in the direction of his hidden stash.

"Oh...that liquor. Well, ah...well, I did see some liquor hidden in some branches and stuff but paid it no mind. Really, it's none of my business, Mr. Rushing."

"Well, Pastor Kinnard, if it bothers ya, I can get rid of it. I'm just storing it for a while. Now tell me, are you gonna tell anyone about this...if ya are, tell me now so I can get rid of it."

BJ dismounted and led his horse up closer to Snake as he started his confession, "I saw that stuff...but don't you bother. Don't you think about moving it. You will not hear a word out of me. No siree...no word from me. Not a word. You can count on me, Mr. Rushing."

Snake could tell that he seemed a bit nervous, but he took that preacher at his word. Snake slapped him on the back and thanked him for being so neighborly. And the story could have ended there had Reverend BJ Kinnard kept his word and said nothing about the unlawful whiskey.

Several days later, Snake was going about his daily tasks when a buddy from town pulled up in his old pickup truck and hollered out at Snake. "Hey, Snake...you home?"

"Is that you, Boba-lu?"

"Sure is, Snake...let me ask ya something. Where's dat stash of sugar whiskey ya got in da woods?"

Snake responded like any great poker player with a solemn face, "Whatcha talking about?"

Boba-lu laughed, "C'mon, Snake. You're one of the best moonshiners and runners in this county. Everybody knows 'bout ya. Now where's da shine? Can't believe ya got some stashed in the woods somewhere while those federal guys are looking everywhere else. How much ya got?" Boba-lu was the kind of guy in Monroe that knew everyone's business and then some. But Snake did not like anyone knowing his moonshine business.

"Don't quite know what you're talking about. Moonshine where? And where are ya hearing about such foolishness?" Snake kept the perplexed look upon his face as he asked Boba-lu this probing question.

"Well, I was down at the store a little while ago, and that preacher that lives close to here was telling everybody about a stash of liquor that he came up on back in the woods well behind your place...or somewhere."

Snake could no longer hold his poker face as he yelled, "He what? That sneakin', lowdown, sorry case of a preacher man. He told me not to move it, that he would not say a word."

"Well," continued Boba-lu, "Ya do have some of that ruckus juice hidden somewhere. He was down there telling anyone that would listen and braggin' about his find, ya know?"

Snake stared right into the soul of Boba-lu and burned a warning into his core being, "Well, now ya know. I'll share a little bit with ya later. But if I find that you...Boba–lu, tell anyone else, they'll be looking for you out in them there woods. Ya hear?"

"Yes, sir, Snake...would not cross ya for nothin'...never do it." And with that Boba-lu crawled back into his rusty old pickup. He wanted to know when he could catch up with Snake and get a quart or so of his divine concoction, but he was a bit too afraid to even ask. He pulled out of the drive and waved back to Snake, who just stood there adjusting his big old hat.

It was no more than a few minutes later when Snake's cousin pulled up into his front yard and yelled out for Snake.

"Snake," his cousin yelled. "Snake, come quick. The preacher man is down at the feed mill spreading a bunch of stuff about ya."

Snake came running out of the house. "Don't say that it's BJ Kinnard running his mouth about my liquor stashed out back of the Boar Run Creek?"

His cousin stopped dead in his tracks. "How the heck did ya know?"

"Boba-lu was here just a few minutes ago and told me the same thing. He said that BJ was down at the store talking the same trash. Let me tell ya, I'm gonna beat the livin' daylights out of that preacher man. And when he is dead, I'll pray for him to be born again, and when he is, I'll beat the life out of him all over again."

Snake was boiling mad. He was kicking up the gravel of the drive and cussing like a drunken sailor. His cousin knew when it was time to leave, and this was one of those times. He got into his truck and went back into town.

Snake sat down against an old oak tree and plotted his revenge. He settled scores, but he did it on his time. He decided to just wait on him until he showed up again. Word had gotten back to the preacher that Snake thought he had turned him in for the liquor he had hidden in the woods. So BJ Kinnard thought that he just might set the record straight and visit the Rushing household on his next trip through the woods.

So, a couple of weeks later, Reverend Kinnard strolled up in Snake's yard looking a bit timid. The pack of dogs always alerted Snake of anyone's coming. Snake came out of the door and tossed his hat onto a nearby rocker. This meant trouble was on its way and things just might get violent, but BJ had no idea of the storm that had been brewing. He tried to look normal as he hopped off of his horse and greeted Snake. "I've been meaning to talk to you, Mr. Rushing."

"Me too," Snake replied as he hit him with a right fist right between the eyes. Blood splattered all over BJ's shirt and face as BJ bounced back like a .45 caliber slug had plastered its lead upon his forehead. He shot right back up into the bed of an old '54 pickup truck that sat in the drive. It was as if he were rocket-propelled from a standing position to an airborne projectile. He fell with a bang onto the hot bed of the old pickup. Snake was even a bit surprised that the preacher man had flown to right up and over the tailgate onto the hot metal bed—just from one punch. The horse took off a'running and never looked back, but Snake was too busy to pay the silly horse any attention.

Snake jumped on the preacher man and began to beat the man silly. In fact, he beat him plumb out of his nicely pressed white shirt and tie. "Ya lied to me...ya lied to me!" Snake kept screaming as he had the preacher man's head in his hands banging it down again and again onto the hot steel of the truck bed. BJ's back was burning from the hot steel, and he was screaming as loud as he could scream, "Mercy…mercy…show me mercy. I am a minister of the—"

BJ never finished that sentence, as Snake's fist again came down on his mouth, loosening several teeth and busting his jaw wide open. Snake knew something was wrong when BJ's jaw fell into two pieces, held on to the rest of his face by a few jaw muscles and facial skin. Snake continue to beat away, pinning him down and burning him severely on the hot bed. BJ still squirmed and squealed though no intelligible words came out of his broken and busted jaw.

Snake moved from beating his mouth to his eyes and continued to beat the man as BJ groaned with sounds only a dying wild animal made. Snake continued to beat his face until his eyes and nose looked like a raw piece of steak that had just been tenderized with a twenty-two-ounce construction hammer. Finally, Snake let the preacher up and looked into what was left of his eyes, a tiny slit in both, and told him with his own clinched jaw, "Don't ever lie to me again, preacher. Don't ever cross me again. Ya hear?"

The preacher could do nothing else but nod his head as he leaned against the tailgate.

"Now get yerself out of here and *never* lie to me again." Jerry shoved him toward the street as BJ shuffled his feet ever so slowly, moving at a snail's pace to the road.

Snake was never really proud of the beating he gave that preacher man. But Reverend BJ Kinnard never lied to Snake again. He walked all the way back home and spent weeks in the hospital recuperating from that beating. Snake often recounted the beating to his buddies.

"Ya know, he shouldn't have crossed me. I guess I should feel real bad, beatin' up a preacher man like that. But ya know what? I really don't."

He continued, "I had asked him in a good honest way to tell me if he was gonna talk. He said no and then lied. So in my way of thinkin', he had it coming to him, and I pretty well put it on him. Well…that's nothin' to brag about…beating up a preacher man, but I had to do what I had to do."

Sometimes the hate mixed with the wild moonshine and bootlegging culture resulted in someone like Reverend BJ Kinnard being terribly beaten. At other times, the moonshiners and bootleggers found themselves in a terrible fix while flirting with disaster.

NEAR-DEATH DISASTERS

Both the moonshining and the bootlegging businesses were very dangerous enterprises that often brought death or disaster to the operator or one of his family. Though the hazards of the business often plagued families for generations, the young folk were still intrigued with the excitement, intrigue, and danger of the sport. Even the Rushings experienced calamities from the moonshine business. Espy Rushing, Snake's father, died in a farmer's pond, no doubt intoxicated from the stuff. But even prior to Espy's death, he experienced many dangerous encounters that nearly took his life.

A typical example of the danger that continually surrounded the moonshiner occurred one December day when the Carolina hills and mountains were blanketed with a thick white snow. Snake was still young and had not yet taken an active role in any of the illegal whiskey operations, though he remembers the story well.

Snake's father and his uncle Dooley were running a still back in the woods, well off of any road or beaten path. They had carefully hidden the still operation and had located it up a stream far from the trails of any sneaky federal revenuer. They had run the still for several months making hundreds of gallons of the sugar whiskey and were delivering it throughout most of Union County. It was common for men to make a few bucks now and then by finding an illegal still and then reporting it to a federal agent. If was difficult for any moonshiner to know exactly whom to trust. Therefore, most kept to themselves and to their own family members who were also involved in their clandestine affairs. As stated earlier, even a large percentage of federal agents and local law enforcers were dishonest and corrupt, occasionally selling jugs, stolen license plates, or even hustling sugar to the moonshiners they were trying to capture. Most all of this corruption centered around money and the opportunity to make additional cash on the side.

It was the middle of December when an old man in the town of Monroe heard a rumor about the approximate location of their still and decided to investigate for himself to see if the rumor was true. After several long cold and frustrating walks along some of the more obvious creeks in the county, he accidentally stumbled upon their operation and quickly made haste to a local officer to collect a few dollars. Strangely enough, he ultimately used the little cash he received to purchase more of that white lightning from another source.

So the old man reported his findings about Espy and Uncle Dooley to Leo Wall, one of the toughest agents in the entire western area of North Carolina. Legend was that no one escaped old Leo. He was fast, mean, and tough. So Agent Wall decided that he alone would bring in Espy and Dooley. Knowing the approximate location of the still, he drove his government car one evening to a location near the stream. He then grabbed his shotgun, loaded his pockets with shells, and started into the woods on the backside of the still location. It was cold with a slight breeze, but the snow kept the noise down as he slowly crept along from tree to tree searching through the distance for any sign of a still. He had walked over a mile when he caught a faint view of the top of an arm from a copper still as it reflected a bit of the bright full moon that made its way down through the pines.

I've got them, he thought to himself. He readied his shotgun and moved even more quietly through the snow. When he was within thirty yards of them, he stooped down behind a tree and listened to Espy and Uncle Dooley chat with one another about the day's run.

He again began to stalk his prey, moving ever so slowly and purposefully through the snow until he was with a few yards of Espy. Espy had just bent down and picked up a sack of sugar when Leo jumped out and grabbed him by the seat of his britches. Uncle Dooley ran off into the woods as Espy's response was to swing that heavy sack around his shoulder. It caught Agent Leo upside the head, knocking him to the ground. Espy knew the consequences of getting busted by this agent. It meant a long sentence in the slammer, and that was the last thing he wanted.

The hunter had his prey in his sights but found himself face down in the cold wet snow. Leo immediately grabbed Espy's pant leg to hold on. His shotgun was lying in the snow about six feet away. Leo was screaming, "You're mine... you're mine." Espy was just bellowing guttural grunts that sounded like any wild animal caught in the trap of a hunter. He was twisting, turning, and jumping as he tried to shake the trap from his leg while the agent just held on more firmly. All the while, Leo was trying to inch in the snow closer and closer to his weapon.

Then Espy twisted with all his strength and kicked Leo right in the ribs. Leo screamed out in pain as Espy brought his boot back again, took aim at the hunter, and kicked Leo hard again, perhaps even breaking one or two bones. Leo yelled, fell back, and released his trap-like hold from Espy's leg. Espy took off like a scared rabbit, running around the many trees through the snow. Leo rolled over, grabbed his twelve-gauge shotgun, and began firing shots at the fleeing moonshiner. Only this time, the agent was not tying to confuse the shiner with noise. He was shooting for the kill, and his first several shots were not far off.

As the shots barely missed their mark, the snow was exploding all around Espy like hidden land mines detonated as he ran. Leo was cussing and screaming at Espy and shooting on the run. They were running through a very hilly area that made running very difficult, especially in the snow. Espy ran up one hill and then flew back down the hill to the next valley below. Occasionally he slipped on the snow and arrived at the bottom of the hill faster as he slid as fast as a little kid on a sled. Leo ran until he was out of breath and walked awhile as he reloaded his shotgun, then he took off running back up another hill to catch up with Espy.

Leo always kept him in his sights, but with the heavy underbrush and the density of the trees, try as he might, he could not put Espy down with his flying buckshot.

His gun blasted, splitting the night air with fire exploding from the end of the hot barrel, sending sparks into the sky. Occasionally, Leo stopped again and rested his gun barrel against a tree, steadying himself, and fired off another round of shells.

Boom, boom, boom.

Reload.

Run until out of breath.

Stop and take careful aim.

Boom, boom, boom.

Leo chased Espy far into the woods and continued the pursuit until his pocket was empty of the many shells that he had packed into it hours earlier. Espy knew his still was destroyed, and he hoped that Uncle Dooley had escaped. But he took no chances that Leo was trying to deceive him by continuing the night run without shooting. Espy ran and ran until he could run no longer. He then sat down in the snow with only the moon as a nightlight. He watched every tree and shadow and finally figured that somewhere in the past half-mile or so, Leo had given up on him. The hunter had failed, and the hunted had survived again. He looked at his legs and boots to make sure that the freezing cold had not made him numb to being hit by some buckshot. But he was fine and perhaps a bit lucky. Not many men could brag of an escape from Agent Leo Wall. Now Espy could.

He walked a large circle around his still and arrived home a couple of hours before sunlight.

Mama was asleep on the couch, and Snake had already gone to bed.

"Woman," Espy whispered, "I'm home…alive…tired…though nearly killed by the old nasty agent Leo Wall."

"Good God, man! Where have you been?"

Espy could hardly catch his breath. "I was nearly killed. Wall found our still. Someone must have snitched. I must have ran for miles in that cold snow as he practiced his shooting, trying to bust some buckshot in my butt. I could have been killed. We've lost the still…I'm sure. Have you heard from Uncle Dooley?"

"Nope, but if the law is on ya, ya better move quick. Your man brought a big load of sugar and put it all in our smoke house. If the law comes here, we're all in trouble."

Espy rushed out of the house, still panting from his life-or-death run. He loaded the sugar and filled his old '38 Ford full of the stuff. By this time Snake had awaken, he watched from the front door as his daddy pulled the truck back out the drive. The frozen top crust of the snow cracked and popped from all of the weight of the sugar. Espy unloaded the sugar at a neighbor's house, and then reached under the seat and pulled out a quart jar of his most recent brewed hillbilly pop. He took a couple of swigs to warm up. Then a few more to calm his nerves from his midnight death run. Before returning home, he finished the quart for the medicinal purposes of putting him to sleep quickly, not that he needed it. He arrived back home around day-break, falling on the couch half-dead from the scary run, half-beat from the fast loading and unloading of the sugar, and half-drunk from the quart of the white lightning he finished before returning home.

Many men were shot dead and killed in similar circumstances, but Espy survived this winter night's incident. Many of the others died terrible and painful deaths, bleeding slowly in the woods after being shot by some federal agent. Shotguns could tear an awful hole out of a man's side, leaving him on the ground bleeding and suffering for many minutes before passing from this world to the next. On this particular winter night, Espy was one of the more fortunate ones.

There were many such occasions where even Snake could have been killed and left for dead. Sometimes the peril he faced was directly related to his illegal moonshining and bootlegging activities. But at other times, his hazardous predicaments were a direct consequence of his own deep-seated hatred and explosive angry temper. A fight at a local beer joint in the middle of Union County and the brawl that followed could have resulted in Snake's death and nearly resulted in another man's death. Such is the life of a modern-day outlaw living on the edge.

The local beer joint was in a rundown concrete block building that had more paint on the outside than mortar between the concrete blocks. The building was fairly decrepit and was called the Pig Pen. It was dirty and dingy and had been a trouble spot for the law for years. Located right behind the high school, it was owned by D. Jay Bailey and run by Bailey himself and several rough-looking thugs that were referred to as the "boys."

Though the Pig Pen sold beer, chips, and peanuts to the local fellows that were just looking for a cold one on a hot summer night, it was really a front for some of the most illegal activities in the county. D. Jay Bailey sold and bought unlawful drugs, bought and pushed illegal 'shine, and sold heroin, cocaine, and marijuana to most anyone that had enough funds to grease his palm. At any one time, he had a dozen or so women hustling on the side and poker games for high cash stakes going on all night long. The inside was a dark and seedy place with a long bar at one end and a door that opened into the rear rooms that held the illegal poker games and the loose ladies. The Union County Sheriff's Department had tried to close it down on many occasions and somehow always failed to find enough evidence to prosecute old D. Jay.

Well, Snake had a younger brother, Johnny, who assisted him in some of his bootlegging. Johnny just loved beer and poker. Though Snake warned him to stay away from the Pig Pen, one way or another, Johnny always ended up there during the late evening. As long as Johnny was losing money, he was welcome at their poker tables. But if he got on a lucky-man's roll and began winning money, they tried to run him off. Johnny also had a temper like his brother. That temper mixed with the exhilaration of a good poker hand along with a healthy dose of hard liquor often resulted in a scuffle in the back room of the joint. As soon as Johnny got to be too much to handle, especially if he was winning and the boys were trying to get him out the door, they called Snake.

The telephone rang in Snake's house, and the request was the same.

"Hey, Snake... why don't you come over here and get your brother. He's raising Cain and causing trouble. You need to get him out of here before somebody gets hurt."

It always aggravated Snake to get calls in the middle of the night about his brother. "Now listen to me, boys, it ain't my job to come and look after Johnny. He's twenty-one years old and can take care of himself. Sell him some liquor to go and send him home. Now, don't call me again."

It was like a broken record as Snake told them the same thing night after night. Then one night the telephone ran at four o'clock in the morning. Snake flung his legs over the side of the bed and walked to the kitchen to answer the telephone as he screamed back to his wife, "That better not be the boys down at the Pig Pen, or I'm gonna kick some butt and it'll be over fast."

"Hello... hello... tell me this isn't the Pig Pen!"

"Hey, man," one of the boys chirped, "ya gotta come over tonight. Johnny's real bad, and somebody's going down."

Snake was furious. "You're right about that. You all are going to get a real beating cause I told ya not to call me about Johnny again."

Then Snake gave the boy over the telephone his final warning.

"You tell D. Jay, if anyone calls here again and bothers me and my family, they're history, 'cause I'll come over there and kick some real you-know-what."

The voice on the other end of the line chuckled, not knowing how serious Snake was. Snake slammed down the receiver on the telephone, cussing and spitting as he made his way in the dark back to his bed.

Well, the next afternoon one of the boys with three other brothers were playing in a poker game with Johnny. Johnny won a large pot with a three-of-a-kind. He tossed three kings on the table, and as the cards spun around and around, he swigged down another shot and pulled the pot of cash to his lap.

One of the brothers turned to Johnny.

"Time for you to go, boy. In fact, you can get home before dark if you leave now...and leave that there cash on the table."

"Whoa now, boys," Johnny reacted, "I'm a'winnin' and not going nowhere."

Knowing that a brawl would arise any minute with Johnny, one of the brothers made the mistake of dialing Snake just one more time. It was around four in the afternoon when Snake's telephone rang.

"Hello," Jerry said as he picked up the phone.

"Hey, Snake...I know ya said not to call...but...huh...I think ya better get down here this afternoon and take old Johnny home with ya. I'm thinkin' that this could get real nasty and..."

Jerry never heard the rest of the brother's comments because he was out of the house in a flash. He jumped into his old van and drove like the mad man he was. He had told them not to call and had given them adequate warning. Now they paid the consequences.

He pulled into the front gravel parking lot and slammed on his brakes, nearly colliding with an old Ford pickup. He was out of his van and up to the door nearly before the engine had stopped running.

He slung open the door and paused for only a second or two as he summed up the situation. The bootleg joint was smoky and dark in spite of the fact that it was still light outdoors. The place was completely full of people. The bar was full of drunks, and each table had its share of intoxicated men and wild women.

A customer once said, "A man can come here, shoot pool, have some fun with a wild woman, play some poker, lose some money, drink some beer, and then buy some milk and eggs for the family before returning home…what a place."

Snake walked into the joint with no weapons but his right powerhouse fist and his left hook, both attached to the end of his arms. He walked right up to the counter and addressed one of the boys serving drinks.

"I thought I warned you last night not to call me again."

The bartender smirked and started to say something like, "You don't tell me what to do" when he abruptly learned otherwise. Snake planted the right powerhouse directly between the eyes, busting the boy's nose. Bright red blood splashed over the bar, mixing with several drinks of the customers. Everyone at the bar scattered, leaving their beer and peanuts behind them. The boy fell back into a large shelf of medicine and the like and bottles went flying. It was as if a bomb had gone off right behind the bar. Before the boy could regain his composure, Snake had leaped over the bar and grabbed him by the throat and lifted him up, slamming him against the back wall.

Ladies were running out of the joint as if it was on fire. Men were scattering and the poker players were looking out the game room trying to determine the reason for all the commotion. No one really wanted to tangle with Snake, and the screaming, yelling, and running were all testimonies to the fact.

Snake popped him time and again right in the face with one hand while he held him against the wall by his throat with the other hand.

"Like I said…"

And he popped him again in the temple, rocking his head back against the wall like a rag doll.

"…I did not want to be…"

Again Snake hit him in the nose as if for assurance that it was thoroughly busted and broken.

"...called again. I thought I made that plain."

Blood was now running from a cut over his eye and from his nose down his face and into his mouth. The boy was crying and spitting out great gobs of soggy red stuff as if he were drowning in his own blood. The last punch of the five or six flurries knocked the boy completely unconscious, and he went a'snoring as Snake dropped him to the floor in the pile of aspirins, pills, and other supplies.

About that time, the boy's brother, one of the four, came out of the rear gaming room cussing and screaming. "What the heck's going on here?"

Snake picked up one of the nearest glass bottles and hurled it his way as he rushed him. The bottle busted all over the wall, shattering glass everywhere. The fellow ran to the pool table and crawled under it looking for some cover, but he found none. Snake grabbed a couple cases of glass Pepsi bottles and started hurling them like missiles back into the poolroom area. Bottles were exploding, and Pepsi was raining down on the pool tables like a mighty thunderstorm. Some had made it out the door while others were cowering under tables or behind chairs. Some had taken refuge behind the jukebox, shaking as the bottles exploded like grenades.

Snake enjoyed the circus and continued chuckin' the glass bottles until the entire two cases were empty. He went through the place wrecking it by throwing packages of bread and turning over the snack and chips rack. He then began tossing gallon milk jugs from the cooler around the joint. Jugs were busting and milk was splattering everywhere. Snake was out of control, and the anger and hatred from deep within was fueling the fight.

He ran back into the poolroom, chasing all the boys in sight. He took one of those big glass Pepsi bottles and busted it open against the jukebox. In the other hand he grabbed a pool cue stick and headed for the closest fellow to cut or whip. Four of the guys went busting out the back door all at the same time, and they nearly got stuck trying to escape. He saw one of the brothers still hiding under a pool table and began beating him unmercifully with the cue stick, trying to cut him with the broken bottle all the while. The poor boy rolled on the floor to the door and jumped up, catching another whelp across his neck as he dove out the door and landed in the grass.

Snake proceeded into the rear game room where the illegal poker games took place and found one of the ringleaders, the man he had beaten so severely behind the counter. He was still bleeding bad and was virtually covered with his own blood. Snake picked the guy up and slammed him right against the wall, knocking most of the pictures off the walls.

"I told ya not to call me anymore...like never. I've told most of your boys to never call my house again...and I hope you've learned your lesson."

The fellow was struggling to get loose Snake continued.

"I told ya I was gonna to beat your butt and here I am. Look there..." Snake pointed to four guns standing in the corner of the room for protection, and then he continued, "You've got four guns standing there and I walked right into your mess and whooped all of you...and I busted you up right behind your own counter. I hope ya learned your lesson."

And with that warning, Snake popped him again in the head, kicked him a few times for good measure, and headed to the door. The war was over, or so he thought. He got into his old van as if he had just finished his daily job and headed home. Back at the Pig Pen, it looked like a tornado had ripped right through the place, nearly totaling the joint. And in fact, a tornado had torn through the place...Jerry Rushing, Snake...the tornado.

Snake returned home with but a few sore knuckles from the beatings he had given out. Things seemed to return to normal, and he heard nothing from the boys of the Pig Pen or the law for several nights. Then the phone rang again. It was the big brother of the fellow he had beaten so brutally.

"Don't like the whippin' ya gave to my brother, Snake."

Snake listened intently and carefully chose his words.

"I don't reckon you do. I wouldn't like it if somebody whooped one of my kin real good."

"Well," the brother continued, "I'm gonna put it on ya, and I mean in a real good way. I'm gonna put a mean hurtin' on ya. I hope your ready for a beatin'."

Snake had heard it before, and it did not move him or scare him a bit. "Go ahead....bigger men have tried." Snake often tired of weak-bodied, big-mouth men talking a big talk.

The brother became angry as he could tell that Snake was not really taking him seriously. He began cussing and screaming over the phone about how bad he was going to whip Jerry. After a few minutes of listening to all the bragging, Snake told him, "Well, ya can't sit there and whoop me on the phone. I know that ya got ten people probably sitting around listening to ya going off on me as you're bragging. Come on over here to my place. We'll have a real private scrap away from friends and family."

Well, the fighting and verbal assault continued to grow and became more heated until the brother finally gave Snake the final threat: "Well, if ya will not come over here for a fight, I'll tell ya what I'll do. I'm gonna shoot and kill your wife and daughter the first time I see 'em on the road. Hear me....I'll kill 'em both dead."

Well, that about did it. Snake could take a lot of abuse, but no one threatened his wife and daughter. "I'll be there in about ten minutes." With that he slammed the receiver down and headed for his back room. He grabbed his 8mm rifle and strapped a pistol on his side. He walked out of the back door and headed through the woods. He knew that they would be looking for him to pull up in his old van. But they never expected him to walk through the woods and cross through the cornfield. It was about three-quarters of a mile. He quickly crossed the woods and entered the cornfield. Every time a car drove by the store on the road, Snake ran as fast as he could run through the cornfield. As soon as the car passed, he hid in the cornfield, silently waiting for the next car to pass.

Now he was the hunter, and that was something he really knew. He finally arrived at the backside of the road where he could keep an eye on the place. He lay quietly on the ground with his left hand securely holding his rifle. He silently watched them as they walked around the store. They had all the lights out, so he could not see them well. But with his keen night vision, Snake could make out most of them. There were sixteen of them sitting around in chairs outside, waiting for what they thought was the prey. Little did they know that they were the prey and were under the careful eye of the hunter. He saw one of the fellows standing beside the store with a shotgun. Each time a car passed the joint, Snake watched the fellow raise his shotgun, expecting the car to be Snake. As soon as the car drove by, he whispered to his friends. "It was not him. . . . but hold tight. He'll be here."

Snake wondered just how many of them had guns and how many more boys might be in the darkened store. So acting out his childhood fantasies, he jumped up right in the center of the road and shouted, "All right, boys, just like Jesse James, I showed up when ya least expected me."

And talk about surprise! Not one of them expected Snake to jump right up in the middle of them out of the dark. They just stood there watching the big brute of a man with his 8mm rifle pointed their way and strapped with a pistol. He looked like a modern-day Jesse James. No one spoke big now because it's a scary thing to be staring down the barrel of a 8mm.

Snake continued with his verbal instruction, as he knew that he had the drop on them and they had been stunned with his quick appearance. "So, boys, you want to rumble; let's get it on. But know this, I don't know who all has a gun in this crowd, so if anyone moves or stands up, I'm gonna blast your guts across this store yard. I came over to whoop all of ya, and we're gonna get the show on the road. Only, I'm gonna take ya on . . . one at a time."

The one boy with the gun started to raise it up, and Snake screamed and warned him, "Pick it up, boy, and I'll blow your brains right out the back of your head." He had quickly leveled his rifle right between the boy's eyes.

"Raise it up, big boy, and let's see the brains fly. Drop it or you die."

Snake kept the rifle pointed at the boy's head and slowly walked his way. The boy still had the shotgun in his hands and had begun to back up. Snake arrived within a few feet of him and then busted him in the face knocking him back into an empty van sitting in front of the store. About that time he heard a car come whipping into the store lot. It was his brother Johnny.

"Johnny, hold them off…keep them back. I want them one at a time," Snake screamed. Johnny grabbed his twelve-gauge and bolted from the car.

"Back off, boys, ya heard him. He said he'd take ya one at a time," Johnny barked the orders. Snake was in the van on top of the boy with the shotgun as Johnny was screaming. He jumped on top of him and continued to beat him relentlessly, hammering away on his face. He must have punched him more than two hundred times. He knocked him out, grabbed his head, and continued to bust on his face. The skin ripped around his mouth like a wet newspaper as blood splashed all over the windows of the van. The corner of his lips busted open, and with each punch the tear in his cheek became longer and longer until the cut nearly wrapped his cheek skin around his left ear.

Though the man was unconscious, Snake continue to beat him as he screamed in his face, "So you want to kill my wife and kid, son? I am going to teach you just what killing is all about. I'm gonna beat you to death." And Snake did beat the fellow within an inch of his life. Eventually he remained in the hospital on a deathbed for weeks with more than 125 stitches in his face just to put him back together again.

Boom, boom, boom. Johnny's shotgun rang through the night. He shot the ground all around a fellow that had moved. Fire and buckshot were all over that dark ground, and the fellow was dancing in the air, as he was bare-footed. He knew better than to move and decided to stand at attention during the rest of the assault.

Finally, Snake crawled out of the van looking almost as bad as his adversary. Blood and small pieces of facial skin and fat were all over Snake's face, shirt, and arms. He looked as if he had been shot with a shotgun. He marched over to the fellow's brother and addressed him.

"OK, big boy, now you want it. Come on."

"No…no. I really like you boys, both of ya. I really like y'all. I think the world of yas."

Snake loved to see them squirm.

"Come on. You wanted to fight. Ya threatened my wife and kid, so let's get it on. I'll fix your face so you'll look just like your brother there." Snake smiled and smirked that little smirk that he seemed to flash at times like this.

Snake continued, "Ya talked big on the telephone. I came all the way down here, and let's not waste my time, OK?"

"No siree...I told ya...I think the world of ya. Now just leave us well enough alone."

"Now listen carefully. If y'ever bother me again or even think of my wife or kid, I'll kill ya all."

He turned to Johnny. "Hey, brother, keep that gun on them. Get back in your car and head out of here. Don't ever come back to this joint. I mean it."

Snake crossed the road and headed back home through the cornfield. He was halfway through the woods when he heard the rescue squad coming down the road to pick up the bloody mess he had left in the van. Snake arrived at the house and heard the telephone ringing.

He picked up the receiver, and the county deputy was on the line. He explained that the sheriff wanted him to make the call. He told Snake that they had been experiencing problems with the Pig Pen for years. A young girl had died from an overdose of dope they had given her after school one day. They just could not prove it. He went on to explain that the sheriff had been trying to close the Pig Pen down for months and just could not do it. However, after the beating, the brothers had taken out a warrant for Snake and Johnny. And the deputy wanted Snake to know that the sheriff had nothing to do with it.

"Really, Snake," the deputy explained, "the sheriff wants you to know that he had nothing to do with this thing. He's sorry, but he has a warrant for you because of this beating. He said that you and Johnny need to come in tonight, real quick. He will let you sign for Johnny's bond, and Johnny can sign for you."

"OK, man. We'll be right in. How bad is the old boy hurt?"

The deputy was nervous about telling him. "He's hurt real bad. He's in the hospital in surgery now. They don't expect him to live. He's in bad shape. When they got him to the hospital, he was talking to his daddy, and his daddy has been dead for over two years. He was also screaming for him mama to fry him some biscuits and all kind of crazy talk. Don't look good."

"Well, Deputy, tell the sheriff that we'll be right up. Good-bye."

When Snake and Johnny arrived at the sheriff's office, they signed each other's bond, and the sheriff was quick to let Snake know that he had nothing to do with this. He had secretly told his deputy not to make Jerry mad or tell him he was under arrest, because he could get mad and tear the place apart.

The sheriff gave Snake the name of a lawyer that could assist him in the court cast. He asked the lawyer to do him a favor and help Snake out. They cut a deal right there in the sheriff's office, promising each other favors, and the lawyer accepted the case. Secretly the sheriff, deputies, and the attorney were glad Snake had gone into the Pig Pen. Once Snake had beaten several of them and literally tore the joint up, it never opened again.

Snake eventually went to court and was quite scared. He was really dreading it. They had him for assault with a deadly weapon with an attempt to kill. He was accused of beating the man with the butt of his rifle. When Snake took the stand, he denied hitting him with any gunstock. He admitted to beating him with only his fist. When asked how many times he had hit the man, he replied as many times as it took for him to drop that shotgun he was holding. They presented pictures of the face of his beaten foe. Snake really couldn't tell that it was a face of a man. He could not tell where the man's eyes were; his face was swollen out flush with the tip of his nose. It had red blotches all over it, and his mouth and cheek were stitched up. Even during the trial, the man was still in intensive care.

The sheriff said that it was a wonder that nobody got killed. Several of the brothers took the stand throughout the day, and then the judge was ready to make his decision.

"Well," the judge started, "you may question my decision, and you are entitled to carry this further up to a grand jury. But I'm going to find no probable cause on all charges. I simply refuse to prosecute anybody that busts a man's head that runs such a terrible drug-infested joint as you boys do." The judge was frowning and staring at the brothers that had placed the complaint for the warrant.

"Not guilty," the judge said, and he leaned back in his big chair and watched Snake breathe a sigh of relief. As Snake was leaving the courtroom, the sheriff called his name, "Jerry Rushing...come over here please."

Jerry crossed the courtroom and faced the sheriff. "Remember, Jerry, when you cussed me and called me names in front of everybody uptown?"

Jerry nodded his head.

"I was your friend, and you didn't even know it. I wanted to shake your hand for what you did. It took a lot of guts, and I just wanted to shake your hand. You used to get down on your knees and make monkey motions at me in town with your hands and face whenever you saw me. That's behind us now. We're friends, OK?"

Jerry nodded again.

Snake knew that the sheriff appreciated him closing the Pig Pen down, and he may have helped in getting the judge to release him. Snake shook the sheriff's hand and smiled a small smile.

"Thanks," Jerry said.

"No," the sheriff responded as he shook his hand vigorously, "thank you!"

Snake knew that he was lucky to be alive. He could have been killed, or he could have killed the guy and spent his entire life in prison. Snake was fortunate and he knew it.

God's Grace on the Whiskey Runner

Sometimes life is confusing. Why do some men die early and some men live very long lives? Why do some experience terrible disasters and face dreadful deaths while others live through their tragedy to tell the story? We may never know the answers to these questions on this side of life. But we do know that God loves the sinner and is always at work in his life whether he knows it or not. Sometimes we are spared from disaster, and sometimes God reaches into our life and sheds His grace upon us. An old song was written years ago about this:

> Amazing grace, how sweet the sound
> That saved a wretch like me.

I once was lost but now I'm found,
'Twas blind but now I see.

Grace is defined as God's unearned and undeserved love that He bestows upon us. Grace is undeserved acceptance and love received from God. It is the characteristic attitude of God in providing salvation for sinners. In spite of the hate and the bitterness of life, God worked in Snake's life and ultimately saved him. Snake received large doses of God's grace throughout his life, even though he had no idea at the time.

The hand of God was upon Snake and kept him alive in the most horrendous of circumstances. Snake's hatred and repugnance were the cause of many difficulties in his life that could have actually claimed his life. There were many occasions when Snake could have been killed and should have been killed, but God had other plans. There was probably no better example of this than the day he drove his car right up under a chicken truck.

Snake had just bought a brand-new 1955 Chevrolet. One evening when he was still young, his daddy sent him up to a fellow's house to buy some illegal whiskey and bring it back home. It was not a long run, and he should be able to get the liquor and be back home within an hour or so. He had not been gone long when a big chicken truck loaded with full crates of chickens pulled to the left as if he was turning into a store. Snake pulled his new '55 Chevy quickly to the right just as the trucker pulled back to the right and ran in front of the fast-runnin' Chevy.

Snake slammed on his brakes and locked them, skidding right under the truck. The Chevy crashed into the side of the truck—the entire top was cut off from the hood to the rear trunk. Glass from the windshield exploded throughout the car, and the chicken truck flipped over, dropping hundreds of pounds of chickens down into the open-air Chevy. The weight of the chickens and coops broke off the steering wheel, causing it to pierce Snake's side. It tore right into his side and penetrated all the way down to the bottom of his intestines, exploding an enormous hole in his abdomen. The chicken manure fell out from the cages and into the car, filling the bloody hole in

Snake's side with awful-smelling stuff. Snake was bleeding profusely. He was pierced like a fish on a hook on that broken steering wheel.

The impact of the wreck tore his elbow up and ground it like hamburger meat, forcing glass bits into the muscles of his elbow and forearm. Snake lay there in the car knowing he was facing death. Chicken manure was everywhere, and the chickens were flying and squawking like crazy. Feathers were floating in the air, and it looked like a December snow. Snake could feel his busted elbow, and he looked down and almost vomited as his stomach wrenched from what he saw. The broken steering wheel was sticking out of his stomach. He slowly began to pick the manure, mixed with thick red blood, out of the gaping cavity in his stomach. He reached down, and his hand went well into the crater until he could feel the soft velvety texture of his own intestines. He gagged from the thought of it and laid his head back.

As a man came up to help him out of his car, he remembered telling the man that he felt that he was going. But going where? When a man reaches the end or believes that the end is near, he knows that he is going. Jerry Rushing did. Ultimately he passed out and did not wake up again until he was on the operating table. He felt the doctor reach deep within his abdomen and pull out chunks of chicken manure mixed with chunks of glass. The doctor reached over and threw the stuff into a metal trash receptacle.

"Am I bad, doctor?" Jerry asked.

"Sure, you're very bad." And then he passed out again.

Jerry Elijah Rushing was one of the fortunate ones. God's hand was on Jerry, and He was not finished with him yet.

Months after the accident, Jerry was in town and happened to pass the Chevrolet lot where his car sat. The wrecker had pulled it to the Chevy dealer and left it in the side yard. Jerry walked up to that car and was surprised that he was standing outside of it alive. It was completely totaled with blood all over the place. Blood, mixed with chicken feathers and manure, and glass covered the entire interior. About the time he was looking at the car a salesman came up. "Young man, can I interest you in one of our better Chevrolets? This here's a bad one. You know this boy got his head cut off... yep, right off of his shoulders."

Jerry just shook his head and replied, "No kidding." Then he walked off, wondering about that close call. Later he shared that the Lord was really looking after him. Without God's protection he would have lost his head in that accident, just like the salesman said. God spared his life and let him life.

God's grace is all around us.

The Bible tells us that God loved us while we were yet sinners and poured His grace upon us in the form of His Son, Jesus Christ. Jesus came that we might be saved through Him. He loved us that much. The Bible says in Ephesians that it is grace that has actually saved us:

> For by grace are ye saved through faith; and that not of yourselves:
> it is the gift of God: Not of works, lest any man should boast.
> —EPHESIANS 2:8–9

Jerry Rushing was a man that experienced God's grace upon his life. He could have easily been killed during the fight at the Pig Pen. He could have been decapitated in that horrible car wreck that tore off the top of his car. But God's grace did shine down upon him and save him from such a terrible death. At that time Jerry Rushing would have gone to hell. Remember his comment in the midst of the terrible chicken truck accident.

"I think I'm going…"

Thank God that Jerry did not "go" that day. But he thought he was going that day. If he had, he would have gone directly to hell, without passing Go. He did not know Jesus as his Savior, and he would not have gone to heaven.

His brother, Johnny, was not as fortunate. He and Snake sometimes clashed with one another, but in a scrap, they fought side by side to the end. But his brother died a terrible death in a car accident that claimed his life early. We do not know where Johnny went or where he is spending eternity. He may have not accepted Jesus in time, but the grace of God was always there for the taking if he ever asked.

So, what about you? Have you accepted Jesus as your Savior? Do you know where you are going? Jerry Rushing did not know back then, but praise God, he does now.

Have you experienced God's grace in your life? Do you have any bitterness or hatred that boils up within you like Jerry Rushing did? All of us have experienced some of this, though few of us go through anything quite as severe and dangerous as Jerry did.

If you have bitterness in your heart, and have hate for those around you, remember that God loves you and has a plan for your life regardless of where you are now.

Why not embrace His love and grace and accept Him today? He will change your life. And when your end comes, you will know where you are going! Say yes to Jesus. Snake eventually did!

CHAPTER 8

The Whiskey Runner's Other Passions

THE OUTDOORSMAN

"**M**AMA, MAMA," THE little skinny boy yelled as he slammed the front screen door behind him, "I've got three more. Look Mama, three more. Am I a real live Daniel Boone or not?"

His mama stood there with a big grin on her face. The little boy liked to see her smile. It sure beat those days when she cried all day about his drunken daddy.

"Well, looky there. Those are the fattest lookin' squirrels I've seen for years. It must be a rough winter a comin' since they've fattened up on those acorns already. Where'd ya get those?"

"Well, I was with Daddy at that still that Uncle Dooley and him just built back behind Uncle Dooley's. It is there at the creek across the hill where those oak trees are so big. Daddy and Uncle Dooley were real busy mixing all that sugar and stuff, and they asked me to stay busy. So, I just grabbed one of those old shotguns that they keep there and headed out to the woods. Aren't they just big and juicy?"

Little Snake spent most of every day out in the woods. Family life was rough on the little boy. His daddy was especially harsh on the little boy, and Snake suffered many cruel beatings from the father who showed so little love, if any at all.

His mama answered him, "Well, Snake, they are big, and I can only hope that they're juicy."

"Mama, do we have enough for some of your squirrel stew with your special gravy? Remember, you've got a couple in the icebox from yesterday. They were bigguns', too." Snake liked fried squirrel, but he really loved his mama's squirrel gravy. Snake was very proud to bring food in for the family even though he was just a little guy.

"Sure, Jerry. You run along and I'll fix it for us all tonight. Tell Johnny to bring me in some of those, potatoes and I'll put 'em in the stew."

So where did this little skinny boy find his sanctuary from such a rough family life? Where did he go to find inner rest from the harsh world of the Rushing clan?

His refuge from the cussing, screaming, and fighting was the woods. His safe haven was out in the green forests of the land around him in Union County.

The little boy grew up loving the woods and the creatures that lived in the woods. At night he loved to listen to the sounds of the crickets, tree frogs, and owls as their hoots penetrated the cool night air. The darkness brought out the calls of the whippoorwills, too. Snake listened carefully to the night sounds and was especially fond of the whippoorwills and their call. He worked on his unique whippoorwill call until he had nearly mastered it as a young boy of five or six. He could sit under a tree and answer back. He smiled a big smile and was proud of his accomplishments when the first whippoorwill answered him back.

He also enjoyed walking in the woods at night and hooting like an old hoot owl. Sometimes an owl answered, but more often he recognized the call of some tom turkey that had roosted in a nearby tree for the night that answered the owl call. Later he used that technique to find roosted turkeys in order to hunt them the following day. He learned that the turkeys that roosted high in a treetop for safety often returned the call of an owl. When he was older, he made an owl call in the woods until a roosting turkey returned that call. Then in the morning, he grabbed his shotgun and set up at the base of some big tree about one hundred yards or so from the turkey. At daybreak, the turkey flew down from the tree and begin to feed. Snake then made hen calls to get the turkey he located the night before to come in close to him, looking for the hen. If the tom came close enough, Snake raised his twelve-gauge shotgun, and the result would be a big turkey for dinner that evening. The woods around Monroe were full of turkey, and Snake took his share home. Wild turkey with giblets, stuffing, and gravy was hard to beat even if it wasn't Thanksgiving.

Snake thrived in the woods. He loved the pungent smell of the rotten bark and leaves as they decayed into the dark rich topsoil of the forest. He loved the sweet fall smell of the acorn crop as the giant oaks began dropping their seeds onto the moist floor below. He especially liked the smell of the woods right after a rain. He often claimed that the crispness of the clean night air could cleanse the soul of any troubled man. In fact all of Snake's senses came alive in the woods like no other place. He treasured the mornings when the sun broke through the darkness, creating a bright red-orange sky that looked as if the entire world beyond the horizon was on fire.

Slowly before daybreak, the owl stopped screeching and the whippoorwill stopped its cry. The night symphonies from the crickets and katydids went quiet, and for just a moment, all was still. The stillness of that time just between the night and the morning always amazed Snake from the time he was a little boy to the time he grew to be an older man. It was deathly quiet. There was tranquility in the woods as all of mother earth stood at a standstill, motionless and at rest, waiting for the command to start the day. And Snake could tell you who of all of the forest's creatures spoke first as if giving the command. It was the simple cardinal.

Snake, as just a young boy, may not have known that the cardinal was the state bird of North Carolina as well as Virginia, West Virginia, Illinois, Indiana, Ohio, and Kentucky. But he could tell you that the male cardinal is identified by its high crest, black throat, and red plumage. The females were olive-green in color, with dull reddish wings and a brownish-pink crest. He could tell you the bright red bird was one of the first birds of the forest to call for the morning. Its quick sharp chirps followed by three or four low to high whistles broke the silence of the forest's tranquility, awakening and ushering in the morning sounds of many other birds.

He was a lover of the outdoors from the time he could walk and catch crawdads in the creek hiding under the rocks from the noon sun. Running and playing in the woods when he was young cultivated a love and appreciation for the outdoors that stayed with Jerry Rushing all of his life. He loved walking down a creek bank watching the beavers swim and slide into the water down some beaver-made mudslide. There was really only one thing Snake loved better than just walking in the woods, and that was hunting in those same woods.

Hunting was a way of life for Union County boys. Whether it was part of their family and culture or whether it was because they had nothing else to do, one may never know. But it was as much of their daily life as eating breakfast or going to bed. It actually went hand-in-hand with the moonshine lifestyle that many were entrenched within. They took the trips to their family still as just youngsters and then assisted their father, uncle, or grandpa with the moonshine operation. Then when things were slow, they entered deep into the woods and hunted for dinner.

Snake often laughed when asked how long he had been hunting or shooting. With a big old grin, he often replied, "Why, I've just always been livin' with a gun in my hands. Come to think about it, I can't remember a time when I didn't have a gun or run out to the woods lookin' for a rabbit, dove, or squirrel."

Many families hunted to live, that is, hunting was a survival skill in order to provide meat for the family dinner table. Snake, though, lived to hunt. He loved to hunt squirrel, rabbit, deer, dove, turkey, duck, and geese. He thought of himself as a rugged outdoorsman that could skin a deer, run a trout line, and live off of the land. He often pictured himself as the tough Daniel Boone type mixed with the characteristics of an outlaw like Jesse James. That is really quite a combination. This combination resulted in the individuality of natural survivalist combined with the criminal distinctiveness of a modern-day outlaw. His daddy summed it up best when he referred to his son as a wild buck.

When he was younger, many of his crazy antics were to prove that he was a man, a wild man that could do anything and everything. On one cold January day, one of the local rivers was slightly frozen over with a crust of ice spanning one bank to the other. Snake and a couple of buddies, Freight Train and Bullfrog, were rabbit hunting and came upon this frozen-over river.

Bullfrog stood on the bank and fired his twelve-gauge into the ice, breaking up some of it into little pieces.

"Boy, I know of some good areas on the other side of this river, if only it were frozen thicker so we could cross over."

Snake shouldered his twelve-gauge and pumped five fast rounds from the nearby bank to the other side opening a large gap across the iced-over waterway.

"There it is, Bullfrog…there's the way over."

Bullfrog, being a bit dense, had no real idea what Snake was talking about.

"There's a way? Whatcha talking about? Ya only shot up the river, Snake, are ya crazy or something?"

"Well, of course I'm crazy," Snake replied. "Crazy enough to race the two of ya over to the other side."

Freight Train was a big, strapping boy. He always looked larger than life and was bigger than any of his friends his age. When he came through a crowd, it was like a freight train coming through, therefore the reason for his nickname.

"Snake, don't cha really be silly. There's no way over to the other side except to swim. Ya saw Bullfrog shootin' at the ice, and you shot it, too. It's much to thin to race on…well…we'd all get wet and find ourselves swimmin' the river in this freezing temperature."

It was around twenty degrees with a fast-blowing wind. There was at least three inches of snow from the day before, and it was frozen, snapping and popping as you walked over it. The temperatures made for a difficult rabbit hunt, but they had been able to shake a few out of brush piles and were able to shoot them before they could escape to the next pile or hole. But before Bullfrog or Freight Train could say another thing, they looked at Snake and were surprised at what they saw. Standing right there in the middle of a snow forest, Snake had tossed off his hat and jacket and was working on his shirt. Off went the shirt, and there he stood half-naked with the moist heat coming off of his hot chest like steam from a kettle.

"Snake," Bullfrog hollered, "what the devil ya doin', anyway? Ya want to catch a heck of cold?"

Freight Train chimed in as well, "Ya, Snake. Whatcha doin' standing there half naked and all?"

Snake just laughed his crazy laugh and sat down upon the frozen snow and began working on his boots. He tossed them aside and pulled off his wool socks, carefully placing them inside his boots. As an outdoorsman, he knew the importance of keeping your feet warm and dry.

"Let's go, boys," Snake hollered back as he unzipped his pants and took them off. He tossed them upon a nearby tree branch and pulled down his undershorts and tossed them onto another branch. He looked real silly standing there in the cold snow with the heat radiating from his body with steam like a sauna. He was rubbing his arms and jumping up and down like a naked crazy man.

"Like I said boys, if ya are real men, you'll race old Snake here to the other side. Last one over is a you-know-what."

And with that dare, Snake ran right down the bank into the cold river and dove head first into the icy water. He swam ten yards or so under water as his two buddies stood on the bank fully clothed and shaking their heads. "Snake...you're crazy! You've finally lost it all! Are ya nuts or what—you'll die a death of colds," they yelled.

Snake finally surfaced and swam straight to the other side. Without hesitation, he jumped out of the water onto the bank yelling, "I won, I won. Boy, you guys are really a couple of girls or what? What about the race?"

Crazy Snake looked like a man that had lost his mind. There he stood stark naked except for a bit of river grass hanging here or there. He was jumping up and down trying to keep from literally freezing. And then without warning, he jumped back into the frigid water and swam as back across the river as he had crossed it the first time.

He ran again up the bank and grabbed friends, partly to tease them for not following suit on his swim and partly to dry off his cold, wet, naked body. He quickly dressed, pulling his clothes back on without giving out any impression of the chill that was going through his body. A typical man would never have made it across those chilly waters, let alone back again without suffering from hypothermia. But Snake was not the typical man. He was a wild buck that never grew too old to sow some wild oats and then a few more. He was always pulling such shenanigans. It was as if he was proving his manhood and his "wildness and unruliness" to those that participated, watched, or ultimately listened to the recounting of his crazy and bizarre adventures.

Snake really liked hunting geese during the cold Carolina winters. On several instances, he was hunting geese, and somewhere in the midst of the hunt, he fired at a flock, only to knock two or three right out of the air. Sometimes they fell right out of the sky into the icy cold river. It might be five degrees outside, but Snake stripped down naked and jumped in the river to get the geese, another of his outlandish antics.

Walking down the street in downtown Monroe, his friends often joked with Snake, "Hey, Snake, what kind of retriever do you take with you when you hunt for geese?" Then they laughed. Sometimes he answered them, going right along with their joke, "He's a great bird dog. He's called a 'Stark Naked Heck-of-a-Man.' Do ya want to see 'em?"

"No...no," his buddies screamed, and they laughed all the way down the street. They knew he was talking about himself, and they knew better than to tease him too much about it. They had heard of that bird dog and did not want to see it in the town square because the sheriff just might haul it in. In fact, Snake and his buddies were known within the county to hunt whenever the notion hit them regardless of the season. The game warden heard about them hunting outside of the season, and try as he might, he chased them all over the county but never did catch old Snake with a goose in his hand.

Snake was not only one of Carolina's fastest bootleggers but was also one of the South's greatest outdoorsman, excelling in both hunting and trapping. On more than one occasion, Snake found himself in the frigid waters of a nearby stream, creek, or brook. This was due to his trapping adventures. Trapping, in effect, is the capture of animals by means of a physical trap that may be designed to kill, injure, or preserve the captured animal. In the early days of fur traders, beaver pelts and other skins and furs of wild animals became the medium of barter and financial exchange between the mountain trapper and the trader. Since those early days, there has always been an almost irresistible lure to follow the ancient sport of trapping as a profession. Jerry E. Rushing followed that enticement and ultimately earned quite a living for years by his trapping skills. His skills as a professional trapper of most any animal of the wild kingdom won him quite a reputation.

In his book *Trapping as a Profession*, author Dick Wood says the following:

> Having the spirit for venture, it is necessary that the trapper should have an insatiable longing for the out-of-doors, the silent places. The person who cannot stand solitude will not make the best trapper. The fellow who doesn't take to the woods as a duck to water, who would not prefer to be in the woods or along a stream, in any kind of weather, to mingling in human society, had better stick close to his fellow men. It is not necessary that a trapper become a recluse, but he should prefer to be out of doors to any other place, and he should have open eyes and ears for everything that goes on in the open. The person who cannot enjoy nature is not cut out for a professional trapper.

Such is the definition of Jerry E. Rushing.

Embedded within his soul was an insatiable longing for the outdoors. He preferred the solitude of a cold winter stream located in the back woods hidden like a moonshine still.

Perhaps the personality of the moonshiner and the trapper are so similar that it should not surprise us that Jerry Rushing was great at both ventures. When he was not making sugar whiskey in some clandestine moonshine operation, he was running the unlawful stuff in the spring, summer, and fall. But when the cold winter days moved in with the snow, sleet, and ice, running moonshine was difficult on slippery roads. And the weather made it difficult to run a still, so Jerry took to the woods and ran trap lines all winter long. Trapping really went along with moonshining, as in both cases you somewhat lived in the woods, coming in from time to time to share your spoils or to see your family.

Jerry treasured his days in the woods running a still, and he especially loved running from the law. He liked the modern-day outlaw image and sensation that came over him when the red lights were flashing behind him and the siren blaring his way. Though he ran over two million gallons of the illegal white lightning, he never got caught while running in one of his souped-up cars. But hunting and trapping were his second love. He worked from early in the morning until late at night running the trap lines along the creeks in the deep woods. As he set the traps under water, occasionally he slipped on a slippery bank and ended up in the freezing water. In fact, he fell into the frigid water at least four or five times a winter. But he stayed in the outdoors, coming in only to catch a few hours of sleep before heading out again.

Though Snake ran on a few hours of sleep a night and stayed either damp or wet throughout the winter, he never caught a cold. It was as if he was immune to any virus that tried to attack him. Others simply said that he was too mean for any cold. It was not until after the winter when he stayed inside more hours of the day that he caught a bad case of the flu. But when he worked the cold and icy creeks trapping, he never even had the sniffles.

Jerry Rushing never had a son to pass along his love for the outdoors, but he had a little girl that was the love of his life. Darlene Rushing was born on February 20, 1960. Jerry loved to take her wherever he went, and she took to the woods like a fish to water. When she was only four, Jerry asked her if she wanted to accompany him on some wild trapping adventure.

"Darlene. Darlene, where are ya, girl?" Jerry yelled throughout the house. He was preparing for another day in the woods, and the sun was bright on this particular day. That meant that although the temperature was around forty degrees, the sun helped brighten up the winter day and warm the January air.

"Here I am, Daddy. Whatcha want?" The little girl was still wiping the night's sand from her little eyes. "Whatcha doin' today, Daddy?"

"Well, I'm gonna fire up that old Jeep and head to the creek to check my traps. If ya want to go, I've got a present for ya...whatcha say?"

The little girls eyes got real big, "A present...a real present? What is it? Can I have it now? Does it walk or move around? What is it? Can ya tell me...pleeeese?" The little girl was firing up more questions than her daddy could answer, so he just smiled.

"Getcher self dressed real fast, and I'll meet ya outside." Jerry had caught a small little muskrat. It could not have been too old. He had been feeding it out in the barn, and it had become accustomed to his handling. Darlene had a real love and affection for all of the wood's creatures. She loved to watch as her daddy ran the trap lines. She sat there in his old Jeep and clapped her hands, hollering, "Way to go, Daddy...way to go," whenever he pulled out a beaver or muskrat from the creek.

She came running outside with a giant smile of expectation on her face. "Where is it, Daddy? Is it wrapped? Can I have it now?"

"Let's get in the Jeep and I'll give it to ya." And the two partners went out together. He helped her into the Jeep, wedging her between the seats and packing her in a big, fluffy quilt to stay warm. Jerry told her to stay put as he went out to the barn and grabbed the little furry muskrat. He had fashioned a small collar around its neck and had it on a small rope.

"Close yer eyes and hold out yer hands." The little girl was almost too excited to even close her eyes. When Jerry placed it in her hands, little Darlene could hardly believe her eyes. "A tiny little bear...such a cute little brown bear."

Jerry laughed as he jumped into the Jeep's seat. "It's not a little bear, Darlene. It's a little baby muskrat.

"Well, Daddy, it's so cute it looks like a little bear...so...I'll just name it Bear."

"Great idea," Jerry responded, and the two headed out to the woods to work the traps together. As Jerry ran the traps, little Darlene played with and loved Bear as if it was a little baby or a tiny kitten. It warmed Jerry inside to see her love little Bear so.

They worked all day together, coming in at night just to stop long enough to skin out the furs and get ready for the next morning. The sun set for the day, and upon its return the next morning Jerry, Darlene, and, of course, Bear headed out for another day of adventure. Those were financially productive days and were some of the most memorable days he had with his little girl.

Jerry could set a trap in the woods to catch just about anything. He trapped red foxes, gray foxes, muskrats, beavers, and raccoons, along with just about anything else on four legs. Sometimes it was legal, and sometimes, like the moonshining and bootlegging, he flirted on the edge of legal into the territory of illegal trapping. It always seemed like the law and Jerry were at odds. It was as if he started making a lot of money trapping, and then the game commission passed a law to put the trapper out of business. One day Jerry checked some of his traps and was returning to his car with four big red foxes. He saw the game warden's car in the distance and immediately tossed the foxes into the trunk of the car as the game warden pulled up next to him.

"Good day, Mr. Rushing," he greeted him, as if part of his job was to maintain a sense of formality to the local trappers. "Ya know that ya cannot trap foxes now."

"Oh, yes, I can," Jerry said directly, never one to mince words. "I've got some brand-new traps, and they are good ones."

"Well, Mr. Rushing, like I was saying, it's illegal to trap foxes now, and I'll probably have to write you up and maybe take you in. You're breaking the law, and I'm here to enforce it."

"Well, Jim . . ." Snake replied, getting a bit irritated with the warden, "let me tell ya something, and we can settle this right up. See that field over there?"

"Yep!"

"Well, do you see where that little road goes through the woods?"

The warden was looking and replied, "Sure . . . so what?"

"Well, I've got a fox trap sitting right there right now."

Snake continued, "So see where the woods come out here at that little peak? I've got a fox trap right there, and there is one in the weeds next to this road up about one hundred yards or so."

The game warden adjusted his pistol and belt and pulled at his government-issue pants, trying to hike them up on his big old donut-eating belly. "Well, Mr. Rushing, I will be here at eight o'clock sharp tomorrow morning to look at those there traps. If you have a fox, I'm gonna arrest ya and take all your traps and take you in."

Snake just grinned that same ornery grin and looked at the warden, and then back to his traps as if thinking about what the warden just said. He could have just picked up his traps and headed home, but he did not have a bent for avoiding trouble. In fact, it was just the opposite. He looked for trouble and embraced any challenge. So in the spirit of this legal confrontation and the warden's threat, Snake offered his proposition to the warden.

"I agree, Jim. In fact, if you want to catch me, you be here at 8:00 a.m. sharp. If there is one thing I know, it's foxes, and tomorrow morning around eight, I'll have me five. And I want to personally tell you something. If you're here at eight and even try to get in my way, I'll just blow your brains right out the back'a your head and right out of this county...OK?"

The warden blinked and then blinked again.

"In fact," Snake continued, "I'll have those traps set here the entire season, and if you come down here again, I'll kill you at eight o'clock sharp. How's that for a deal?"

The game warden went back to his truck, tossed his hat onto the passenger seat, and drove off. Snake kept his word and was at his traps the next morning at 8:00 a.m. sharp. He pulled out another three foxes out of the traps. The game warden was nowhere to be found. In fact, Snake trapped that entire set of woods all season and never saw Jim again. Many a fox came out of those woods and field that winter, and the game warden was nowhere to be found. Old Jim must have been busy. Or perhaps he just did not want to share his brains with the adjacent county.

A Champion of the Competitive Bow

Snake loved hunting and could shoot a shotgun, rifle, and pistol better than anyone else in all of Union County. But he was also a champion with a bow. There was something special about walking through the woods and stalking a rabbit, coon, or a large whitetail deer holding nothing but a recurve bow and arrows in your quiver. And there was something about hunting with a bow and arrow that took him back to the roots of an earlier existence in the Appalachian Mountains.

Several generations back, the Cherokee had hunted the western parts of North Carolina and Tennessee utilizing a bow and small arrows fitted with flint arrowheads. They were very successful in their harvesting of game, even with such primitive methods. When he was young, Jerry loved to pretend that he was a little Cherokee boy as he quietly walked through the woods with his bow in hand.

"Mama, Mama," Jerry yelled as he ran into the house excited. "Look what I got here . . . it's one of the biggest rabbits I've ever seen."

"Wow, and I guess you are going to tell me you shot that with your bow and arrow?" his mama replied.

"Sure, Mama. Just like an Indian. You should have seen me. I sneaked up on that old rabbit, hid behind a big oak tree, and about the time he put his head down to chew on some clover, I let him have it. Awesome, huh?"

"Absolutely awesome, little buddy. Why don't you go outside and skin it, and I'll prepare some fried rabbit with brown gravy for dinner tonight."

Little Jerry not only grew up in the woods assisting his various family members with their moonshine operation, but he also grew up with a bow in hand. It became necessary in the future as his trips to the federal penitentiary and his probation made it illegal for him to possess a firearm. Therefore, the use of the bow and arrow either in the woods or for protection was his major source for hunting and for defense . . . other than his brute force of course.

Jerry opened up a bow shop where he sold and outfitted bows, arrows, and other archery accessories. On March 14, 1973, the North Carolina Bow Hunters Association was first incorporated as a nonprofit organization in Monroe, North Carolina. Jerry Rushing was one of the original directors of the association and is still listed on the incorporation charter as one of the first "incorporators."

His wife, Dean Rushing, began running the bow shop, and they ultimately opened the Sherwood Forest Bow Club, which gave both bow shooters and hunters the opportunity to shoot at an outdoor open range. It was at that time during their life that Jerry's wife, Dean, found one of her true loves, aside from Jerry himself. As she worked in the bow shop and ultimately ran the Sherwood Forest Bow Club, she became as good as Jerry with a bow and arrow. She seemed to have a natural talent for intuitive shooting. She used no sights or beads, but shot from the "feeling." It was not unusual for Jerry to enter local, state, or national bow competitions to compete with other bow shooters throughout the area. But ultimately, it was his wonderful wife, Dean, that excelled in bow shooting.

In fact, Jerry admitted that his wife ultimately became much better than him with a bow and arrow. She assisted young hunters and shooters with their shooting style when they came into the bow shop. She became well known throughout North Carolina as one of the greatest female bow shooters in history. Ultimately she won more than four hundred local, state, and national competitions.

At one time, Fred Bear of Fred Bear Archery fame tried to coerce her to leave Monroe and travel as a representative of the Bear Bow Corporation. Though it was an honor to have received such a request, it would have been very difficult to pull herself away from her husband and daughter, Darlene.

Even today, both Jerry and Dean are known to have picked up a bow from time to time and placed an arrow in the bull's-eye of any particular target. In fact, at the twenty-fifth anniversary of *The Dukes of Hazard* convention, which was held at the Bristol (Tennessee) Motor Speedway, there were several in attendance who asked Dean Rushing to illustrate her handling of a bow and arrow. After much coercing, she surprised hundreds of the attendees by picking up a bow, fitting it with an arrow, and eyeing one of the downrange targets. With the grace of a beautiful southern belle, she released the arrow, and it found its way to the very center of the bull's-eye beyond. Cheers went up from the crowd as she casually smiled, and placed the bow back into its holder, refusing to continue her archery exhibition.

The love of archery still permeates the very soul of both Jerry and Dean Rushing, though they shoot and hunt less now with their bow than they did when they were younger.

A Daredevil at the Racetrack

Snake loved hunting and could shoot a shotgun, rifle, and pistol better that anyone else in all of Union County. And his skills with a bow are nearly legendary. However, when he was not running whiskey, he was no different than the rest of his bootlegging friends. He was either bragging about his fast souped-up cars, which he used for bootlegging, or he was racing them to prove his point. Ever since the Whiskey Rebellion in 1794, men of the South have argued their case for making homemade whiskey and selling it without any government intervention.

It was not really a case of right or wrong. Most figured that if the government could sell whiskey, why couldn't they? Prohibition gave folks the reason to make moonshine so they would have their liquor to drink. And bootlegging gave them a way to earn a living by selling it and transporting it as if they were legal distributors. Then the Great Depression hit, and many of the poor farmers and mill workers suffered with little or no money just to put food on the table, and that was an amazing motivator to attempt moonshining and bootlegging as a way of life. It was the first opportunity in years to make money and to make lots of it fast.

Their corn was more valuable in the liquid state and easier to transport than the typical truckload or bushels of it. The business of bootlegging really was a family business as the older men oversaw the operation and the younger men provided the brawn for the more physical labor. It became a means of survival, especially in western North Carolina. The bootlegging of corn liquor could provide a comfortable income for a farmer's family if he could avoid problems with the law.

Southern Appalachia has been described as "a pocket of courage." During the Korean War, there were only three Medals of Honor from the New York area among millions of people, whereby there were three Medals of Honor in rural Wilkes County, North Carolina alone. The Scottish-Irish descendants in Appalachia were a very tough people and were survivalists with the guts and courage to buck the system. And it was within this bucking of the system that led to bootlegging, and it was the fast cars of bootlegging that led to stock car racing.

Most racing historians agree that the birth of NASCAR and the early racing of stock cars eventually can be traced to southern Appalachia and the racing of early bootlegging cars. The South has always been known for their ability to spin tales and pass on stories daily from one generation to the next.

Once bootleggers began telling their stories of getaways, shootings, and close calls with the law, it naturally led to some healthy competition among their ranks. Who had the closer call, and whose car was really the fastest? This competitive spirit led to a need for a proving ground to determine just who had the fastest bootlegging car. Bootleggers took great pride in both their hot cars and their ability to drive them fast and hard. They needed very fast delivery cars to make their getaways from the federal revenuers, and they made many modifications to achieve this means.

A direct influence of the modifications to bootlegging cars can be seen in some of the design of stock cars even today. Consider the fact that early bootleggers removed the rear seat and the passenger seat in order to make maximum room for the liquor. They then loaded the whiskey in cases all the way up to the windows. Today the stock cars still have no passenger seat and no rear seat. The bootleggers even stacked the cases right up to the right side of the driver to create a brace to hold the driver in the seat. This was before the installation of seatbelts. Then, due to the weight of the whiskey, the mechanics of these moonrunners installed extra-heavy-duty suspensions in order for the cars to balance their load while sticking to the road on sharp turns at high speeds. Today, successful NASCAR race car owners install expensive suspension systems to allow their drivers to maneuver the sharp turns at their high speeds.

The early days of running 'shine would require a completely different gearing system to allow quick acceleration in order to get a jump on escaping the law. It was not uncommon for a bootlegger's car to achieve speeds up to 95 miles per hour while still in first gear and then be able to accelerate up to 115 miles per hour still in second gear. And finally, the doors today are fixed similar to the welding of the doors during the moonshine heydays. A welding of the driver's door made certain he would not fall out of the car on high-speed curves when the complete body would be stressed, causing the driver's door occasionally to pop open.

Fast cars in the South were a symbol of freedom, a way in which the lower working classes could beat the old social order. The races got bigger and bigger, and the boys began to bet on who had the fastest cars, which meant some of the racers could leave an informal race with extra money in their pockets. Bootlegging was a weekday job, and weekends were saved for arguing about who had the fastest car. Some of the first races were held on Sunday afternoons. The bootleggers showed up at the races with the same cars that they had run whiskey in all week.

Bootlegging's biggest boom was between the 1930s and the 1950s. As the moonshine industry began to slow down, the sport of racing exploded upon the scene. By the early 1950s, crowds were begging to attend the races, and one race organizer had the idea of fencing the events and charging admission for the tickets. It was into this lifestyle first of moonrunning and then racing—that Jerry Rushing was born in 1936. He was running whiskey before 1950, and began racing his fast whiskey-running cars during the beginning heydays of the racing era. Sometimes Snake had his bootlegging car full of whiskey and still went to the tracks to race.

"Hey, Snake...whatcha doin' here tonight?" one of his friends yelled as he saw Snake pull up in one of his fast getaway cars. "Oh my gosh, what the heck you doin' with whiskey here at the track, Snake? Why, if those agents come snooping around, you're sure to get busted," he whispered with a strain in his voice.

"Grab a couple of boys and help me unload this stuff fast. We'll put it over there in the corner and cover it up with tires. I've got a run to make later tonight, but I wanna win a race first, and then I'll be on my way."

Before his buddy could complain, Snake handed him a quart jar of some of the Rushing's stuff. He put it up to his lips and sucked down a belly full of that sweet mountain dew. "Good stuff, Snake...y'all make the best...so, where do ya want that stuff?" It took but a quart of 'shine to buy some help and assistance from his buddies at the track.

Snake hid the liquor in some tires, ran the race, pocketed the winner's money, and then ran his whiskey two counties over. This was typical of a Saturday night in Union County at the racetrack. Nearly every car entered in the race was a bootlegger's car that had been souped-up for running white lightning, and they ran just as fast and hard on the track as they did during the week from the law. Both were fun, both were extremely dangerous, and both paid good money.

Snake begin driving before he was twelve years old. By the time he was thirteen years old, he was fast and mean and running whiskey, though it was small stuff for his daddy. He took to the road, and the faster the better. His first race was when he was fifteen years old. He loved stock car racing. Just the speed alone got in his blood. Add to it the smell of the gasoline, the danger of the sharp curves, the odor of burning rubber, and the element of competition, and you had a sport that enticed any youngster.

Snake was as rowdy in a stock car at the races as he was behind the wheel during a whiskey chase. He drove like a maniac. Drivers called him crazy. If he took a notion to wreck a fellow driver that looked at him funny, that fellow had no chance of survival.

One of the busines bootleggers in Union County, Snake likes to brag about one of his busiest months. He had run thousands of gallons of whiskey all over western North Carolina while outrunning federal and local agents without ever being caught. In that one month, the law chased him thirteen times, an average of a little more than three chases per week.

During the same month he won five races and pocketed more money than most of the residents of Union County make in a year. He was living high on the hog, as he used to say. He had the respect, or in some cases, the fear of most of Union County. He loved to pull into the bars and watch the guys and gals run to the door as he raced his high-compression engine while parking in the lot. Even the town drunks took a certain pride in knowing that Snake was part of their southern heritage. And he was proud as well.

Snake spent most of his time during the good weather months either running whiskey or racing his fast cars. He enjoyed them both. While loading whiskey for a run, he'd be bragging about the last race.

And at the next race, he had a crowd of buddies spellbound as he spun his famous Rushing tales about his last whiskey run. He especially loved telling the boys at the track about the twenty-two law officers that were assigned to him during one month. He loved the attention. During that month, he loaded up his whiskey and left at night for the delivery. As he passed the local store, the fellows looked out the window and said, "There he goes again!" He was a legend and really ate it up.

One month a total of twenty-two law officers staked him out and followed him every night for thirty days. On many occasions, Snake had sugar to deliver to the still but obviously could not go to its location with lawmen on his tail. Some nights he drove around for two or three hours before he lost them, and then he made his sugar delivery. They never caught him and never followed him to the still. Finally they gave up their unsuccessful sting operation because they were wasting too much manpower and money just chasing him around the county. It was a huge success for Snake and an embarrassing state of affairs for the federal agents.

Right after that sting operation, agents finally busted one of Snake's other still operations and destroyed it. Whether they followed one of his boys back into the woods or whether someone snitched, he never found out. On that particular Saturday night, Snake was racing at the track, and he experienced his own catastrophe. He had raced for years enjoying the excitement of the stock car competitions and had experienced his share of wrecks, but he had never been hospitalized until this one.

He was racing one of his faster cars with a HEMI engine when he lost control and did what they call a "double-mother." Most of those in the stands that saw the accident thought that he had been killed. It had been a rough race all night with a lot of bumping and hitting. He had two large rubber donuts that had been burned on both sides of his car when he took a fast corner and was bumped again in the rear. His car swerved to the right, and Snake corrected to the left, only to lose control. He ran into the fence and flipped several times until he came to rest right in the middle of the spectator's parking lot.

His buddies ran out to the car, which was totaled. All the windows were busted out, and the front left tire and wheel assembly had broken off the frame and had come to rest on top of an old Chevy. The crowd was screaming, and many ran out into the parking lot for a closer look. Snake lay unconscious in the car, cut and bruised and looking as if he had taken his last ride. There were few signs of life to those that first made their way to the car. The radiator was hanging on by a hose, and hot water and steam was shooting several feet into the night air.

The ambulance finally arrived, and the emergency crew worked hard to remove Snake from the terrible wreckage. He did not wake up from the accident until he was in the hospital. He had broken his neck and immediately underwent surgery. He was in intensive care for days before he was finally moved from the South Carolina hospital, where the crash occurred, to a North Carolina hospital that was closer to his home. When he arrived at the North Carolina hospital, he was shocked to see one of his moonshining buddies, Spot, in the bed next to his. He told Snake of the federal agent's bust on the night of his accident. The agents had found the still and used dynamite to destroy it completely. The federal agents then searched home after home and each barn and outhouse, looking for the cache of illegal whiskey. Though they never found it, they did arrest Spot.

Spot had escaped from the still when the federal agents showed up, but later in the night they caught up with him and searched his car, finding a pint of illegal whiskey that he had from a previous race night. They confiscated his car and booked him for the still. Strangely enough, that had given him a migraine headache, which had landed him in the hospital and in the very room of his moonshining buddy Snake.

Eventually, Snake healed from that terrible racing accident, bought another car, and was running whiskey again as fast as ever. Though he may have had some ideas of praying when he woke up in the hospital and thought he was dying, the saying was proven true that "vows made in storms are seldom kept in calm waters." He was soon back as mean and as nasty as ever, terrifying every lawman that dared to chase him. It would be a long time before Snake's life changed for the better.

SNAKE GOES HOLLYWOOD

Back in the 1950s, when the moonshine and the bootleg business was booming and Snake was running the illegal stuff each night, no one would have believed that eventually this rough backwoods character would end up in some of Hollywood's most interesting movies. But he was never one to be underestimated, and Union County could not hold him back. So just how did backwoods Carolina moonshinner and bootlegger ultimately become a Hollywood star? Well, it first started with his country songwriting ability. Jerry had always loved music, and he loved to write songs relating to the backwoods moonshinning and bootlegging that he knew best.

After writing several songs, he happened to hit upon one that was autobiographical about big rigs running moonshine down the line. It was an interesting song, as it was a ballad of sorts while at the same time having an interesting tune. He was prompted by many friends to take the moonshining song to an agent. The agent was so impressed that he asked Jerry to carry a tape recorder and record as many of his past moonshining experiences as possible. From hundreds of such tapes came the Hollywood motion picture *Moonrunners*, which was actually the story of Jerry Rushing's life. It was produced and directed by Guy Waldron, who collaborated with Bob Clark.

According to Jerry, "Bob Clark told me that they were working on a movie script and wanted me to write down all of my experiences that I had had both as a moonshinner and bootlegger. I had been in prison several times and had been in multiple wrecks running moonshine, but I had never been caught. I had also raced in a number of early stock races, and decided that this might be fun working with the movies. I did not necessary want to talk specifically to an agent, so I talked into a tape recorder instead and collaborated with him on the movie *Moonrunners*."

The opening credits of the film *Moonrunners* state the following:

> Although the characters here are fictitious, some of the events are based upon incidents of the life of Jerry Rushing, who also served as a technical advisor.

The movie *Moonrunners* that was produced in 1975 was the beginning of Jerry's acting career. Jerry Rushing served as a technical advisor for the movie and stared in one of the roles as well. He also performed much of the stunt driving throughout *Moonrunners*.

Jerry enjoyed seeing his life's history on film, but he enjoyed even more the glamour and excitement of the movie business. Over the next twenty-five years, Jerry Rushing appeared in over sixty TV projects and Hollywood movies. He has preformed with the likes of Tony Curtis, Kathy Ireland, Rosanna Arquette, Teresa Russell, Jeff Daniels, Morgan Freeman, Sissy Spacek, Bo Hopkins, Dennis Quaid, Mark Hamill, Gary Busey, Jodie Foster, Robert Mitchum, and Johnny Cash. He has played a variety of roles in many movies.

The following is a partial list of movies in which Jerry Rushing has appeared:

- ★ *Moonrunners* (1975)
- ★ *Whiskey Mountain* (1977)…Sheriff
- ★ *Seabo* (1977)…Redneck, aka *Buckstone County Prison* (1977)
- ★ *Wise Blood* (1979)…John Huston
- ★ *Living Legend: The King of Rock and Roll* (1980)…Chad
- ★ *The Last Game* (1980)…Coach Nelson
- ★ *Carny* (1980)…Tucker
- ★ *The Nights the Lights Went Out in Georgia* (1981)…L.C.
- ★ *Final Exam* (1981)…Coach
- ★ *A Day of Judgment* (1981)…Sheriff
- ★ *Dogs of Hell* (1982)…Carl Dunnigan, aka Rottweiler
- ★ *Murder in Coweta County* (1983, TV)…Herring Sevill, aka *Last Blood* (1983, TV)
- ★ *Night Shadows* (1984)
- ★ *Albert's Gang* (1984)…aka *Mutant* (1984) (UK)
- ★ *The Fix* (1984)…Redneck, aka *The Agitators* (1984)
- ★ *Door to Door* (1984)…Redneck One
- ★ *The Baron and the Kid* (1984, TV)…Teaser
- ★ *Marie* (1985)…Gas station attendant, aka *Marie: A True Story* (1985)
- ★ *Track 29* (1988)…Redneck
- ★ *Black Rainbow* (1989)…Bud Orwell

✳ *Escape* (1990)...Heavy #1
✳ *Bandit*: "Beauty and the Bandit" (1994, TV)...Uncle Jim
✳ *The Journey of August King* (1995)...Gudger
✳ *A Good Baby* (2000)...Wallace

Though he also made a TV appearance as Ace Parker on *The Dukes of Hazzard*, perhaps his favorite project was playing in the TV program *Young Daniel Boone* in 1977.

Jerry spent several of his years traveling to movies sets throughout Carolina, Kentucky, and Georgia, as well as traveling back and forth to Hollywood for a variety of acting roles. His last movie was *A Good Baby*, in 2000. More than sixty television and movies appearances are fairly impressive for a backwoods moonshiner and bootlegger from Monroe County.

Jerry still has a twinkle in his eye when someone says, "Oh, I remember seeing you in *The Dukes of Hazzard*," or "Sure, Carny was one of my favorite movies. I remember you in it."

A Spiritual Void

Leo Tolstoy once said that within each man is a "God-shaped blank," and that man spends most of his time trying to fill it with all types of activities and experiences. The void is within man's soul, and it cannot be filled except by the God that designed such a void into mankind.

This void in a man's life is the inner motivation that leads all men to question their future and the reason for their own existence. Peace, joy, and contentment with our own lives can never be obtained without God. He has created this within all of creation. Though we can try to achieve happiness and try to experience a life filled with purpose and significance, it is impossible without God.

Jerry Rushing found this out for himself, though it took him many, many years. He tried to fill this void with the moonshining passed along to him by his father and grandfather. Then he moved to the fast-paced life of a bootlegger. Though this dangerous and adrenaline-producing endeavor was exciting and he loved the running, it never filled the void. Without God, no activities, no relationships, and no job or hobby can really fulfill your life. Life becomes an empty pursuit of significance with many unanswered questions.

Why am I here anyway? Is there any purpose in life? Is there any purpose in life specifically for me? If you have asked these questions, you are in a large crowd, because sooner or later every man will ask these questions.

Jerry tried to fill this void with the outdoors. Though God created all of nature, nature without God is just a collection of trees, birds, and wild animals. We can enjoy them and enjoy nature, which is their home, but they are unworthy of worship. Only the Creator of those things deserves worship.

Jerry then tried to fill that void with hunting and trapping. They are exciting activities and can fill a man's life from sunrise to sunset. But in the quiet of the night or in the calm of an early morning before the cardinal awakens the forest, man will experience the void. These things can never fully fulfill a man's soul. Jerry tried with his competitive bow shooting and then with the notoriety that comes with being a movie star.

He was a modern-day gun-slinging outlaw and was feared by many.

He raced with the legends of the fifties and ran with some of the most notorious public enemies of his time.

But his heart was empty, and it continually needed more and more excitement to simply try to fill the void. The world is deceiving in that it will parade false hopes in front of you regarding the way to happiness, peace, and contentment. But in the end, any hope of finding the true answers to life slips through a man's fingers like sand in the desert.

Men have a natural bent toward striving to find anything that can fill the void but God. That search for meaning leads men into a world of darkness. Jesus is quoted in the Bible in the Gospel of John:

> And this is the condemnation, that light is come into the world, and men loved darkness rather than light, because their deeds were evil. For every one that doeth evil hateth the light, neither cometh to the light, lest his deeds should be reproved.
>
> —JOHN 3:19–20

Jesus is explaining here that the Light (Jesus Himself) has entered into the world. He came some two thousand years ago because He loved you and me and also evil and wicked men like Jerry Rushing. But though Jesus came into the world to love us and save us from our sins, men naturally loved the darkness. When men look to other worldly solutions for the void in their life, it will always ultimately lead them toward deeds of evil. Jerry Rushing loved the darkness and hated the light. He was filled with hate and rage that often exploded on anyone that got in his way.

How have you tried to fill that "God-shaped void"? Have you tried to fill it with excitement as Jerry Rushing did? Have you tried to fill that void within you with sinful activities that only bring pleasure for a season? Trust me. The devil will toss every idea your way to try to fill that emptiness.

Do you feel empty today?

In the still hours of the night when all is calm and you are lying in your bed, wide awake, do you wonder if life is even worth living?

If you are experiencing the emptiness that Jerry Rushing experienced, why wait? If you are sick and tired of being sick and tired, if you have become weary of experimenting with life's counterfeit treasures and are aware of that void within you, why not find real happiness, contentment, and fulfillment today?

Ask Jesus into your heart, and ask Him to fill your void with His love, grace, and forgiveness. For the first time in your life, you will stop running.

You may not be running whiskey as Jerry Rushing did. But believe me, you are running. He is waiting. Tired of running? Stop today. Jerry Rushing did.

CHAPTER 9

The Whiskey Runner Serves Time

COLLIDIN' WITH THE LAW

THERE IS A popular shirt worn by children today with the message imprinted on the back that says, "Does not play well with others!" Well, that pretty much summarizes old Jerry Rushing. He got along with his mama and occasionally got along with his brother, Johnny. He regarded as friends his uncle Dooley and a few of his racing and moonshine buddies. Other than that, Jerry Rushing more often than not stood alone. He was a bad-tempered and strong-willed individual who simply had his own way of doing things. He was respected by most of Union County for his ability to outrun the law and deliver whiskey. Among the poor rural folk, anyone that could buck the overly oppressive government system and make a living was more of a hero than an outlaw. Those who did not respect him feared him. A man only crossed Jerry Rushing once, and then would be lucky to tell the story. One way or the other, he stood alone with few close friends that he could trust, and he stood alone against any authoritative government figure.

Jerry did not respect, did not like, and never got along with anyone associated with law enforcement. It did not matter if they were from the local sheriff's department, some neighborhood town police officer, North Carolina's game wardens, or federal revenuer agents sniffing around the county. He disliked them all. In fact, he hated them. He mocked them, made fun of them on the streets, and outran them while carrying whiskey. He saw the law as the enemy. As just a little boy, he knew that it was the law that busted up his granddaddy's stills, exploded his daddy's moonshine operations, and tossed his friends and relatives in the local or state slammer. Life was basically a war against every legal authority figure in his life.

It was the Rushings against the federal agents as they poked their Washington noses into the South's business. Almost sounds like a return of that great and sad War between the States. There was a tremendous animosity against this federal intervention. Many of the agents themselves were dishonest and corrupt, taking money on the side. It was not unusual for some to be selling unlawful sugar, whole-saling plastic whiskey bottles, or turning their head on a whiskey run for some cash or corn liquor payoff.

Many agents just flashed their badges and told a jug seller that he was setting up a moonshine sting operation and they would load his truck up with jugs without anyone signing for them. The sale took place without any of the required information on the books. Sometimes crooked federal agents bought sugar in the same way, using their authority as federal revenuer agents. Days later they sold the jugs or sugar to moonshiners like Jerry Rushing. Many of the revenuers made more money weekly on the side from moonshiners than their typical federal paycheck.

Many of the agents made extra money selling metal state car tags. A bootlegger changed his tags often. Jerry paid federal agents ten dollars per tag. He had one agent that could deliver tags from different states nearly weekly if Jerry needed them. Some came from the sheriff's office, and many came from confiscated cars that other bootleggers or moonshiners were caught in.

One time a deputy sheriff came driving up to Jerry's house and began to chit-chat about the weather and hunting and other sundry topics. Jerry did not like any lawman, and he figured he was up to something. He finally cut to the core.

"So, I know you're not scheduled here for some pastoral visit from the local church. Cut to the quick, Mr. Deputy Man; just whatcha wasting yer time for standing here talking to me?"

"Well," the deputy started slowly, "I am here on a officially authorized appointment from the sheriff himself, though it's an 'off-the-record' type of visit, ya know."

"No, I don't know...so tell me what the heck you're talking about. If ya have something on me, just try to book me and take me in, but it's gonna take you and a dozen more stronger than you."

"No...no," the deputy replied. He didn't want to make this trip anyway, and now he was getting a bit nervous, actually facing this notorious outlaw face-to-face.

"The sheriff just wanted me to come out and talk to ya."

"About what, Deputy Man?"

"Well, about a little whiskey."

Jerry knew he would get around to the point sooner or later. "I don't know nothing about no whiskey."

The deputy continued at his own known risk, "I can make ya looks real good. Me and the sheriff can do that for ya."

Jerry was getting aggravated and irked from this conversation. He pressed his six-foot, four-inch massive body closer to the little scrawny deputy and replied, "Is that right?"

"Yep...we can make ya'all look real good...we could be real good in turning our head and telling the fed's whatever you want us to tell them."

"So...tell me..." Jerry replied, "just what does the sheriff know 'bout me? Tell me that!"

"Nothing really, I mean he hears all the stories like the rest of Union County. But really, he knows nothin'. I mean he doesn't have anything on ya'all yet. But he's lookin' real hard."

Jerry pressed up closer to the deputy as the deputy slowly inched toward his sheriff's car. "Well, you go back and tell Mr. Sheriff

SmartyPants that he's gonna have to get a helluva lot smarter than he is now for me to give him anything. Now get out of here before I whoop ya good and tie ya up like a dead deer on the top of that there sheriff's car and deliver ya myself back to your office."

It scared the officer that he jumped into his car, accidentally hitting the siren and light switch as he did. He ran out of the drive and down the street as if he was on another official sheriff run with lights flashing and siren running. Jerry had many such confrontations with lawmen that wanted to make extra money by compromising their values and playing both sides of the fence.

That just rubbed Jerry wrong. He may have been rough, tough, and ready to shoot you dead if you crossed him, and he may have run more moonshine than any other Carolina bootlegger, but he had ethics. There was a certain southern morality in his business dealings, and he ran his operation in accordance with principles, even if they were based on a backwoods mentality. He did not lie, and he delivered what he said he would deliver. And he hated federal or local agents on the take as much as he hated lying preachers.

Both Jerry and his brother had their share of scrapes even with the local sheriff's department. On one cold evening, just a week or so before Thanksgiving, Jerry received a phone call from Johnny.

"Hey Jer-bud, it's old Johnny here, your one and only favorite brother. They got me and Turkey on battery charges from this here fight early tonight and locked us up here in the slammer. Can ya come up and sign my bond? I don't want to spend the night here again."

Jerry had heard the story before, "Johnny, do you have any idea just how cold it is tonight? I don't wanna come out tonight for this."

"Please, Jerry. Turkey and I'll go stir-crazy, and he can't call his old lady 'cause if she even finds out, he's in a big hurtin'. Will not happen again…honest…I'll never call ya again."

Well, Jerry had heard a drunk's promise before and finally agreed. "I'll be up in a jiffy. Don't go anywhere and don't cause anymore trouble."

Jerry jumped in his truck and headed to the sheriff's office. Little did he know that they were prepared for the worst. Johnny had gotten off the telephone and had told them that Jerry was fighting mad and was coming up there to whip up on them all. He told them that he was coming into the office with one of his automatic machine guns and was going to tear up the place. The deputies were discussing the situation and wondering who might pull their weapon against the wild man first and shoot to kill if needed. About that time, Jerry strolled right into the front door.

"Howdy, guys...where the devil's my brother? Get him out now," Jerry barked with a scowl.

"Well...well, uh...uh...," the first deputy began to stutter, "how's ya...a...ya...a...doing, Jer?"

"OK. So where's Johnny and Turkey?" Snake barked again.

The deputies were staring at his big long coat. He looked like an outlaw with that long brown coat, and his big cowboy hat. They kept staring at the big coat suspecting the machine gun was concealed under it.

"So Jerry, what's the big coat...for?" Now both were stuttering.

"Well, for starters, it's cold outside. And I've also got a job to finish. I'm hauling liquor and I've got another fifteen cases in the car right now. I'm gonna to deliver it tonight. Don't think of stopping me if you guys want to see your mamas tonight."

The deputies on call nervously looked at each other and then asked Jerry to sign the bond.

"Ya got crops to assign to this here bond?"

Jerry stared at him and said, "Just give me the bond. I'll sign it, and nobody dies tonight. Now!"

Moonrunners had no crops. In fact, they didn't have much in their name. That kept the government from confiscating it. But though they had little assigned in their name, they often had plenty of money. As long as they made their white liquor, the money flowed.

Jerry signed both Johnny's bond and Turkey's bond, and the deputies released them from the holding cell. As Johnny passed one of the deputies, he turned and jumped in his direction, "I'd aught to just punch you into tomorrow."

Jerry had enough foolishness for one night and shoved Johnny to the door. "Start more trouble around here, and I'll slap you plum out that door."

Johnny rolled his eyes, and the three walked to the door. Jerry turned to the deputies and, with that famous Rushing smirk, said, "Good doing business with ya'll. Now stay out of trouble." And he laughed his big old laugh all the way out to the truck.

Jerry's appearances were a common sight at the local sheriff's office. On another occasion when Johnny was booked for a fight, Jerry visited the office to get Johnny out of the slammer. He was furious that he again had to visit the jailhouse. He was upset with Johnny and more upset with the crazy cops that kept picking Johnny up. Jerry busted into the offices, slamming the door back against the wall and nearly breaking the glass.

"Which one of you idiots picked him up this time? Who wants to learn a fast lesson right here tonight?"

He eyed a state trooper that he had a previous issue with and started to head toward him.

"How about you and me having a little tumble?" Jerry asked, ready for a fight.

He was pounding his fists, heading toward the trooper when the old boy started stammering, "Now, Jerry, you don't want to hit me. Hitting an officer can get you in gobs of trouble. In fact—"

Before he finished his plea, he took off like a rocket running out the front door. "Don't hit me...don't hit me," he screamed as he fled. The other deputies from the radio control room came running out and stopped dead in their tracks as they saw Jerry standing tall at the front counter. He was swearing and throwing their office papers into the air that had been neatly stacked by the night officers before they begin their nightly beat.

"Let 'em out now. I'm gonna beat someone's tail end tonight!" Jerry started toward them, and they took off running, unlocking the holding cell that had Johnny. They continued running out the back door. Jerry heard their car start up and the gravel fly as they headed out the drive.

It was quite a sight. Here stood Jerry in the middle of the sheriff's office as if he owned the place. He had the entire sheriff's department to himself. He thought about using the radio and sending out some "butt-kicking" messages, but he knew the deputies would be fired if the sheriff ever heard about this incident. He figured that they had been scared enough, so he just packed up Johnny and had a good laugh as he remembered the terrifying looks on those young deputy's faces as they headed through the door. They were afraid of him, and that made Jerry feel good.

Their punishment for locking up Johnny again was the fright they just experienced when they thought they were meeting their Maker. Jerry, being the southern gentleman that he was, never spoke a word of this to the sheriff. But he did wink and smile at the old boys whenever he'd see them. They knew what he meant, and that's all he wanted. He liked it that way.

It was only a matter of time until the two opposing forces at work within this southern county, the law, and Jerry Rushing, ultimately collided. And collide they did. Jerry was only seventeen years of age when his first conflict with the law occurred over a minor infraction. But this minor infraction resulted in a young boy serving eight long months in prison, and the seeds of hate and anger were planted.

HATRED GROWS IN PRISON...THE FIRST TRIP

Jerry Rushing was always a prankster. When he was young he was full of himself, always the joker and jester in the crowd. He loved to pull tricks and jokes on anyone he could. He was not yet evil-minded or mean-spirited. He was just the typical run-of-the-mill moonshiner's son that loved life and the outdoors and occasionally got bored. From time to time he and his buddies played pranks on the local school. When they were not hunting or fishing, they climbed the tower and tied the clapper to the bell so it would not ring. This always caused laughs throughout the school, and most attributed strange acts like this to Snake and his friends. These things might have caused some inconvenience to school administrators, but never were they done with any evil intent. It was just a fun sort of activity for young kids who were otherwise bored. Bored, that is, if they were not helping their family with making 'shine or busy running some of the fresh brew.

But on one occasion, Snake and his buddies went to the school when there was little else to do. Snake's uncle Dooley was busy building another still, and the boys had fished the previous day. There was no real agenda until they noticed a door open at the local high school, even though the school was typically closed during the summer. So with nothing else to do, Snake and his buddies, along with several other boys, entered the school to look around.

Perhaps they should have never trespassed, but they found the open door an invitation and simply walked right in. They didn't really feel that they were doing anything wrong since the son of a teacher and a son of the principal accompanied them. Snake almost felt as if they had a hall pass since they walked in with such dignitaries, two sons of the school's staff.

"I can't believe this," Snake commented. "It seems like there should be some teacher screaming at us to get to class."

"It's so quiet and eerie," another commented.

"Should we really be here?" someone else said.

"We'll just walk around and then leave...we're causing no real harm to nobody," Snake commented as they continued to walk the halls, pushing and shoving like most teenage guys do.

When they got to the cafeteria, one of the guys who was always hungry or thirsty said, "Let's check out the kitchen. I'm thirsty."

That's all it really took; it seemed like a harmless recommendation. Since it was summer, most all of the food had been cleaned out and all that was left were a few half-pints of milk and a box of saltine crackers. So the boys decided to have a little party in the kitchen and chow down on the milk and crackers. It was not the kind of snacks that they may have ordered at the town café, but there was something special and funny to these boys about dining on crackers and milk in the middle of summer in the school kitchen. So they dined and partied and had a good old time, until the law showed up at the front door.

It was 1953, and Snake was only seventeen years old. He was young and full of spunk and loved having a good time. He was the center of attention and liked it that way. He was not ready for what he faced. Apparently someone had come by the school and noticed the front door open and had called the sheriff about it. When the sheriff arrived, he called for backup when he heard the laughing and screaming of the boys reverberating within the halls. He was not sure what he would face and was expecting the worst. Little did he know that there were but a few boys eating crackers and drinking school milk. When the deputies arrived, they walked slowly through the long halls wondering what they would find. They were surprised to only find the boys drinking milk and cracking jokes. They ordered the boys to stop and stand against the hall. Then they marched them outdoors and questioned them individually. Quickly the deputies were able to determine exactly what had happened. The sheriff pulled the deputies aside and quietly gave them directions.

"Listen up, boys. What we have here is a classic breaking and entering along with the theft and use of government property," the sheriff instructed them.

"But, sir," one of the deputies reasoned, "the boys said the school was open. They didn't break in at all, but just walked in the front door. And the only thing they did was drink milk."

The sheriff had his own take on the situation and was fully ready to use this for his own benefit.

"Now listen to me, guys. You don't really know who we've got here. One boy is related to the principal, and another is related to one of the schoolteachers. We'll question them real good, but it would be real bad to arrest them. It would make the judge and the county folks upset with us. But the other boy is a Rushing. He's part of that moonshining and bootlegging family we've been having trouble with. I want to book that kid big time. It'll look good for all of us and will teach them old Rushin' boys not to mess around with us."

So that was exactly what happened. Snake knew something was fishy when he looked around in the sheriff's holding cell and didn't see any of those upper-class boys. He took the brunt of the situation, and they made an example out of him. In actuality, they sent a message to the entire Rushing clan that they would continue to clamp down on their family moonshine activities. And young Jerry Rushing would pay the price.

He went before a local Union County judge who immediately booked him in a state prison for eight months. This was an extremely harsh sentence for drinking school milk, but the judge and the sheriff's office were working together on this bust. It was one of the few times they could actually get a Rushing. So he jumped on the chance, and a young Jerry Rushing was handcuffed and taken into the harsh climate of a state prison, where he lived for mroe than eight months with some of the most hardened criminals.

So what made Jerry Rushing so hard-hearted, mean-spirited, and cold? And what turned his fun-loving, prank-pulling youthfulness into a tough and cold individual who saw himself as a criminal with a grudge to carry?

He felt that he was imprisoned for drinking a little milk. He was locked away by a sheriff looking to make a name for himself. They had yet not been successful in capturing a Rushing in the moonshine business, but now, they had one. Jerry grew to hate the local law that had put him away. There were eight long months for that seed of hate to grow. The internal grudge expanded, and the hate spread like a growing cancer within him. He came out of prison wanting to make them pay for the life they had stolen from him. He walked out the fenced-in prison focused on his major objective—to make those lawmen, and all other lawmen, live a life of terror for the injustice he had suffered. And for years to come, he did terrorize the two deputies, the sheriff, and every other lawman he encountered.

And to think that it all started with a simple half-pint of school milk and a few crackers.

HEADED TO PRISON AGAIN...UNTIL THE PREACHER STEPPED IN!

Though Jerry spent his share of time in prison, he was never caught making moonshine, and he was never caught running the illegal brew. It is said that Jerry Rushing ran over a million gallons of unlawful whiskey alone in his favorite car, *Traveler*. And though the law chased Jerry for literally thousands of miles through all of Carolina, they never came close to catching him on the road. And though he assisted in the production of thousands of gallons of whiskey with numerous stills located all throughout Carolina, he was never caught making the stuff. He was chased and shot at on many occasions, but he was never caught.

It was the early sixties, and Jerry was still heavy into moonshining and bootlegging. It was always a battle with the law. If he built a still, the law might finally catch up with him and destroy it completely. He would lay low for a season, and then go out and build another still at another location and start the production of the corn whiskey all over again. The federal revenuers heard of the location of one of Jerry's stills and totally destroyed the operation. Fortunately, Jerry was not caught during the raid. However, they did center in on one local boy that had worked with Jerry for years.

Jerry continued to run the whiskey for the next two years and had several other still operations hidden all over Union County when he was awakened in the middle of the night with men beating at his front door. One of his moonshine buddies involved in that still operation that was busted over two years ago had apparently given the feds the name of Jerry Rushing. The revenuers had a warrant of arrest against Jerry Rushing on charges of fraud, liquor tax, and manufacturing. They decided to rush his home and take him by surprise at 4:00 a.m. They knew the wild stories of Jerry Rushing and were not taking any chances. They pulled up to his home with twenty officers and five police cars. They surrounded the house before they started wildly banging on the front door. Their typical raid was based on a surprise tactic with lots of noise, whether it was raiding a still or rushing a house.

Jerry's wife, Dean, first heard the commotion and elbowed Jerry. He jumped out of the bed, running to the door while eyeing his shotgun that sat over the mantle. Should he jump for the gun, or continue his race to the front door? The beating of the door sounded as if they were actually trying to break it down. Jerry's first view through the window revealed several police cars with bright, flashing lights illuminating his front yard and the woods surrounding his house. So he left the shotgun hanging where he was and continued to the door. Upon opening the front door, the agents rushed the house, screaming, yelling, and waving their loaded guns. They warned for Jerry not to make a move, or they would shoot immediately.

With twenty agents rushing the front room screaming and all, it was pandemonium at the Rushing place. Agents immediately put handcuffs on Jerry and began informing him of his rights.

"So what's the case? Ya haven't caught me in anything. Tell me, what's this all about?" Jerry was as confused as he was angry. It was 4:00 a.m., and his wife was crying and walking around the house in total disbelief. Jerry and Dean's little girl, Darlene, had wakened from all of the commotion and was crying and running for her mama. "So, tell me...whatcha got on me? You can't just bust into my house in the middle of the night."

One of the federal agents responded to Jerry's questions.

"Your buddy squealed on you, Mr. Rushing. We have sworn testimony from him that you were involved two years back on that still we busted. Oh...by the way, we can bust into your place anytime in the middle of the night. Here's the arrest warrant, and here's the search warrant. The judge is behind this, and this time, Mr. Rushing, we've gotcha."

Jerry really could not believe it. He was being booked on a still bust that was over two years old. They must have caught one of his buddies and squeezed him for leads, and then cut a deal for additional information leading to Jerry's arrest. He was seldom, if ever, really scared, but when twenty agents burst into his house with a federal warrant, he knew he was in big trouble. If a buddy had squealed, he would really have a tough time beating this rap. He had years of moonshining and as many years of bootlegging without a single charge, and he had to be stung by a so-called buddy that talked. Now he was in trouble, and he knew it.

They looked over the house while Dean held their little girl, attempting to console her from the shouting and screaming. They began to lead Jerry out to one of the police cars when Dean hollered to Jerry, "Jerry, please don't leave them here with Darlene and me. Tell them to go."

Jerry, already handcuffed, turned to the ten or so officers that were going to stay behind and thoroughly search the place.

"Boys, you've got her very upset. If I were you, I wouldn't stay in this place. She's awfully nervous, and in her condition and with the guns hidden all around this place, she's likely to lose herself and shoot one of ya any minute."

The officers heeded Jerry's warning, and with a nod of his head, the infamous Jerry Rushing was led to jail. Dean sat on the couch, which she often did, and cried. It was tough loving a man like Jerry Rushing. It was difficult living with the danger and uncertainty. It was painful to continue to try to make a good life for your family when Jerry was always running against the law, and this time, the law had caught up with him. The house was lonely without Jerry. Both Dean and their little daughter had trouble falling back to sleep that night. Jerry was gone, and they were left alone. It was quiet and foreboding, and the two of them did not fall back to sleep until about the time the sun was rising again that morning.

Several months later, Jerry's case came before the courts. The judge was a tough one and quickly found him guilty of all four counts—conspiring, fraud, liquor tax, and manufacturing. There were cries, sobs, and screaming from his mother, wife, and other family members when the judge found him guilty.

The federal judge turned to him and stared for a minute or two.

"I sentence you, Mr. Jerry Elijah Rushing, to three years in the federal penitentiary for these four guilty counts. You will be held in local jail until such time whereby you will be transported to the federal penitentiary in Tallahassee, Florida. That is all." And with that, the judge stood up and left the courtroom, leaving the family members crying for the man they loved. Jerry was immediately taken from the courtroom and ushered down the hall to a holding cell until he could be transported to a local jail, where he would wait until they sent him to Florida.

Dean, Darlene, and other family members went back home crushed by the judge's decision. They had to survive for three years with Jerry all the way down in Florida. All they could do was hope for the best and pray. Dean just sat day after day on the couch and cried. It was a very hard time for the Rushing family. But she pulled through this—that was the kind of woman she was. She stood by her man because she loved him. There was simply no ifs, ands, or buts. He was her husband, and she loved him. She stayed with him and raised Darlene.

One day ran into another day as the courts prepared for Jerry's departure and his ultimate transfer to the Florida federal prison. Then without any forewarning, two agents came into Jerry's cell and told him to call his wife and have her pick him up. He had been sitting in that holding cell for eight days waiting to be moved. He had told Dean and Darlene good-bye and had prepared himself for the three-year stay, as well as anyone could prepare for something like that. Jerry was shocked as he walked out a free man. He could hardly wait to find out what had happened.

"So what's the deal? Is this a joke?"

One officer smirked and replied, "We'll getcha again, Rushin'. Just wait. I guess someone got to the judge. You've gotta pay a fine, and you'll be on a five-year probation. Just get out of here!"

Jerry did not need to be told twice. He left in a hurry, anxious to get out of the place. Later he found out what had happened. He had acquired a friend several years back who happened to be a local pastor of a nearby church. Jerry had tried to attend that church, but for several reasons had stopped attending. However, he had remained friends with the pastor and still remains friends with him to this date. The pastor's name was Reverend Bradley Doles.

Pastor Doles had a big heart, especially for Jerry and his family. He recognized the good in Jerry, regardless of how deep it was buried. He knew that Jerry had a good family and that his wife, Dean, loved God and Jerry. He felt sorry for his little girl, Darlene, because he knew how difficult a life could be for those family members of a bootlegger. He knew that Jerry spent many nights a week running whiskey while leaving Dean and Darlene alone in their house. He knew how Dean's heart broke every time Jerry left the house to run the whiskey.

So with no outside intervention, Reverend Bradley Doles visited the judge on Jerry's behalf. Whether the visit was a result of Dean's prayers and calls for help or whether the visit was simply a result of his concern for Jerry and his family, we may never know. But we do know that Reverend Doles visited the judge and pleaded for Jerry's life.

"Hey, judge. Thanks for seeing me. I wanted to chat to you about the Jerry Rushing case."

"Too late, pastor," the judge responded. "He's already had his day in court, and he was found guilty and sentenced to three years in a federal prison. It's a done deal."

"With all due respect, judge, this is killing his family. I know the other boys you busted with Jerry have no family and are just bad apples. But Jerry Rushing, in spite of the legend that surrounds him, is a good family man with a wonderful, godly wife and a little girl that's only three or four years old. "

The judge took a long deep breath and asked, "Well, pastor, what do you expect me to do 'bout it?"

"Well, Jerry's a good family man, and I care for him a lot. This could be the end of Jerry and his family. You heard them crying and all when you stated his sentence. I was sitting there in the back, and it was just terrible. Can you lighten the sentence just for me? I promise that I'll stay up with him and try to keep him out of trouble."

The judge thought for a moment or two, and then agreed to the pleas of Reverend Doles. "I won't give those other crooks that we busted with that same still bust any break, but I'll work with you on Mr. Rushing. What are you asking for?"

"How about probation? Please?" Reverend Doles never minded pleading for a friend.

Finally the judge agreed and changed Jerry Rushing's sentence to a fine and five years of probation. Jerry did not know for years why the judge changed his mind until he got a letter from Reverend Bradley Doles explaining how he had gone behind the scenes to plead for Jerry and his family.

Without the pleading of this pastor, Jerry would have spent three years away from his family in prison. He was glad that they canceled his prison trip, but he was soon back to his old lifestyle. Habits of old bootleggers are hard to break.

Jerry knew this as well as anyone.

THE LAST TRIP TO THE SLAMMER...THE THIRD TRIP

There comes a time in every man's life when ultimately he reflects on who he is, what he is doing, and where he is going. Jerry Rushing was no different. Born a moonshiner, he embraced the whiskey-making lifestyle from the time he was born. He ran whiskey when he was as young as twelve years old, even if it meant only running to his uncle's place to fetch his father another pint or two of the homemade brew.

Jerry had lived the fast life of the bootlegger and had become the modern-day outlaw he had dreamed about when he was a little boy. He had run more cars through the backwoods of Carolina hauling whiskey than most whiskey runners. He had never been caught and perhaps owned one of the most famous bootlegging cars of all time, the Chrysler 300-D named *Traveler.*

The lifestyle was harsh and rough, not only for the moonshiner or the bootlegger but also for his entire family. The extreme danger, the run-ins with the law, the fights, the shootings, and the explosions of anger were beginning to take a toll on the entire Rushing household. Both Dean, Jerry's wife, and Darlene, Jerry's only child, loved him and stayed beside him on every turn, but life was increasingly getting more difficult. The anger and hatred in Jerry's heart toward the law were growing daily. The brushes with the law on the backwoods highways were becoming more dangerous and more risky. Jerry knew that something ultimately was going to give. It had to.

The anger toward any lawman that began to grow from his first prison trip was now explosive. He went out of his way to wreck a lawman or send him over the mountainside on a chase if he had a chance. But there was another aspect to Jerry's life that showed a certain evil was getting completely out of control. On more than one occasion, Jerry's hatred toward an individual was so great that he could imagine a certain catastrophe overtaking that person, and it would actually occur. It really didn't matter whether it was a past bootlegger that had "snitched" on one of his operations, a "warring" moonshining family he was having difficulties with, or simply one of the local lawmen or federal agents that was hot on his trail.

It surprised him at first. He simply thought in his mind of some harm that should happen to them. And only days later he found out that it did actually happen. It was a bit spooky and almost scared him. The evil was out of control and spiraling Jerry Rushing to ever-greater depths of darkness. And he began to realize it.

There comes a time in a man's life, either through a spiritual experience or through the pressure of a certain catastrophe, when he reflects on his life and makes changes for the better. Jerry Rushing knew that if he continued in the moonshining and bootlegging business, he might ultimately kill someone. He would then spend the rest of his life behind bars, away from the family he loved. If he did not kill someone, he might eventually be killed himself. Really, neither were options he wished to embrace. So he made a change.

Jerry Rushing took his wife and his daughter and headed north in an attempt to leave the past behind. All of his links with bootlegging friends and family, as well as the local moonshiners, centered around the town of Monroe and Union County. Jerry packed it all up and left Union County and his associations with the past behind. He and his wife and daughter packed up their belonging and headed northwest through Charlotte, past Statesville, and relocated outside the small town of Taylorsville. They purchased property and built a simple log home on the side of Whiskey Mountain in an attempt to create a brand-new life.

Jerry then invested himself and his love for the outdoors and hunting into a new business adventure, Chestnut Hunting Lodge. He advertised in several local magazines and began to build the hunting lodge business, Hunters from all over the East Coast could book daily or weekly hunts with the old-time moonshiner right there on his property outside Taylorsville, North Carolina.

They came from all around to hunt wild boar or the beautiful whitetail deer that was prolific throughout the area, and to listen to the stories of the ex-moonshiner and bootlegger. Occasionally friends and past associates visited him at his new place, asking for advice regarding their own criminal or outlaw activity. Occasionally they requested Jerry's assistance in some unlawful business dealing, often having something to do with bootlegging or moonshining.

But Jerry stayed true to his word and his new-charted direction. Though he often listened to his old buddies and, though occasionally, Darlene would see a glint come to his eye, he would always reassure his family that the bootlegging portion of his life was over and he was attempting to write a new chapter in the Rushing life.

Darlene married and had a little girl who was the apple of Jerry's eye. They named her Brandy. Brandy loved to play with her grandpa, ride around in his trucks, and walk the great outdoors like her mama did as a little child. Brandy was just a little girl when Jerry's life again came crumbling down around him. Brandy loved to stay with her grandpa and was at his home that evening watching TV while Jerry sat at his desk working on the schedule of his hunting lodge business. Jerry's wife was not home, as her daddy had come down with Alzheimer's and she was staying with him and assisting with household chores. The night was quiet, and there was a calm and peace inside that log cabin as little Brandy sat on the floor watching one of her favorite programs—until the knock came at the front door.

It was not really unusual for someone to visit the Rushing household. Because of Jerry's past and background and because of his many different criminal activities, it was also not unusual for someone to come back and attempt to take revenge on Jerry. Folks had tried to rob him before, right in their home, and they had been the victims of several break-in attempts.

Because of that, Jerry kept a rifle over the mantelpiece in a sincere effort to just protect his family. But on this night, the knock on the door was a little different. It startled Jerry, as it seemed harder and louder than usual. He most likely would have not answered the door immediately, but little Brandy had been sitting between Jerry and the door watching TV, and, as most little children would, she bounced to her feet and headed to the door. As the two visitors saw the little girl approaching the door, they immediately opened the door and abruptly walked in. Brandy in a little girl's voice smiled at the two men and said, "My papa will be here in just a minute."

But before she could get that out of her mouth, the men rushed right past her and headed toward Jerry. The knock on the door had startled him, and the abrupt entrance of the two men shook him even more. Now Jerry could easily take ten men in a brawl, let alone two. But on this particular evening Jerry was not fearing for his own life as much as he was fearing for his little loved one, Brandy, who stood in an explosive situation between him and the two strangers now standing in the middle of his home.

Before Jerry could get out of his mouth, "I will be with you in just a minute...," the two men had crossed the room and mumbled something to Jerry about being from the agriculture department.

Jerry knew that there were no agents or employees of the agriculture department in his part of town, plus it would be odd for them to identify themselves in such a way. Their plain clothes did not reflect any official status, and he could only assume that two men from his past had abruptly rushed into his home to harm himself or his family, or to rob him. Jerry immediately pulled his rifle off the rack on the wall. He swung it their way as he screamed with an anger representative of his evil moonshine past, "What the heck you here for, and what do you want with me?" Then he turned to little Brandy, "Quick—get behind Papa."

While he was swinging the rifle around, getting the bead on one of the men, the other pulled out some sort of ID from across the room and began to show it to him. However, in the excitement of the moment and from the distance across the room, Jerry could not really make out the identification at all. In the meantime, one of the men had crossed the room and moved nearly upon Jerry. Still being in shock from the abrupt entry, he felt that he had no option but to haul off and lay a barn-buster right up the side of his head. He whooped on him pretty good. The man hit the wall, spun around, and hit a post in the middle of the room. As Jerry drew the gun back to hit him again up the side of the head, the man began to run backward and fell to the floor. His associate took off screaming, jumped over the couch, and, in his fear, wet his pants trying to get out of the door. He opened the door behind the couch and ran through it, slamming it behind him.

However, in his excitement, he had opened the wrong door and found himself in the middle of a little bathroom off the foyer of Jerry's log cabin. Jerry screamed at the man in the bathroom, still believing they were criminals or outlaws from his past. He had one bleeding on the floor and the other one locked in the bathroom with the rifle pointed in his direction. He could only hear a slight whimper from inside the bathroom, "Don't shoot, don't shoot . . . please . . . don't shoot!"

Jerry felt no more comfortable about these two men as he still didn't know who they were. But he felt more comfortable with the situation. Through Brandy was frightened, she was safe and behind him, and he had one man on the floor and the other man hiding in the bathroom with soiled britches.

Jerry was afraid that the fellow in the bathroom was armed and could shoot through the door. So he began to scream, "I want you to walk out of that bathroom right now with your hands high. Let me warn you, and I won't warn you again…if you try to come out of that bathroom and get to the front door, or if you dare think that you can come out of that bathroom with anything in your hands or with your hands hidden, I will blow your brains out this cabin wall and all over the side of this mountain. So if you want your brains in your head, get yourself out here…now!"

Little Brandy was now terribly frightened. She loved her papa, and her papa had two men at gunpoint and ready to kill them both. She just kept saying, "No, Papa don't, don't don't…no, Papa don't, please don't, please don't." But by that time he was very angry and ready to kill both of them. They began to stutter. And then the man that had soiled himself finally came out of the bathroom slowly and obviously humiliated by the situation. He began to stutter, "No, no, no, don't, don't shoot, buddy, don't, don't, don't shoot…we are really from the agriculture department."

"I don't believe it. I don't believe it for a minute. What are you two guys running in here for without even lettin' me answer the door and scaring me and my little girl? You barged right into my house, and that's breaking and entering. Let me see your ID."

The man with the soiled britches handed over his ID, reaching into his pocket very slowly. Jerry took it into his hand, keeping the gun pointed at both of them at the same time. Now Jerry began to breathe a bit more calmly. He still was not certain these men were, though their IDs did identify themselves as officials of the agriculture department. Nevertheless, as far as Jerry Rushing knew, they could have fake IDs. But he did feel more comfortable that he had the situation under control with one man bleeding and one man humiliated with soiled pants. Jerry began to interrogate them as an attorney might before a jury trial. " So what have you come here about, and what do you want?"

The agent with the bloody nose looked up and began to explain, "Well, we came to talk to you about your hogs. We want to make certain that you know everything is fine and those wild boars have no disease and all…you know. It is important that we check those for you."

If there was one thing Jerry could do, he could determine the truth from a lie. He could separate a man "shooting straight" from a man "feeding you a line," and he knew without question that these boys were lying. Whether they were real agriculture agents or not, he didn't know. But he did know one thing. They were lying about the hogs.

"Well, I know you're lying, I don't know what you're really here for, but I know that you are lying. See, I have already talked to several agents from the agriculture department, and they have already been here. They have checked on my hogs and told me that they were fine and none of them had any disease. I have talked to the state man and everything is cool. Everything is fine."

Well, those two boys started to stuttering awfully bad about that time, and Jerry still didn't know if they were agents up to no good or whether they had fake IDs and had come right into his house to do some harm. He decided that he didn't care what the situation was, and he pointed his rifle into the face of the fellow sitting on the floor.

"Let me tell you something, boy. If you and your buddy here don't get your tails out of my house and off of my property by the time I count to ten, I'm going to fill you so full'a lead you'll won't be around to tell the story! Now get outta here."

The two guys jumped up, and they looked like something out of *The Three Stooges*. They were running into the post, into the walls, and bouncing off the couch and each other as they struggled to get out of the front door. They thought that they were running for their life.

"I will tell you something else, whether you are agents or not," Jerry yelled. "I am calling the sheriff now and I am taking out a warrant on both of you for breaking and entering because you walked into my house without us opening the door. Your butts are on the line." The two agents jumped into the car and raced off of Jerry property as fast as they could go.

Jerry could not help but chuckle to himself, because the old rifle hanging on the wall was not loaded. It was funny how a man's self-confidence can make the biggest difference in any type of confrontation such as that. Jerry handled that rifle like he was capable of taking either one of their lives, yet they were really in no harm, at least not from the rifle.

It didn't take Jerry Rushing very long to find the real truth behind the situation. They were agricultural agents were employed by the state of North Carolina. They checked on farmer's crops as well as various types of livestock, like those that were hunted on Jerry's property. However, they were not at all on a mission to check Jerry's hogs out. Jerry had already met with state agricultural officials, and they had given him a clean record regarding his entire hunting operation. But these two fellows were working an illegal operation on the side.

They were stealing equipment and feed from the state storage area. They had stolen a large load of feed and needed to bring it down to his area of the state to some folks who raised horses. They needed a reason to travel to the western part of the state to deliver the stolen horse feed. Therefore, they had simply logged in at their office that they were coming to Jerry Rushing's hunting lodge to check on his hogs. However, they were hauling a stolen trailer full of stolen horse feed to one of their clients near Taylorsville, and they were using Jerry as an excuse to make the run.

It was a strange coincidence, but Jack, one of Jerry's workers, had seen the two of them early in the day park their truck and long trailer over at a local church. It was loaded with the feed at the time, and one of the fellows assisting them happened to be Jerry's friend. He ultimately told Jerry what had happened. Though the man was involved in the loading and unloading of the horse feed, he had no idea that they were going to visit Jerry regarding his hog business.

The two men had hoped to walk in, say a few things to Jerry, and then walk out. However, the entire episode escalated into a massive brawl and resulted in the two agents being scared to death and running for their lives. Once they got on up the road, they began to think about the last thing that they heard Jerry scream, and that was that he would be contacting the local sheriff and taking out a warrant for their arrest for breaking and entering. They also began to realize that they indeed opened the door and walked directly into his home. They began to be concerned for their job. The last thing they needed was to get fired from their jobs.

So they decided to trump up a charge on Jerry Rushing. Three days later they took out a warrant on him for assault on a federal officer, assault on a state officer, as well as kidnapping and several other charges. They listed that he had held him at gunpoint for over eighteen hours and had threatened their lives as well as beat them severely over and over. Jerry knew that they were only in his home five to ten minutes at the most. But it was his word, and the word of a scared little girl, against the word of two government officials.

Jerry would have his day in court.

It took the agents over two years to get their case before a jury trail. Jerry and his family were living through these nightmares, only this time it was not brought on specifically by bootlegging or moonshining. Jerry had been in trouble a lot with the law, and he knew this would be part of the court case against him. Now here was a fellow that had been trying to turn his life around and even relocated his entire family to a new town, and now he was in trouble again. The day for the court case finally arrived.

He went before a jury in federal court. They placed the two officers on the stand, and they began to testify about their eighteen-hour ordeal of being held at gunpoint. One lie led to another and then another. They called in other agents, officers, and game wardens to try to prove their case. The game wardens were slipping in and out of the courtroom and were beginning to share previous testimonies with many of the new witnesses that they were calling.

Darlene, Jerry's daughter, did not know a whole lot about the law. But she just happened to get up from the courtroom and walk out into the hall. There stood a federal marshal that had been previously sitting inside of the courtroom. He was briefing other state officers regarding the testimony that had previously been shared, which is illegal. When the federal marshal saw Darlene walk toward them, he grabbed the future witnesses and took them back into the judge's chambers for a briefing that lasted over forty-five minutes and then brought them back into the courtroom.

The federal prosecutors continued to bring up their previously "briefed" witnesses, and they began sharing almost word for word what the previous witnesses had shared. But the jury was sharp; the jury looked right through the lies, the set up, and the collaboration of the witnesses and found Jerry not guilty. His family was ecstatic.

Jerry had a new confidence in the legal system, which previously had always dealt him the wrong set of cards. He was proud to be an American and proud that the system, however flawed, had proved his innocence. He was excited to start life again until the judge issued his final statements.

The entire courtroom became silent as the judge picked up his gavel and hammered it three times furiously upon his desk. All eyes focused on the judge as they expected him to thank the jury for the hard work and issue some statement of warning to Jerry Rushing concerning any future confrontation with law officers.

But the next words out to the judge's mouth shocked the entire courtroom.

"In light of the testimony that has been shown in this case and in light of the severe beatings, kidnapping, and assault which the officers endured at the hands of Mr. Jerry Elijah Rushing, and in spite of the decision of acquittal which has just been handed down by this jury of twelve, I find Jerry Elijah Rushing guilty on all counts. The sentence shall be twenty-one months in the federal penitentiary."

Gasps and cries went up from the entire courtroom. Dean and Darlene were totally flabbergasted. Nobody could believe what the judge was saying. Obviously the agents were fighting for their jobs. In the event that Jerry would have been found innocent, then their stories would have held no weight and they both would have been fired. There was collaboration between the agents and officials as well as the judge, and ultimately the judge handed the guilty sentence to Jerry Rushing in order to save the both jobs of the two agents.

Jerry's attorney immediately objected, "Your Honor, Your Honor, with all due respect, this man is innocent. You have heard the testimony, which at best has been a collaboration of storytelling by a number of witnesses, and he has been 100 percent acquitted by a jury of his peers of this community. More than twelve people looked at the evidence and have found him innocent of all charges. You simply cannot do that. Your Honor—"

But before Jerry's attorney had the opportunity to address this any further, the judge immediately interrupted him with his gavel and, staring straight toward the table of Jerry and his attorney, stated, "Oh, yes, I can. Mr. Jerry Elijah Rushing has been found guilty by this court and has been sentenced to twenty-one months in the penitentiary. In the event that you would wish to appeal this, sir, you know how the federal appeals system works."

Two agents handcuffed Jerry and led him from the courtroom. His family fell into each other's arms in total despair, not believing the turn of events. They knew that Jerry was trying to turn his life around and had completely relocated to Taylorsville in order to do this. They knew the rough life that they had lived, and they were hoping for a better day. They also believed Jerry's story regarding the five-to ten-minute incident and were totally aware of the collaboration of the witnesses, yet the law had again struck at the heart of the Rushing clan.

The hope for the legal system, which had just been birthed in Jerry's heart, quickly sank to dark despair. His hatred for the law now grew toward the agricultural agents, the federal and state agents, as well as the game wardens. They too had been involved in the collaboration of witnesses against him. The hatred continue to grow in his heart as he felt that he had been wronged by the system, wronged by the judge, and let down by the courts.

Jerry was immediately transferred to the Butner Federal Penitentiary, north of Raleigh, North Carolina, as his attorney filed the paperwork for the federal appeal. From inside the concrete walls of prison, Jerry continued to plead with his attorney to appeal his case to a higher court and let him know when his court case would be scheduled. He had a hunting lodge business to run, a family to protect and provide for, and a new little granddaughter to embrace and love. But the system let him down again. Though the appeal paperwork was documented and filed with the courts, an unidentified federal agent placed a telephone call to his attorney.

"You're a pretty good lawyer and fairly wellrespected in town. If you want to keep your law practice in the state of North Carolina, the best you can do is to stay out of that courtroom, drop the federal appeal, and leave Mr. Jerry Elijah Rushing exactly where he is."

The lawyer buckled to the system and did not even represent Jerry on his appeal. In fact, the appeal was dropped, and the appeal courts considered nothing at all. Jerry sat within his prison cell at the Butner Federal Penitentiary for more than eighteen months. It was another low in the life of Jerry Rushing. Eighteen months in a federal penitentiary is a long time for a man to sit away from his family for a crime he never committed.

Jerry's inner hatred and anger now focused more directly on the agricultural agents of the state and game wardens, both of which teamed up against him in the case. Jerry wasted more than eighteen months of his life away from his wife and family.

Why? He was found guilty because the two agents had a job history of twenty-five years and did not want to lose their jobs. It was a sad way to start your life over again, and it was an incident that Jerry Rushing would never forget. The eighteen months in prison proved to be a hard life where Jerry met many men, some of who deserved the incarceration and others who did not.

Jerry Rushing was in prison because of the two officers breaking and entering his home. He only reacted to the surprise entry. Interestingly enough, Jerry's cell was not far from a TV evangelist by the name of Jim Bakker, who resided in the same penitentiary, after he was found guilty on a variety of financial dealings.

Jerry sat in jail while his wife struggled to run the family business alone again. The legal system just did not seem fair, and it filled Jerry with many questions about life, God, and why he was there. It would take a divine intervention from God for Jerry Rushing to ever get over it. But ultimately, Jerry saw God's hand in his situation.

And with God's help, he came to grips with it.

In Bondage to Sin

Though Jerry spent time in the bondage of various jails or prison cells, he spent more time in another bondage, a type of bondage known to all man. That is the bondage of sin. The Bible tells us in Romans 3:23 that "all have sinned, and come short of the glory of God." I have sinned, Jerry Rushing has sinned, and you have sinned. Sin is just missing the mark regarding God in our lives. He has a will for how we are to live, which the Bible reveals. If we do not live according to His dictates in His Word and according to His will for our lives, we fall short—and that is sin.

The Bible also tells us what we earn for sinning against God:

> For the wages of sin is death; but the gift of God is eternal life
> through Jesus Christ our Lord.
>
> —ROMANS 6:23

This means that for the sin that we have lived, our wages (or what we earn and deserve because of it) is death. That is separation from God both in this life and in your future life. If you have sinned and God has not yet forgiven you of that sin, you are experiencing a spiritual death right now even as you read the words on this page. You are separated from God, and you do not have fellowship with Him. You are living for you, and your life is empty and void.

Don't you feel the emptiness? Haven't you tried to fill that "God-shaped void" in your life? You can't, because only God can fill it. Not only do you experience those wages—*death*—now on earth, but also you will experience eternal separation from God when you leave this world, because without Him, you will go to an eternal hell and spend the rest of your life in terror and anguish.

But thank God that Romans 6:23 did not end there, because it continues: "The gift of God is eternal life through Jesus Christ our Lord." You do not need to accept the wages of your sin. Jesus paid those wages and carried your sin on His back when He was nailed to the old rugged cross. Salvation is free and is for the taking. You just need to ask Jesus to forgive your sins and to come into your heart. God's free gift to you is eternal life. There is no need to leave this world without Him.

When we sin, we are in bondage to the devil and his world. Though Jerry Rushing was in bondage, or prison, for several years, he was in another type of bondage for a long, long time. And that is the bondage of sin.

The Bible talks about this:

> Even so we, when we were children, were in bondage under the
> elements of the world: But when the fulness of the time was
> come, God sent forth his Son, made of a woman, made under

the law, to redeem them that were under the law, that we might receive the adoption of sons. And because ye are sons, God hath sent forth the Spirit of his Son into your hearts, crying, Abba, Father.

—Galatians 4:3–6

In this scripture, the Bible is talking about the bondage of sin. Paul is saying that when he was young and in sin, before he invited Jesus into his heart, he was in bondage. It was no different, in many ways from the prison that held Jerry Rushing. He was in the same bondage of sin. Sin is like chains of bondage, weighing us down with the evils and cares of this world. But Jesus came to overcome the world and to set us free. In the passage from Galatians above, the Bible tells us that in the fullness of time, or when the time was just right, God the Father sent Jesus, His Son. Why did He send His Son?

He sent His Son simply to redeem us. What does redeem mean? It means to buy back. Jesus came to pay the price for your sins that you might not need to live in bondage, in the prison of sin. Jesus paid the price and bought you back. What was the price He paid? The price was His very life by the shedding of innocent blood for you. It was as if He sat in your electric chair. The wages of your sin was death. You were on death row in your prison of sin. Jesus came to your spiritual prison door, gave you the key, took your place in the electric chair, and paid your sentence with His death. You only have to take the key and open your cell, and you will be set free. What is this key? It is your acceptance of Jesus as the One who paid the ultimate sacrifice. Why not use this key today and allow Jesus to set you free? Your price was enormous. It was His own life and blood, but He paid it.

You can be in a state or federal prison and yet be free, free in Jesus and free from the bondage of sin. Or you can be physically free, outside of any prison walls, and yet be in bondage, the bondage of sin. Whether you are sitting in your home today or sitting in a prison cell like Jerry Rushing was, why not today pick up the key (Jesus Christ's love for you) and use it today to set yourself free?

Accept Jesus today and accept His death as the substitute for what you deserved. Ask Him to forgive you for the sin that has kept you in bondage these many years, and He will set you free today. Jerry

Rushing accepted Jesus' death for his sins. He is free today from any physical prison cell, but more importantly, he is free from the bondage of sin that had chains around his soul for so many years.

Accept Him today. Do not wait.

Tomorrow just might be too late. You do not want to leave this world without those "wages of sin" being paid for. If you do, you will be found wanting, and you will pay those wages ultimately in hell for all of eternity.

Similar to a television commercial but focusing on Jesus instead of a credit card...

"Don't leave home (this earth) without Him."

Take the step...Jerry Rushing did.

CHAPTER 10

God Changes the
Roughest of Hearts

GOD'S FIRST TOUCH

THERE IS AN old saying that talks about the conscience in a man. "Conscience is a three-pointed thing in a heart that turns around when you do something wrong, and then the points hurt a lot on the inside. But if one keeps on doing bad, the points of your conscience eventually wear off, and then it doesn't hurt any more."[1] When Jerry looks back, he is certain that his conscience did not really bother him regarding making whiskey. He was taught from the time he could walk that if the government could make or oversee and approve the making of whiskey, why couldn't the common man?

Making whiskey from your farming grains was nearly as old as the Appalachians themselves, where the early moonshiners lived and farmed. Whiskey making and the legal consequences with the law enforcers was just a part of the Rushing household. Since it was passed down from generation to generation within his family, "the points of the conscience" eventually did wear off, and there was no sense of right or wrong at all in his mind.

The more that little Jerry grew up, the more he became immersed within the illegal moonshining culture, including the running of the 'shine. The federal revenuers' major objective in North Carolina was to find each moonshine operation, destroy it completely, and imprison the moonshiners and anyone else that had a part in the operation from watching the fire, to mixing the mash, to hauling the sugar from the house to the still. In some situations, an entire family and as many as two generations could be tried and found guilty all in one courtroom sitting, sending the whole family to jail for a season.

It could be argued that the first step toward embracing criminal activity and selecting it as a lifestyle was in the actual manufacturing of the white lightning. And of course, all moonshine had to be delivered unless the 'shiners were going to consume all of their product and profit before ever leaving the woods. Therefore, the bootlegging of the illegal whiskey became an important part within the whole operation.

It was bootlegging that eventually captured the heart and passion of young Jerry Rushing and put him at odds with the local lawmen. Thus came the second step toward making a life of crime his profession of choice. Small compromises eventually lead to larger compromises, dulling the conscience of a man until most any criminal activity could be embraced as acceptable.

The Bible says a lot about a man's conscience. Consider the following scripture regarding the conscience:

> Now the Spirit speaketh expressly, that in the latter times some shall depart from the faith, giving heed to seducing spirits, and doctrines of devils; speaking lies in hypocrisy; having their conscience seared with a hot iron.
> —1 TIMOTHY 4:1–2

This Bible verse is clear that in the latter times, which one could argue is and has been upon us, many will be led away and depart from God's goodness and faith in Him. They will listen to other spirits and doctrines of the evil master of the world. They will speak lies. Then the Bible shows us as to how man can stoop so low.

It is possible for a man to continue on his own course of destruction until ultimately the points of his conscience are dulled. Actually, from a spiritual perspective, his conscience is seared, and he no longer has a sense of right and wrong. Jerry could beat a man within inches of his life and actually enjoy it. How? His conscience was seared to the things of God, and he no longer could perceive that internal compass that God gives man to lead him on the right path. Without a perceivable conscience, man is lost without God's divine intervention.

Consider some definitions of conscience within a man and the important role of a man's conscience in his daily life:[1]

> Conscience is a walkie-talkie set by which God speaks to us.
> —JAMES J. METCALF

> Conscience is God's presence in man.
> —EMANUEL SWEDENBORG

> Conscience is the inner voice which warns us that someone may be looking.
> —H. L. MENCKEN

> Most of us follow our conscience as we follow a wheelbarrow. We push it in front of us in the direction we want to go.
> —BILLY GRAHAM

As seen from these quotes, God uses man's conscience to guide him, direct him, and keep him on the right path. The conscience works in a man whether or not he knows that God has implanted it within him. Unless, of course, it has been seared and the points have been dulled. With Jerry Rushing, it had been seared and the points had been dulled. Without a conscience, Jerry would run his own course in life. And without God and a working conscience, he would eventually crash.

Though Jerry's conscience was dulled from a young boy and he seldom attended church, he did believe in God. He had heard some Bible stories when he attended grade school and first learned how to

---

1. Bible Illustrator, Version 2.0, Parsons Technology.

read. Those early Bible stories stayed with him throughout his life. His family was not known to attend any church unless, of course, someone died and the family would gather for the funeral. His Granddaddy Atlas attended a primitive Baptist church that met for preaching about once a month, but that was about the extent of any church attendance. His Granddaddy Atlas never joined the church due to some feelings about the members, money, and hypocrites.

So Jerry grew up thinking that most people in the church had as many problems as he did and that many were hypocrites who lived for God on Sundays but lived like the devil during the week. It is funny how harmful and destructive feelings like that can be passed on from generation to generation.

As Jerry got older and his brushes with the law became more dangerous and his life as a modern-day outlaw continued to flourish, he began to get a sense that his life was out of control. The moonshine business and the bootlegging business were thriving. Most folks in Union County knew that Jerry Rushing was one of the fastest bootleggers in the county. His notoriety was spreading, and he had just about reached the fame that he dreamed about when he was young.

He was no real Jesse James, and he knew it. But he liked the role he played and saw himself as a feared desperado with a fast car, lots of homemade whiskey, plenty of cash, a big, black Stetson cowboy hat, and the admiration of his lawbreaker cronies. But then things got too big too fast, the close calls got closer, and the danger of his running became more hazardous. His temper exploded more often, and his existence had become a treacherous life of daily fights, brawls, and battles that often resulted in someone getting hurt real bad. Ultimately someone could die, and he did not want that for his family.

His family was living the same hell that he was experiencing. It was a harsh life, and the bootlegging kept him on the road most every night. It was not good for his wife or child, and he needed to make a change. He knew that his life and the life that he had prepared for his family was going from bad to worse. He had to make a change.

He figured that a change of scenery would help his plight and get him away from the negative influences that had always plagued him and his family for years. So he moved his family to Taylorsville,

North Carolina. Jerry and his family liked the new area, and the move away from the center of Jerry's moonshining business immediately had positive effects on the whole family. But Jerry knew he had to make other changes to stay alive and be there for the family he loved. Though he had not shared his feelings much with his wife and daughter, inside was a great love for both of them.

The first step toward change with anybody is the acknowledgement that change is necessary. Jerry had taken the first step. A certain brokenness in a man's soul does not necessarily result in salvation, but it is a very necessary step toward God. Jerry wanted to change. He needed to change, and he was prepared to change. Martin Luther once said, "God creates out of nothing. Therefore until a man is nothing, God can make nothing out of him." Though a piece of Jerry Rushing still wanted to embrace his youthful illusion of being a modern-day outlaw, the authentic Jerry, under the tough shell, loved his family too much for them to suffer any more.

He had about reached the bottom. Now God could work in his life.

Jerry knew that he had been in too many scrapes and accidents to still be alive unless some hidden eternal power had His hand upon him. God had extended His hand to the bootlegger many times. Jerry had seen the hand reach through the muck and mire of his moonshine lifestyle. At the lowest times when his very life and existence hung in the balance, he may have even considered reaching out for that hand. But in the end, he always backed away from God and decided to continue running his life "Jerry's way."

But toward the end, he knew that he was being broken and that unless he made some change, he might eventually cross the line and his life would break in a thousand pieces. He did not want his loved ones to experience this. Jerry was broken and confused. Now God could begin His work to change Jerry from the inside out.

Several times, Jerry shared with his friends why the change took so long in his life:

> I wanted to change, but pride in a man is a terrible thing. I had a bunch of pride. I always wanted to be the tough guy that bowed down to nobody. In Union County, I was like God. I was the "Godfather" of the underworld illegal activity. If anybody

wanted anything done, they would call me. If they wanted anything moved, legal or illegal, they called old Jerry Rushing. I was the king.

When I drove up, I was respected and revered. I was respected and admired, though mostly by the criminal element throughout that part of Carolina. That's a hard thing to lie down. I would want to give up the bad stuff and then I would run back to it again. I had a lot of pride...man. A lot of pride. And that pride just about took me down. I thank God it didn't but I had to lose the pride first. That was the hardest.

Though the change was not overnight, the acknowledgement that he needed to change combined with the understanding of the sin of pride in his life was the catalyst for the transformation that ultimately would occur. Proverbs 16:18–19 says, "Pride goeth before destruction, and an haughty spirit before a fall. Better it is to be of an humble spirit with the lowly, than to divide the spoil with the proud." The pride was coming down. Just maybe, Jerry Rushing would not be the Jesse James of our times, at least not anymore. He was now ready to accept that fact. The alteration of his complete being did not occur immediately, and Jerry had many difficulties and setbacks to overcome, but the change was beginning.

God was using many people to reach this bootlegger. During part of this evaluation of his inner being, Jerry had come in contact with a pastor that he took a real liking to. This pastor was a hunter and loved the outdoors almost as much as Jerry. His name was Reverend Bradley Doles. Reverend Doles had argued to keep Jerry out of prison and invited him to his church. Though Jerry tried to attend the church as part of his "about-face," he was met with a stuffy group of Christians who felt he was just too bad to attend their church. Upon entering the church, everybody turned around and stared. One woman even made a comment to Jerry that he had some nerve coming into the church after doing all the bad that he had done. He was facing more of these difficulties and setbacks. Perhaps these parishioners forgot that Jesus really came for the sinner. God has always loved the prodigal son. God has always loved the men that were far from him. And God had always loved Jerry Rushing. His love was being poured out upon

Jerry's life, and ultimately it would make a difference. God never gives up on those He loves. And God always answers the prayers of His saints. And there were people praying for Jerry.

One was his lovely wife of many years.

THE PRAYERS OF LOVED ONES

Shelby Dean Polk was only twenty-two when she said, "I do," and embraced with a kiss the man she loved. She had fallen madly in love with Jerry E. Rushing, and it did not really matter what he did for a living. The vows she agreed to that very day included "for better or worse, for richer or poorer" and so on. She made that vow in the presence or her friends and family, and she meant it. She was not one to break a marriage vow. She had committed to him as his wife, and she would be the best wife she could be.

She committed to the "better or worse," and God knows that at the time, she probably had no idea just how bad the "worse" would get. She stood by him during the court cases, and she was a strong woman during his prison times. She stood by him during all the moonshining, and she never wavered during his dangerous bootlegging runs as well. She once turned to Jerry and reminded him that there were at least seven years that he left home every night in *Traveler* when she never expected to see him again. That is tough on a woman. But she loved her Jerry and would stand through thick and thin. She was always by his side. She never expected her life to be as difficult as it finally became when he was involved the deepest in the moonshine business. She had read the fairytales as a child and believed in the "they lived happily ever after" scenario. But it was difficult to accept as true when thing really got tough.

Dean did not expect heaven, but she did not expect hell, either. A German proverb says that marriage is either heaven or hell. Through most of their early marriage, while Jerry was immersed within the illegal whiskey business, the marriage was heck. The peace of their home was often violated whenever some of the moonshine business went bad. Fights in the front room, Jerry shooting out the front door, attempted robberies, attempted break-ins, and a variety of other troubles were just part of their everyday life.

If it were not for prayer, perhaps the marriage would never have lasted. In fact, if it were not for Dean's prayers, perhaps Jerry Rushing would not be alive today. Dean had her wishes. She wanted to be far from the moonshining business. She wanted to be through with the evils and the dangers that surrounded every aspect of the unlawful whiskey business. She wanted to be free from the embarrassment that surrounded her whenever she went to the market. And perhaps the wish that she turned Godward more than them all was the simple wish, "Lord, please keep my husband alive and bring him back home."

Some nights he only had a few cases to deliver and would be home shortly after midnight. However, on other occasions, his runs might take him completely out of the county for the entire night. If he crashed or flipped his running car, he might not be back until well after the sun had come up announcing another day. When he pulled out of the drive, Dean never knew what to expect.

Darlene has vivid memories burned into her mind of her mama just sitting there. Each night was the same. Her daddy would spend time loading up and then would spend additional time planning his trip. Then after dark, he would pull the big Chrysler up into the drive and perhaps load a revolver or shotgun to hide in a coat or stuff under the seat. Then after saying a very brief good-bye, he would head out the front door, fire up that Chrysler, and head out fast. Dean would sit upon the couch and watch the Chrysler as it disappeared around the last bend. Then the tears would start to flow. Her mama would cry and cry. She was a very strong woman, but even for her, sometimes, the strength would just run out.

She would imagine life without Jerry. Her imagination would run wild as her mind would play and then replay the past incidents that Jerry had bragged about to all his friends. She knew of the close calls and the flipping of the cars and the wrecks that nearly claimed his life. She had heard of the shots that barely missed and had seen Jerry when he had returned with bullet holes in the Chrysler that had to be filled in and painted before the next morning. She had watched Jerry nearly die in the hospital when he crashed into the chicken truck and the steering wheel had impaled Jerry's abdomen and pinned him to the front seat.

She knew of the stakeouts and the federal agents' burning desire to bring her husband in, either dead or alive. She had felt that pain, and each night she experienced it all over again and again. At first, she tried not to cry, but she soon gave up and the tears could not be controlled. She felt abandoned and alone. She wanted to be strong for herself and for Darlene, but she had already taken a lot for a woman—and now she could take no more.

Many nights she would sit on the couch and stare down the road where she had last seen the Chrysler. *If he would only come back now,* was often her wish. But that wish would not be granted because once Jerry had left the house on a run, he would never return until the delivery was complete. She knew just how stubborn Jerry was and that it could ultimately lead to his demise. He would outrun the law and never get caught if it killed him trying, he would often say. She would ask him to not talk like that. But she knew just how hard-headed he was, and she knew how he had aggravated and humiliated all of the agents with his fast and cocky driving and that they would stop at nothing to bring him down.

So Dean would sit. She would think and try to cleanse her mind of the potential dangers as her vivid imagination ran wild. The tears might fall for hours and then turn to prayer, as she would ask God for a simple favor. "Bring my husband back to me." That was her wish turned Godward. She just wanted her husband back. She would pray, cry, and then pray again.

On many occasions, Darlene would sit next to her mama with her arm around her shoulder, and her prayer would be the same. "God, please bring back Daddy." Darlene often wondered how her mama really did it. She knew that she seldom slept well at night with Jerry out running the whiskey. She did not sleep alone as she would worry about who might come up to the house or shoot their way during the dark of the night.

So they would cry and pray together. How can love be so strong a bond that such a lovely southern lady would stand so strong, so alone for so many years? "Don't let my Jerry die," was her constant cry. "Don't let my Jerry die." Jerry himself would often wonder how he would escape from such terror on his midnight runs.

Many bootleggers died around too sharp a corner, running just a bit too fast. Many were caught or run off the road, dying a painful death in a fiery explosion when they would lose control of their car, run off a bank, and the car exploded with the sugar whiskey fueling the fire from within. Jerry had as many wrecks and flips as the rest of the bootleggers. There were as many roadblocks and bullets lodged within inches of him in the steel of that old Chrysler as others had experienced. But there was a difference between him and the other drivers. He never got caught and he was never killed, though many times he came awfully close. He knew it too and would often brag about the close calls.

"I could'a died last night," he might brag. "That was as close to death as I've ever come. How'd I got through that, I'll never know. That was a close one."

But there was one more difference between Jerry and many of the other bootleggers that met their Maker on some backwoods country road. The other bootleggers did not have Dean and Darlene running side by side with them. Sure, they may not have been in the car, but their prayers were active and strong. Their prayers went out of that little house in Monroe and were carried by angels to God himself. God then dispatched the angels that were needed, in compliance with the loving wife's prayers, and they traveled alongside Jerry on most every run. He may not have been aware of the divine protection, but they were there.

Maybe Dean and Darlene were Jerry's angels. Their prayers were sent heavenward so that he would change his life for the sake of his family. Dean never wavered. She loved her man and prayed many a prayer for his safe return. God is a God of answered prayers. And Jerry lived to tell the story because he had a woman who, a woman who cared, and more importantly a woman who prayed. And he had a woman that cared. And more important than anything else, he had a woman that prayed.

James 5:16 says, "Confess your faults one to another, and pray one for another, that ye may be healed. The effectual fervent prayer of a righteous man availeth much."

James tells us to pray for one another. Dean and Darlene were certainly doing that. Then the Bible tells us of a promise. The prayer of a righteous man (or woman) is powerful and effective. Jerry was a very fortunate man to have such women in his life who would bathe him in such powerful prayer. He came back every night and is alive to tell the story today. We should thank God for godly women in the lives of men. Many men would be in hell today if not for the powerful intercessory prayer of a loving wife or daughter.

Jerry Rushing would be, and today he knows it.

GOD BEGINS TO MOVE AND THE RUNNER STOPS RUNNING

When God begins to move in a man, He really begins to move. Jerry knew that the evil within him was growing. The hatred was stronger than before, and he began to thrive off of the hate he felt for others. He couldn't wait for another opportunity to bust someone or knock someone out. He loved to fight, and he began to sense that this was wrong. He felt as if he were headed to a point of no return. He began to think that he was just too evil to go on. He wondered if the God of the heavens had just given up on him. When he began to think evil thoughts and then they would happen, he became more frightened of his capability to do evil things.

He saw a man in town pushing a woman around and yelling at her, perhaps in a marital argument. Jerry jumped out of the car and took his bumper jack and beat that man until he could not stand up. The woman was crying and screaming, and the town folks were yelling for a policeman in the midst of the brawl. Then when it was over, Jerry got into his car and drove off as if he had completed his business and was on his way.

He saw a man slapping his child for misbehaving, and he parked his truck in the middle of the street, jumped out, and began beating the man with his bare fists. All the while he was screaming at the man about never beating a child again. Perhaps this hatred could be traced to his early childhood beatings at the hand of his father. Regardless, he had not predetermined any of these beatings or planned them like a moonshine run. They were all immediate and uncontrolled hatred and anger explosions that would occur without warning. Afterwards, Jerry would begin to feel that he was completely out of control. If things did not change, he would ultimately kill someone or someone would kill him in the battle.

He continued to thrive off of evil and his confrontations became more dangerous as his hatred continued to grow. On one occasion, Jerry and his buddy Hal were in a beer joint in Charlotte, North Carolina. Someone either said something that offended Jerry or looked at Jerry wrong, and immediately a full-fledged war broke out. Jerry and Hal busted all eight of the guys before the police even arrived at the place. They then grabbed their bumper jacks and went to work on the police just for fun. Within minutes, they had 'whooped up' on all six cops. They grabbed the bleeding bodies and dragged them out to the parking lot and stacked them on one another like logs on a bonfire. All six officers were knocked out cold. Jerry and Hal quickly got back into their car and drove off before they could be recognized.

It was events like this that began to show Jerry that he was about to go too far and perhaps never return. He wondered if he was almost over the hill. He knew that he was too evil and that he could no longer control this evil that was at work within him. He didn't fear death, but he loved his family too much to allow them to continue to be hurt week after week. He knew something in his life had to change.

Once Jerry moved away from Monroe and his old buddies, he then had a spiritual experience that would begin a change in his life. He would never be the same. He was not in a church but was alone considering the evil that he felt within. He knew he could no longer control the anger, and it scared him. It is at times like this when God can reach a man. When we are tired of running, we are more susceptible to hear His still, small voice. When a man is sick and tired of being sick and tired, God can change him.

In a way that only God could do, He let Jerry Rushing know that he was going to hell. He exposed him for what he was—an angry, evil man that had always run from God. He was not only a whiskey runner, but he was also another kind of runner. He was running from the only thing that could give him hope, God himself. And God was beginning to move. It began as a still, small voice within . . . *Jerry Rushing—you are dying and going to hell.*

Jerry had never been afraid of dying before. But this did shake him. He knew that he was going to hell, and all of a sudden, hell and dying and the possibility of him spending eternity in a place like that frightened him. It is funny how God can get our attention. He will let a man nearly bottom out, and then when he has nowhere to turn and no place to look except up, God's hand is there.

In reality, God is always there, and His hand is always extended to men. It was always extended to Jerry Rushing. But in the midst of his sin, his moonshining, and his bootlegging, he had never recognized God's hand before. Now he was desperate. He recognized for the first time the evil that lived within him. He even wondered if he was too evil for God to change. He began talking to God in his own way. "Help me...please help me."

Was this the modern-day outlaw looking for help? Was this the Jesse James of Union County that needed God's help? Yes, it was. It had been too many years with too many heartbreaks and near-death experiences. But he was looking for help. The prayers of his lovely wife and daughter were breaking through to the heavens, and the angels were surrounding that old bootlegger and he was turning his heart toward God. It was still evil and hard, but the process had begun. God was softening the heart, and Jerry was beginning to lean toward Him.

Many of his friends have asked him about his initial sense that God wanted to change his life. His best explanation of it comes, perhaps, in his own words:

> I was thinkin' about all this evil in me and all the things I had done. Then out of nowhere, it was like God showed me, on my inside, that I was headed to hell. Jerry Rushing was evil, bad, and full of hatred and the time had come. I remember thinking that if I didn't change, I would die and go to hell. All of a sudden, hell was a real place and I was going there. I just got this funny feeling. I really feel like God was putting this in my mind so I would know what He was thinkin'. I was in real trouble and now He was my only hope. Maybe, just maybe God could help me change.
>
> Had I gone over the edge to a point of no return? I didn't

know for sure, but I did want His help to change. I wanted to be around for my family. I knew that something was changing inside of me, though I didn't know exactly what it was. I knew that God was beginning to work on me. It was a real strange thing.

I had never feared nothing before, and then I began to fear dying and going to hell. It was a strange thing. It was like He just showed me, "Something's gotta give or you're gone." That thought kept going through my mind. Something's gotta give or I'm gonna be gone, and that means hell. I began to think back of all my wrecks and the shootin' and all and I'm still here to think about it. But I never died, and I began to think about that. Did God keep me alive? Will He help me change? I finally felt inside that God wanted me to know that He would help me if I would but reach out to Him.

Jerry Rushing knew that something had to give. He could no longer live this life. He knew that he needed to do something fast. He knew that he could not keep doing what he was doing, or somebody would get killed—it could be him. He decided that he would take another important step. It had been years since Jerry Rushing had attended church. But now he was desperate. He felt as if he had to give his heart to the Lord in order to make the change. He had tried to make the change before and was not able to do it in his own power.

Sin is just like that.

It is bondage that once it gets its chains around a man, it takes God and the power of the Holy Spirit the break that bondage. So Jerry decided that he needed God, and he would go to church to find Him.

So in the year of 1988, Jerry found his way down his mountain and around the winding country roads to a little Baptist church. He was running the backwoods roads, but this time the law was not after him. He was not running whiskey. He was running to God. He had felt God's hand upon his shoulder, and he was coming home. He knew he had to do it, and God and all the angels in heaven were standing at the portals watching. The heavens rejoice over a sinner coming home, and this was a sinner that the devil had in his clutches for years. The seasons of hate, anger, and rage would soon be coming to an end. Jerry was coming home, and God the Father was standing at the altar to accept him as soon as he entered the church.

The pastor preached, but Jerry did not hear any of the message. He just sat there and cried. He cried and cried. But this was another change. Jerry had never cried real tears before. His tear ducts were closed, and he had used eye drops ever since he could remember, because his eyes would get dry and itchy. But now he cried, big, salty, wet tears rolling down his cheeks for the first time. They rolled down his cheeks to his chin and dropped upon his shirt, making a large wet spot right below the collar. But he didn't really care. At the conclusion of the preaching, he got up and ran to the altar.

God had been working in his life, and he knew he needed God. There was no question about it. He went forward and told the pastor he needed help. He knelt down and prayed the sinner's prayer, asking God to enter his life and exchange his hate for love. The church just went wild. They had been praying for this wildman of the Carolinas, and here he was. They just could not believe it. The church had been hoping that God would turn his life around, and on that particular Sunday morning, Jerry Rushing walked right into that church to give his heart to God.

They immediately asked Jerry if he would join the church and he said he would if the folks would have him. So Jerry, his wife, Dean, his daughter, Darlene, and his granddaughter, Brandy, were all baptized at one time in that little church. Three generations of Rushings baptized into Christ on the same day. It had not happened before at that Baptist church, and it has not happened since. God had performed a miracle in Jerry's life, and his whole family would never be the same.

GOD SOFTENS HIS HEART IN PRISON . . . ONE MORE TIME!

So God finally got Jerry's attention and was ready to help him change. He had committed his heart to the Lord, and this entire life was new to him. He understood that he was a born-again Christian, but he had some doubts if this would really work. He had heard of conversion experiences, and he did not want to live for God on Sunday and live like the devil during the week. He was serious about his newfound Christianity and wanted it to stick.

But Jerry had never walked this path before and was a bit confused as to the next step. He began to pick up the Bible and read it for the first time in his life. He read verses from the Psalms when King David was confused, and then he read in the Book of John where Jesus talked about eternal life. He had started reading God's Word for himself and had started to apply some of this when the situation exploded in his home that night with the agricultural agents. Though he knew that he was in trouble, he never in a thousand years thought that he would be convicted on those trumped-up charges. The jury acquitted him, but the judge reversed the acquittal and sent Jerry Rushing to prison.

It shook Jerry for a time. He was changing, not fast, but he wanted a changed life—then he was convicted and sent to prison for eighteen months for a crime he did not commit.

Why did it happen? Why did the judge reverse the jury's decision?

He had plenty of time in the federal penitentiary to consider an answer to those questions. And with time, he did decide why that might have happened. He began to believe that he was there for a purpose. Let's have Jerry explain it in his own words:

> At first, I was surprised to get the sentence of twenty-one months. I was angry. But as I began to think about it, I came to think that it happened for a purpose. If I hadn't been stopped for a while, maybe I would have been as bad as I ever was. Changing me was a tough thing for God...maybe. I was mean and evil, and in prison, I couldnt get in much wrong. So I continued to study the Bible. I got in a Bible study and studied every day, nearly all day long. I worked in there, but my job only took me an hour or so every day. So after that, I just went back to my cell and read the Bible.
>
> I was about to go too far, and I think God used that prison time to slow me down and get me in the Bible. I was just too busy on the outside and never took the time to read the Bible much. Within thirty days, I would have probably just gone back to my old lifestyle. Now I couldn't. I was in prison and had nothing to do but read God's Word. Without reading the Bible, I would have never known what was going on in my life and that God really loved me all the while I was running. Probably the best thing that

ever happened to me was going to that prison for a time. I at least know something about the Bible and all that I'd never known without being in there. I read the Bible completely through.

I remember thinking that at least now I have the time to read the Bible and the time to study God's Word and just maybe this would last. I didn't want to try God, just to go back to my old lifestyle again. I wanted this to stick. I wanted not only to change, but I wanted the change to last. That's why God let this happen. It would take over a year of reading the Bible to change this tough heart. I guess that I was just a tough case.

He really knew that I needed to get close to Him, and that's why He let this happen with the judge and all. I was in prison for a reason...to get closer to God so that when I got back out with my family and all, I would never go back to the old life. I'm glad God did that for me. I needed the change.

Salvation is everlasting, and once a man gives his heart to God, God is committed to keeping him as one of the saints. The Bible tells us that the Holy Spirit is given to us as a deposit and that the Holy Spirit will guide us in all truth. But though Jerry Rushing gave his heart to the Lord and was committed to living for God, he was nervous about the pull of the world on his life. The anger, hatred, and rage had lived within his soul for so many years, Jerry wanted to make sure that it never returned.

God could have touched Jerry in such a way that he would have been completely healed from all of this evil. However, God works in mysterious ways. Though He did not send Jerry to prison, certainly God used that time to heal Jerry as he spent each and every waking hour in His Word. God's Word can heal us and wash the world and its evil completely out of us. And in Jerry Rushing's case, it took thirteen months, or approximately 390 days, of spiritual cleansing through continual reading and studying of God's Word.

God is faithful and needed to get Jerry Rushing to a place where he knew that he would never again return to his ungodly lifestyle. Jerry's love for the Word continued to grow, and his love for God continued to grow. By the time Jerry was released from prison, he indeed was a new man and had the Word of God within him to sustain him from life's daily challenges.

Jerry Rushing was no longer a criminal or outlaw. That was the past, and today Jerry Rushing is a new man.

He loves the Lord. Let Jerry tell it again in his own words:

> When I decided to accept God, I never looked back. I mean that I laid all of this stuff down that I used to do and quit. I mean I slammed quit it once and for all. Now, I don't mean that I don't occasionally lose my temper or something like that. But God's still working on me. But I never, never returned to my old ways. This thing with God really did stick this time, and I've never been the same.
>
> I do love the Lord. I know that Jesus was the only person in the world that could save my evil and wicked soul from hell. Well, He took my sins away and took the mean, cruel hatred out of me. Sometimes I can slip and start thinkin' like I used to. But I am committed to living a life that He would want me to live. I remember telling God that I would lay it all down, the whiskey makin', the bootlegging, the outlaw stuff I would dabble in...I would just hang it all up. I told Him I could not quit on my own. I needed to have faith in God that He would do it for me. If it was not for Him, I would be dead today.
>
> He changed my life, and He is my Savior. I'll tell anybody. So...it looks like my life is drawing to a close. Sometimes it feels like it just might be right around the corner. Like God's got me ready for my next journey, to actually meet Him and make my last run...my last run home. If it's really right around the corner, I want to be ready when the time comes. I am ready and I'll stay ready.
>
> There ain't nothing worth sending your soul to hell over. Nothing! Sometimes I think about how hard it is to live a good life. With my background, sometimes it is a struggle, and if I didn't have God, I just couldn't do it...period. Never happen...just never would happen. I've tried to do it on my own and failed. Without God, I just could not live, man, just could not do it.
>
> I always pray and hope that I am living a better life now than the past. For my family, I really want to live a better life for the rest of my life. I know my family wants this for all of us. I know that I put them through hell. No, I am sorry for the things I did. I hate it, but that's all behind me now and forgiven. But even though it's forgiven, I often worry about the stuff I put them

through. Someday I'll be in heaven, and it will all be behind me and I will never have to worry about it anymore.

Ask me about my hope and my prayer right now…well, it's to live a good life for God and my family and then to get to heaven. I really want to wind up there. I've run to long and life's been hard, but to finally get to heaven…well, that'll be my last run.

TAKE JERRY'S STEP…RECEIVE JESUS TODAY

Jerry Elijah Rushing needed Jesus. Only Jesus would satisfy his soul and put an end to his running. If you too have run from God, you need to stop and accept Him today. If you have lived a life of sin and rebellion like Jerry, you need to stop and turn to God. Only God and His love will ultimately fill that God-shaped void within you. If, while reading the pages of this book, you have stopped, reflected, and identified with Jerry, you need God.

Perhaps you are not a moonshiner or a bootlegger, but you still need God. Jerry took the steps down to the altar of Dover Baptist Church several years ago, and his life has never been the same. You may not be in a church, or you may be in prison and not able to get to a church immediately. That does not concern God. You can stop the running today and turn to God by following the simple steps below:

Step one: Realize that God loves you.

He sent His Son to die just for you. Jesus paid the penalty for your sins by hanging on the cross and dying for you. Have the faith to believe it. Tell Jesus now that you do believe that He loves you. Embrace the love that the Father has for you and thank Him for that love:

> For God so loved the world, that he gave his only begotten Son, that whosoever believeth in him should not perish, but have everlasting life.
>
> —JOHN 3:16

Step two: Admit that you are a sinner and your sin separates you from God's love.

Man was created to worship God, but we all have a will. Many times, a man's will is stubborn, and he will choose to go his own way, just like Jerry. Running your life apart from God results in sin. This sin separates us from God:

> For all have sinned, and come short of the glory of God.
> —ROMANS 3:23

> For the wages of sin is death [separation from God]; but the gift of God is eternal life through Jesus Christ our Lord.
> —ROMANS 6:23

Step three: Believe that Jesus died for your sins and rose from the dead for you.

Accept the fact that you are totally separated from God due to your sins and that only Jesus and His supreme sacrifice can save you from eternal damnation in a fiery hell. Jesus Christ paid the price and died in your place. Only through your personal acceptance of His death and resurrection can you finally experience God's love and secure salvation for your soul:

> But God commendeth his love toward us, in that, while we were yet sinners, Christ died for us.
> —ROMANS 5:8

Step four: Accept the fact that Jesus is the *only* way to God.

There are many that would tell you that there are other ways to God. Other religions show a variety of methods to secure your salvation. However, the Bible is very clear that there is only one way to heaven, and there is only one way to find the forgiveness of your sins:

> Jesus saith unto him, I am the way, the truth, and the life: no man cometh unto the Father, but by me.
> —JOHN 14:6

Step five: Accept Jesus as your personal savior and receive Him into your heart.

Receiving Christ means repenting from your sins. Repentance means turning from your old ways and turning toward Jesus. You are accepting and trusting Christ to come into your life and to forgive you for all your sins and to make you into a new spiritual being. This is where the phrase "born again" comes from. Your spirit is actually reborn and you are no longer separated from God.

> But as many as received him, to them gave he power to become the sons of God, even to them that believe on his name.
>
> —JOHN 1:12

You can receive Christ into your heart right now. God knows what you are thinking and feeling, and that is more important than the actual words you speak. But here is a suggested prayer that will assist you in talking to God:

Dear God,

I come to You in the name of Jesus who died for my sins. I admit that I am a sinner and have run from You. I am very sorry for my sins and the life that I have lived. I need Your help and Your hand to guide me in the future.

I personally believe in my heart that Jesus died for my sins (like He did for Jerry Rushing) on the cross and shed His blood that I might live and have eternal life.

You said in the Bible in Romans 10:9 that if I confess the Lord and believe in my heart that You raised Jesus from the dead, then You will save my soul. Well, I confess that right now.

I believe this in Your Word and confess it to You.

I confess Jesus as my personal Savior and as the Lord of my life. I believe that Jesus is Your Son and that He died for me. I believe that You raised Him from the dead. I accept Jesus right now as my own personal Savior, and I believe right now that I am saved, born again, and going to heaven.

Thank You for dying for me and loving me.

In Jesus' name I pray, amen.

Now thank God that He has saved you just as He saved Jerry Rushing. Find yourself a good Bible-preaching church and attend next Sunday. While you are there, let someone know what just happened to you.

Begin reading the Bible as Jerry did. Find out what it says about living a life that is pleasing to the Lord. Pray for your family, and pray to God daily.

If you have prayed the prayer above, you are now a Christian, and God has a special place in heaven prepared just for you. When you get to heaven, look up the old bootlegger-turned-Christian. Jerry Rushing would love to know that his life and God's love richly poured out upon him had a positive effect on your life.

Always remember that God loves you and has a plan for your life. He loved Jerry Rushing and turned his life completely around. What God did for Jerry, He will do for you.

Believe it!

Epilogue

AS WE CLOSE this final chapter in the saga of the Jerry Elijah Rushing story, allow Jerry Rushing himself and his daughter, Darlene Tarlton, to share with you their direct thoughts and prayers. Reflect on Jerry's story with the pain, the hatred, and anger that followed him during the moonshining and bootlegging. Then reflect on the change that Jesus Christ brought to his life as he allowed God to change his ways, heal the hurts, and wash away the anger.

As you sit back and read the words of both Darlene and Jerry, let their prayers and thoughts enter deep within your soul and touch you just as if they were sitting with you today, expressing these thoughts directly to you. These are their words, and if they were there, they would speak them to you just as they are recorded here on these pages. You will find a love in these words that reflect the love of God for Jerry, the love of Jerry for his family and fans, and the undying love of a daughter that always loved her bootleggin' daddy.

The Love and Prayers of a Daughter...Darlene Tarlton

The very first thing I really remember about the whiskey business is the sweet, beautiful aroma of ripe bananas. I must have only been three years of age or so, and I was at my grandma's house. It was very dark outside, and I remember the back porch having a huge pile of bananas piled up on one side of it. Many of the folks were carrying them outside from the porch. Though I was too young to recall all of the people that were involved in moving this giant pile of bananas, I can still remember to this day the sweet aroma of them on the back porch.

Being just a little tot, I was walking around wondering what our family was doing with a truckload of bananas. I simply love banana pudding, and I can remember thinking, "Wow...somebody is making a awful lot of banana pudding." I guess that was the way little folks thought. It was not until I was grown that I found out that all of those sweet ripe bananas were going into a large batch of my uncle's banana brandy. That was just the way of life for us at the Rushing household.

By the time I was born, many of the very old whiskey makers had passed on. The only one left in our family that was handing the tradition of moonshinning on to my dad was my uncle Dooley. He was a wonderful man in my eyes, and he was always so sweet and nice to me. I will never forget one of the first times in my life that I struck a business deal with someone regarding something that I really wanted, and this was with my uncle Dooley.

He always wore a big black felt hat, and most of the time I remember seeing him sitting in a straight back chair in the middle of his yard. One day we had gone to his house, and I remember seeing him with his big old hat sitting in the big chair. Only this day was a little different. He had two beautiful baby kittens on his lap, and I can remember thinking that they were so pretty. I always loved animals and especially loved little kittens, and I wanted one of those kittens so bad. I went over to my uncle Dooley's lap and petted and loved those little kittens and told him how much I would love having them. Uncle Dooley turned to me, smiled, and said, "I will make a deal with you, Darlene. If you give me that old baby bottle of yours that you always carry around, I will give you both of these kittens."

Well, I wasted no time handing over my little bottle. I came home that night with two of the prettiest kittens my mom had ever seen. Ultimately, Mom said that the only time I ever said anything again about wanting a bottle was occasionally at night just before bedtime. She would always say to me, "If you want your bottles back, you will have to take those kittens back to Uncle Dooley." She said that I would turn right over and go to sleep and never ask for the bottle again.

Many people will tell you that moonshiners were tough and mean, cared for no one, and had no heart at all. But my daddy was a moonshiner and one of the fastest bootleggers in all of Carolina, and I don't believe that is true. I believe that old moonshine men really had hearts, it was just that the heart was buried down so deep inside of them that many failed to see it.

Moonshiners just refused to let people know that they ever had real feelings. I believe that they had feelings down deep, but never let them out and certainly would not let you know how they felt about things that were not manly. They just refused to let people know that they had feelings down deep inside. My dad was a very hard man, and he and Uncle Dooley were a lot alike.

From the time that I was a very small little girl, I saw my dad as a real strong man. I knew that he was very hot-headed and that he often acted like he did not have any feelings for anything. I don't know, for some reason men back then thought that showing feelings might make them weak. They often thought that having a heart would make them less of a man. It was a tough life being a moonshiner. So, most of the time they suppressed their feelings and showed no heart at all.

It was tough in the Rushing household even when I was a little kid. It was nothing strange for a fight to break out in our house anytime during the day or the night. I will have to say that I never saw my dad start trouble, but if somebody brought trouble to him, he never backed off. It did not matter who the person was or what the trouble was about. If someone would come onto our property and try my daddy, he would accommodate them with all the trouble that they could handle and then more. Things like fistfights and brawls breaking out anytime in the night were common occurrences at our house.

It would often start with Daddy just getting loud. Somebody would come into the house about his moonshine business, bootlegging, or his hunting and trapping. First Daddy would start getting loud, and I knew what was about to start to take place. Once Daddy lost his temper and starting screaming, it would not be long till he would be knocking someone out or tossing them out the door. My mama would be crying again, and I would be running to my room to hide until things would quiet down. During the early days, I hid in my room quite often.

Though fights like that were common occurrences in our household, it would actually be over quite fast. Either Daddy would punch someone out, run him off the property, or literally pick him up and throw him out the door. After the fight, we would often go back to whatever we were doing beforehand. By the time I was five or six years of age, I became used to the fighting, yelling, screaming, and the hiding in my room until the storm had passed.

As I got older, I would often think about my mama and the love she would show toward Daddy. I will never understand how my mama handled all of the problems that would occur at our house. Something was wrong and something was going on all of the time. But this is the way my daddy was brought up. He really never thought that how he lived or what he did would affect the family around him. He had grown up in the moonshine culture, and bootlegging and fighting were part of that culture.

This is how his daddy and his grandpa lived their life, and it was just part of their family history. They were all hard men, they fought, they made whiskey, and they ran it to whoever would buy it. It was a way of life, and in their eyes, this was what life was all about and how life was supposed to be.

It was not a moral issue, legal issue, or a right-or-wrong issue. Their life had been like this for over three generations, and they were walking in the footsteps of their ancestors.

They really had no idea that what they were doing was wrong.

It was the lawmen that were wrong in their eyes. The government, which felt that they were losing a lot of money from nontaxable whiskey, made it illegal, and therefore federal revenuers came after folk like my daddy. But the typical moonshiners felt that they and their family folk before them had been making whiskey way before there was a law against it. It was no more than a job for them. Moonshining was something they did from morning to evening, and during the night hours they ran the whiskey to the buyers. Daddy, just like his ancestors, could not see any reason to change and saw nothing wrong in it.

My earliest recollection of my mama was her sitting on the couch looking out the window and crying when my daddy pulled out of the driveway. It made no real difference to my daddy how many times my mom sat on the couch and cried. It was his way of life, it was his business and job, and it was the way he provided for his family. Nevertheless, my mom always sat on the couch crying. In her head she felt that when she saw him drive out the driveway, it most likely could be the last time she would ever see him again alive, and she loved that man.

If he was not killed during some horrendous bootleg run, perhaps they would catch him, and the next time she saw him would behind bars. But if did not matter how tough life was in the Rushing household or how many times mama would sit on the couch crying and praying, she stayed by that man. I respect my mama more than almost anyone in the world. She is a wonderful woman. No matter what went on in our house or how difficult life became or whatever my daddy ultimately got into, she stood there next to him. She used to always laugh and tell folks that she took good care of both of her children, meaning both my daddy and me.

It really never mattered how rough and tough the situation was, due to the moonshining and bootlegging, one simple touch of my mama's hand would always take care of me and make me feel better. I can remember as a small child climbing up on her lap and, in the midst of terror, feeling so safe. Even now as an adult, I often wish that every child had a lap like that where they could climb up on and feel such security. It never really mattered how rough life got in our moonshining family, my mama always made the world a very wonderful place to be, and she still does. Even today sometimes I wish I could curl up on my mama's lap and still feel that love, tenderness, and security.

Please do not misunderstand me. My daddy was a very good man. He always made sure his family was taken care of and that we always had a very warm home and plenty of food on the table. I have fond memories of when he would take me hunting and trapping with him many days throughout the winter. We would actually spend hours together looking for arrowheads after a heavy rain. My daddy taught me how to find my way out of the woods if I ever got lost. Following in my daddy's footsteps, I learned everything I ever needed to know about survival.

I still have two little water wheels that my daddy made me out of corn stalks back in 1968 went I was just a little tot. We would often take them outside and set them up in the ditches after a good rain, and the water would turn the wheels. I would laugh, and I still remember seeing the joy on my daddy's face. I have many wonderful memories like that. Though life could be scary for a little child submerged in the moonshine culture, my childhood was filled with good times and many happy times.

In my eyes, there was nothing that my daddy could not do. He was one of the greatest men that ever walked, and I loved him with all of my heart when I was little, and I still do today. Though times were rough throughout many of our early years, not one time in my life did I ever stop loving my daddy! (I guess my mama and I are just alike in that department.)

I was never raised in church, and I guess that is no surprise. The many things that I learned about God were actually from my mama. She would often read me Bible stories, and she had a painting of a guardian angel helping little kids cross a broken bridge. (I still have that painting and the Bible storybook with me to this day.) She told me that God's angels were always with me. She would stress to me, especially during tough times, that God would always take care of me.

I always wonder what the folks at the church down the road from our house were doing on Sundays. My daddy often said that they were just a bunch of hypocrites and that they hid behind the Bible. I often heard him say that they went to church on Sunday but lived like the devil during the week. This was Daddy's way of thinking for the first twenty-eight years of my life. Now that I am older, I look back and see that my daddy was really right about some of them.

Going to church and reading the Bible was something that I never saw my daddy do. But somehow I always knew that he believed in God. We never attended church until 1988. I know that God had offered Daddy His hand many times before in his life, but Daddy would never take the offer. He was stubborn, hard, and cold toward the things of God. But thank God, God never gave up on my daddy. Finally, Daddy couldn't turn and couldn't run anymore.

One Sunday he said, "I am going to church with you today." As we drove down the driveway Daddy said, "Kid, I don't know what I am going to do or what I am going to say today, but God is dealing with me strong and I have got to go."

We walked into the church, and from the time that Daddy sat down on the seat, tears were rolling down his cheeks. It was the second time that I ever saw my daddy cry. The first time was when his brother was killed in a car crash. Preacher Elbert Goble gave the alter call, and my daddy stood up and walked down that long aisle. He fell on his knees and asked Jesus into his life. All through the church people were crying and shouting and thanking God. See, they had been praying for my daddy for a long time.

That day Daddy took God by the hand.

The great man that I loved so much had never been more of a man than on that day when he walked down that long aisle and gave his heart to Jesus. The day my daddy took Jesus Christ by the hand and opened his heart up to salvation was the greatest day in all of our lives.

In October 1988 our family joined Dover Baptist Church. We were all baptized the same evening: Jerry Elijah Rushing, Shelby Dean Rushing, Mary Darlene Tarlton (myself) and Brandy Nicole Tarlton Dillard (my little girl). These were only names among other names in Union County until we gave our hearts to Jesus right there in Dover Baptist Church. It is not important that anyone else knows our names or who we are. It is only important that Jesus Christ now knows our names and has written them down in the Book of Life and that now we all know Him.

All is forgiven. All is forgotten.

Jesus finally let His children safely cross that broken bridge and we are all safe now.

It does not matter what side of life we are on, we will always be together.

I love you, Daddy!

Your little girl,

Darlene Tarlton

THOUGHTS FOR MY FAMILY... BY JERRY

Well, I know that I have had a pretty tough life. The life of a moon-shiner and bootlegger is never an easy one. It was a combination of hard work and danger, and it was the thrill and danger that excited me as a kid. My granddaddy made moonshine and my daddy made moonshine. It was my uncle Dooley that taught me about the stuff. I never thought about it bein' right or wrong. It was just what I did. I was born into the moonshine lifestyle. It was the only thing I knew to do, and the only thing my family did basically was making home-made 'shine. My daddy introduced me to running before I was even a teenager. He had me jumping into the car and running here and there picking up whiskey for him and occasionally some sugar. It was always excitin' to me.

As a little boy, I always looked up to outlaws like Jessie James and Bonnie and Clyde. Maybe it is just the excitement of the fast life. Some boys jes' might grow out of that, but I never did. I lived the life of a modern-day outlaw and ultimately paid a price—a rough family life and time wasted in the hoosegow.

I would like to say I never have any thought to return to that old life, but I really can't. Sometimes I think that I would like to make one more run, but I won't do it. I left that life behind. I know that in 1988 when I gave my heart to Jesus Christ, the old Jerry died and the new Jerry Elijah Rushing was born again. This is true, and I thank God that He changed my life. Though I am committed to live my life for God, the old Jerry occasionally wants to rise up and run 'shine just one more time. But I will not.

I knew that life was getting too rough to live and that I might go over the edge and not return. I knew I had to move my family to outside of Union County if I was really goin' to change. Occasionally some of my old friends (or those that I thought were my friends) would travel from Monroe to Taylorsville to talk to me about some of their most recent criminal actives. Some of 'em needed assistance in moonshining and others in bootlegging stuff. Some were even into other criminal kinds of stuff. Once they would leave my house, Darlene, my daughter, would often tell me, "Now, Daddy, you know you don't want to hang around those people. Those people kept you into trouble for a long time and they are up to no good." I know that I would often remind her that I had no intentions to returning to my old lifestyle, though she would tease me about seeing a twinkle in my eye when I would start thinkin' like my old ways.

Sometimes when I look back on the life of Jerry Rushing, I am really surprised of all I did. I guess I would agree with Darlene, my daughter, that inside of a man is a certain amount of good and some feelings toward his family and people. Though I did love my family, I probably never did tell 'em in the early years. I guess that I lived such a life of evil and wrong doin's that not only was my conscience seared but my feelin's were covered up, too. I was a rough and tough criminal outlaw. It was far from me to express any feelin' of care, love, or concern at all. Durin' the early times of my life, I was full of hatred and anger, and I was ready to whoop anybody that got into my way for any reason. That's just the way I always remember bein'.

If I did have feelings, they were so far buried under the anger and the hate. Prior to accepting Jesus Christ, I couldn't find them at all. Sometimes I am surprised that I took pride in beating up a man within an inch of his life. I'd even laugh about leaving him bloody, hurt, and cut, sometimes lying on the street and other times out in the woods. Doesn't really seem like me at all now. But I lived that life, and many times now as I think about some of those things, I am sorry for the things I did.

Usually the greatest sadness I feel is toward my family. Though

I knew that my wife, Dean, really didn't embrace the bootlegging lifestyle, part of me really didn't care. It was my life; it had been my daddy's life and my granddaddy's life. I had every reason to walk in their shoes. I wanted to earn the title of "modern-day outlaw," and I would sacrifice almost anything to make that happen.

Though my wife would sit on the couch praying and crying each night as I ran whiskey through most of Carolina, I really didn't pay her much attention because I had such a passion to do what I wanted to do. Now days I regret that. I often think that if I could turn back the hands of time, I would have done it differently. I would have changed my life earlier and let my wife know that I did care and that I did love her.

As I look back, I know that I created a lot of bad stuff for my wife to live through. She lived through the pain and the sorrow when I got into trouble. Whether it was breaking my neck in racing or the many crashes where I barely lived to tell about it while bootlegging, she stood by me. She always believed in God and always believed in angels. Perhaps she was my angel sent from God to stand with me when I never cared about God or anything else. She loved me when I was unlovable, and usually I was. She cared about me when I cared about no one else.

There were many times when she could have left me. I spent months in prison while she lived alone, many times in fear of the past and the guys I ran with. Even when I was home, she lived in fear in our own home. Many times fights would break out in the middle of the house with folks causin' me problems, creating chaos in her otherwise peaceful world.

When I think about this sometimes outdoors, I often wonder why she stayed. Maybe she loved me that much, and maybe God had her next to me to help save me. I am sorry that I caused her so much pain and put her through so much hell in my earlier years. If I had it to do over again, I'd want to do it differently. I love her today, and I want to love her more tomorrow. I never want to lose sight of the fact that when I was unlovable, she loved me. I guess God's a lot that. There were many times in my life where God offered His hand to me and I refused. There were also many times in my life when I lived through horrible situations, often wondering if God even cared.

Though I often caused most of my own trouble, sometimes I felt that God was standing in the wings waiting for me to stop running and waiting for me to turn to Him. I have to admit that though most of this is behind me, there are many times when I think about a fast bootleg race with the law. I loved smelling the whiskey or burning rubber tires. But at least now I know that those feelings are the old Jerry. Those urges to do that are not the born-again Jerry Rushing. The new Jerry is different. I used to just hate. Now I really feel God's love and want my family to know I love them.

Though I never expressed it in those earlier days, I had a love for my wife, Dean, and my only child, Darlene. I regret that I didn't actually tell 'em this during our younger years. However, though I may have thought it and sometimes felt it, it just never came out of the hardened and callous heart that I had. I always did love them, and one of the worst fights that I ever got into was because a local boy threatened to kill my wife and daughter. I remember screaming at him while I beat his face, "You want to kill my wife and daughter... let me show you what killin' actually feels like."

If it wasn't for God lookin' after me, I could've killed many men and been in prison the rest of my life. I'm glad that didn't happen.

As I look over the many dangerous situations I got myself into, it is a wonder I was not killed a thousand times. It was as if I had nine lives like a cat. Each time I survived a near-death catastrophe, it only lead to my own pride and ego as being an outlaw that could not be put down.

I spent many hours in the woods with Darlene, and we both have a love of hunting and trapping and the outdoors. But I do regret that I did not outright tell her that I loved her when she was little. I am sorry for the many nights of hell when the fighting from the bootleg business would erupt in the midst of our home. I am sorry for the nights that she spent hiding behind her bed as I fought with many of the outlaws that I ran with. Both she and Dean deserved a better life than that. But here I am, and I cannot turn back the hands of time. I can only go forward. I know that without God's hand on my life,

I could have been killed many times. In fact, without God standing beside me and sparing my life, I should have been killed. I owe much to the prayers of both my wife and my daughter, and I thank 'em for their love even through the tough times.

So what does a man do when he has lived such a life of horror, causing pain and anguish on the family that he loves? You press forward. You leave the past behind you and thank God daily for giving ya the life that He has given ya and for sparing ya from the past evil. I love Dean and Darlene, and I thank God for them. I really believe that without 'em and their tears and prayers, this old Rushing boy would have been lost forever, and I would be going to hell. But because of them, I escaped the bootlegging and moonshining grips that many just never escape. I escaped with my life, my wife, and a wonderful daughter, and I escaped with the hope of an eternal life that Jesus Christ has given me.

I also thank God for my one and only grandchild, Brandy. In her very early years, she even experienced many of the horrors brought on the family through my hatred and anger and stuff I did. I really love her immensely, and she is one of the three most important women in my life.

I will never forget the night when my entire family was baptized together in a little church right here in Taylorsville. Dean, Darlene, Brandy, and myself were all baptized at the same time. If I had a final wish for my family, my hope would be that they would never forget the power of Jesus. Only Jesus and His love can take a rough and tough bootlegger like myself, remove my cold heart, and replace it with a soft heart of love. Though I can still occasionally lose my temper, become excited, and allow the "old Jerry" to raise his head, my prayers are that God will continue to change me.

My prayer for Dean, Darlene, and Brandy is that they will always love God and never forget the legacy of the Rushing family. Not the legacy of bootlegging and moonshining, but the new legacy of a "new spiritual birth" that Jesus Christ offered to us when He changed my life. I want them to remember the "new Jerry Rushing," the new husband, the new daddy, and the new granddaddy and never forget God's goodness to me. Without God, Jerry Elijah Rushing would not be here today. It's only by God's grace and His hand that I have survived the many difficulties that I have endured. I thank God for His love and for His forgiveness as He wiped my slate clean. I also thank God for my family's forgiveness as they have embraced me and loved me. Now I not only feel love toward them in my heart, but I can express it by saying I love you.

So...

Dean, I love you.

Darlene, I love you.

Brandy, I love you.

Never forget that!

THOUGHTS FOR MY DUKE FANS...BY JERRY

When I first got into the entire bootlegging and moonshine stuff, I never dreamed for a moment that I would be one of the most notorious bootleggers in all of Carolina. I was merely living my life the way I knew best, working and putting food on the table for my family. It was just a job to me. Delivering bootleg whiskey to me was no different than delivering milk from house to house. It was just a little faster and more dangerous.

I never thought that there was a life outside of bootlegging and moonshining. We lived a fairly quite backwoods existence, and I was just walkin' in the footsteps of the generation before me. Somewhere along the line, like in my first prison adventure, hatred and anger began to grow against all lawmen. Growing up in my family, one had a hatred for lawmen because they were the "bad guys." The lawmen would break up your stills, destroy your whiskey, and put you in jail for doing the only thing you ever knew how to do, and that was to make corn whiskey.

We knew the law said it was illegal, but so were a lot of other things. Most of the lawmen we knew were crooked and profitted as much from the moonshine and bootlegging as we did. The only difference was they were on two payrolls, the federal government and some bootlegger that paid them off. Many got money for license plates, sugar, free rein on a certain highway, or gallon jugs to store the stuff. I never did respect them much then, and don't now.

When I began to write my songs about my bootlegging and my moonshining experience, I never dreamt that one day they would turn into a movie that would turn into *The Dukes of Hazzard* television show. My life was a rough and tough life, and though we put away money from the moonshine business, I was always looking for a better opportunity for my family. Writing songs seemed like that might be the ticket. But the ticket did not lead to Nashville, but rather led to me making a movie called *Moonrunners*.

As most readers may know, *Moonrunners* was a movie that was made about my life. The opening credits say, "Although the characters herein are fictitious, some of the events are based upon incidents in the life of Jerry Rushing, who also served as technical advisor."

I made several tapes regarding my life as a moonshiner and bootlegger, and the movie was based on many of those experiences. I was excited to be able to document my life and make a little bit of money off something more than running fast cars loaded down with whiskey. I was also excited to be able to play a small part in that movie. I guess that is when the movie and TV "bug" first bit me. It was exciting to meet other movie stars and see how movies were made. When *Moonrunners* was completed, it played all over America, but I really never expected where it would lead to. Some of the characters in my personal life, who were portrayed in the movie *Moonrunners*, were then translated into a variety of fictitious characters in the TV comedy *The Dukes of Hazzard*.

It was exciting to see the first television episode shoot as Bo and Luke fairly accurately represented my brother Johnny and me. Uncle Jessie of *The Dukes of Hazzard* represented my Uncle Dooley, who taught us everything about moonshinin' and got Johnny and me first into the business of bootlegging. And, of course, who could forget Daisy Duke, who played one of my cousins that occasionally helped Johnny and me out when we got into trouble. Boss Hogg as well as a variety of deputies that were always on the take within *The Dukes of Hazzard* also was a reflection of real-life characters in my moonshining and bootlegging family history.

Since I had been a felon, I could own no guns, so I shot bows for much of my hunting and occasionally for protection. This was also reflected on *The Dukes of Hazzard* program. My main bootlegging car, however, was not a 1969 Dodge Charger but a 1958 Chrysler 300-D modified for both the race and fast bootleg hauling. Its name was not the *General Lee*, like *The Dukes of Hazzard* program, but rather *Traveler*, which was General Lee's horse.

The similarities between *The Dukes of Hazzard* and my personal life really end there. Though the characters and many of the story lines somewhat accurately portrayed and reflected my life and times, my life was certainly not a comedy. There was little joy and laughter in my life, and never the love and hugging that was shown on *The Dukes of Hazzard*.

Obviously, *The Dukes of Hazzard* was written for a television audience, and even when it hit the television airways, it received quite a bit of negative press regarding the acting and the storylines. But it seemed to become a hit with people all over the country.

I enjoyed *The Dukes of Hazzard* as the popularity grew on television. I also enjoyed the part that I played as Ace Parker, the repo man. We never expected *The Dukes of Hazzard* program to have such a strong following throughout America some thirty years later. Just this year I attended the twenty-fifth annual *Dukes of Hazzard* celebration at the Bristol Motor Speedway. This is put on each year by Ben Jones, who played Cooter in the show. Thousand of people showed up at the racetrack for the convention from all over the country. Men trailered in their specialized *General Lees* and displayed 'em throughout the convention site. It was a two-day event where thousands of people shared stories, gathered for photographs, and were able to embrace one another some thirty years after the television show. Catherine Bach (Daisy Duke), James Best (Roscoe P. Coletrain), Ben Jones (Cooter), and myself, as well as many others, were there after all of these years signing autographs and passing out photos to fans.

If I had a real wish for the many *Dukes of Hazzard* fans, it would be that they not only continue to enjoy the fun and the joy that it brought to many of us over the years, but that they would see through the fun and comedy to this real-life story of the man behind the story. Bootlegging was never a comedy, and moonshining certainly was not as well.

Actually, it was the opposite. It was a life full of danger and difficult for both the bootlegger as well as his family. It was a rough life outside of God and outside of His purpose for my life. It was a life that filled me with hate, anger, and bitterness that only a loving God could change.

If I had another wish for the many *Dukes of Hazzard* fans, I would hope that they would not only embrace the life of Jerry Rushing as the man behind the story, but they would take the next step and view the life of Jerry Rushing as the man behind the message. And the message is this:

> Without Jesus Christ in your life, it doesn't matter whether you are a moonshiner, bootlegger, or Sunday school teacher, your life too will be hell and will be without the peace and joy that only Jesus can give.

As the fan of *The Dukes of Hazzard,* you may not be running whiskey or operating a moonshine still in the back woods, but if you do not know Jesus Christ as your personal Savior, you are a runner. You are running from His purpose for your life, and you are running from His love. If you would examine your life as many times I have examined mine, you would see where God's hand has reached out to you in a loving way and you have purposely avoided embracing His love.

My hopes and wishes for you are that you would embrace that love and grab hold of the hand that is reaching to you. Stop your running today. I ultimately did. Always know this, I am glad that the comedy, which represented parts of my life, has brought you some joy and happiness. However, you can only experience eternal joy and happiness if you receive Jesus. Embrace Jesus as your personal Savior, as I did, and walk with Him today.

And always remember, this old bootlegger and moonshiner is praying for you.

God touched me and changed my life. He can change your life, too. Just give Him a chance.